Library of
Davidson College

HARRY LANGDON

The Comedian as Metteur-en-Scène

JOYCE RHEUBAN

Rutherford • Madison • Teaneck
Fairleigh Dickinson University Press
London and Toronto: Associated University Presses

© 1983 by Associated University Presses, Inc.

Associated University Presses, Inc.
4 Cornwall Drive
East Brunswick, N.J. 08816

Associated University Presses Ltd
27 Chancery Lane
London WC2A 1NF, England

Associated University Presses
2133 Royal Windsor Drive
Unit 1
Mississauga, Ontario
Canada L5J 1K5

Library of Congress Cataloging in Publication Data
Rheuban, Joyce.
  Harry Langdon. The comedian as metteur-en-scène.

  Bibliography: p.
  Includes index.
  1. Langdon, Harry, 1884–1944. 2. Comedy films—
History and criticism.   I. Title.
PN2287.L283R5   791.43′028′0924   81-65868
ISBN 0-8386-3111-8   AACR2

Printed in the United States of America

Contents

Acknowledgments		7
1	Introduction: The Issue of Authorship	11
2	Background	17
3	The Character	54
4	The Performance	103
5	The Mise-en-Scène	119
6	Film Form	127
7	Langdon as Metteur-en-Scène	145
8	Langdon, Lloyd, Keaton, and Chaplin	189
9	Footnote: Arthur Ripley and the Dark Side of Langdon's Comedies	205
Filmography		228
Bibliography		238
Index		242

Acknowledgments

The author would like to thank the following people for their kindness in sharing their knowledge and recollections of Harry Langdon: Gertrude Astor, Edward Bernds, Priscilla Bonner, Frank Capra, Edward Finney, Dorothy Granger, Ruth Hiatt, Donald A. Langdon, Gladys McConnell, Hal Roach, and Jules White.

The author would also like to acknowledge the very generous assistance of William K. Everson in all stages of the preparation of this book, as well as the guidance of Annette Michelson, which also represents a significant contribution to this work.

Other valuable sources of information and assistance in the preparation of this book were: the Library and Museum of the Performing Arts of the New York Public Library at Lincoln Center, the Margaret Herrick Library of the Academy of Motion Picture Arts and Sciences, the Film Study Center and Library of the Museum of Modern Art, the Study Center of the Department of Cinema Studies of New York University, and the Theatre Collections of the Free Library of Philadelphia and the Harvard College Library.

HARRY LANGDON

1
Introduction: The Issue of Authorship

The matter of authorship is commonly an issue when the object of analysis, as here, is a product of the American commercial film industry. Authorship of Hollywood films generally consists of the contributions of many influences and collaborators. In the case of the films of Harry Langdon, this issue has been particularly complicated by misinformation and misconceptions that have been uncritically accepted and passed on as fact in the historical and critical literature of American silent film comedy.

Langdon's influence on the mise-en-scène of the films in which he appears as a performer has been overlooked, and the originality that is evident in the films he directed has been ignored. Even Langdon's origination of the comic impersonation and performance style exhibited in his films has been denied. Frank Capra and Mack Sennett are probably, directly and indirectly, the original sources of most of these misconceptions. Sennett and Capra have traditionally been considered the sole authorities on the subject of Harry Langdon by virtue of their participation in the production of many of his films.

Sennett was the famous American pioneer film comedy producer who first featured Langdon in twenty two-reel comedies, three three-reelers, and one feature-length comedy, *His First Flame,* while Langdon was under contract with the Sennett studio from 1924 to 1926. Most of Langdon's Sennett comedies were written, with Arthur Ripley, by Frank Capra. During that period, Capra was employed as a gag writer. Of the six feature-length comedies produced by the Harry Langdon Corporation, Capra wrote *Tramp, Tramp, Tramp* (1926), with several other writers, and directed *The Strong Man* (1926) and *Long Pants* (1927)—for which Ripley receives story credit—before leaving the company following a disagreement with Langdon during the production of *Long Pants*. The other three feature-length comedies produced by the Langdon Corporation, *Three's a Crowd* (1927), *The Chaser* (1928), and *Heart Trouble* (1928), were directed by Langdon and written by Ripley.

In the autobiographies of these men—*King of Comedy* by Sennett, published in 1954, and *The Name above the Title* by Capra, published in 1971—Harry Langdon is identified with the childlike character he impersonated on the screen. Sennett and Capra are the two sources of that by now commonly ackowledged characterization of Harry Langdon as naive, slow-witted, and spoiled by his success as a child is spoiled by an overindulgent parent. Sennett claims that as Langdon's salary went up, so did his self-esteem. According to Sennett, Langdon subsequently became involved in business and marital adventures and was equally inept in both.

Recalling how Langdon's rapid success in Sennett comedies soon led to a million-dollar contract with First National, Capra remarks that only a year before, Langdon was playing the honky-tonks and that he was ill prepared for his sudden success. Capra also claims that his own departure from the Harry Langdon Corporation, in which he was then employed as Langdon's director, was precipitated by one of Langdon's "tantrums," which Capra describes in some detail.

Both Sennett and Capra declare in their autobiographical accounts that Capra was responsible for conceiving and sustaining the comic characterization personified by Langdon in the films with which Capra was associated (though Capra shares credit with Arthur Ripley). They also both disqualify Langdon in terms of any creative contribution to this formative procedure on the grounds of his intellectual and emotional immaturity. Describing the production of Langdon's Keystone comedies, Sennett recalls:

> Langdon was as bland as milk, a forgiving small cuss, an obedient puppy, always in the way, exasperating, but offering his baby mannerisms with hopeful apology. Frank Capra's enormous talents first showed themselves when he saw all this as something that would photograph....
>
> Under Frank's easy guidance Harry soon became a Keystone star in two-reel comedies.[1]

Capra writes that Langdon's screen characterization came to him in a sudden flash of inspiration that was precipitated by a casual, chance remark by Arthur Ripley (seemingly in much the same fashion that song standards are conceived in Hollywood film biographies about famous composers). According to Capra, the theme or key to Langdon was innocence, and this

Introduction: The Issue of Authorship

was something, Capra asserts repeatedly, Langdon never understood. Talking about his part in the production of *Tramp, Tramp, Tramp*, Capra says:

> I gained Langdon's confidence and respect with my vetoing of gags that violated the character Ripley and I had created for him. It was amazing to me that neither Langdon nor [Harry] Edwards really understood, or took seriously, this integrity of characterization—which made Langdon what he was.[2]

Both Sennett and Capra blame the commercial and critical failure of the Langdon comedies that were made after Capra's departure on Langdon's incapacity, without Capra's guidance, to sustain the characterization which had proven so successful in his previous films. The failure of those films is thus offered by Sennett and Capra as confirmation of their claims that Langdon had no understanding of the character he personified on the screen. Sennett and Capra also assign responsibility for the demise of the Harry Langdon Corporation to Harry Langdon as producer. Their conclusion is presented as confirmation of Langdon's ineptitude.

Similar accounts and descriptions of Harry Langdon by others are hearsay. Their authors merely paraphrase the readily available accounts of the personal experiences and impressions of Sennett and Capra. In his October 1967 *Films in Review* article "Harry Langdon," Vernon L. Schonert reproduces the majority of Sennett's commentary on Langdon in direct quotations. The segment on Langdon in James Agee's well-known and frequently quoted *Life* magazine essay "Comedy's Greatest Era" appears to be based largely on interviews with Capra, from which Agee quotes directly, and with Sennett. The entire discussion of Langdon in Bill Treadwell's book *Fifty Years of American Comedy* is a closely paraphrased version of Agee's reports of his interviews with Sennett and Capra. In their book *Clown Princes and Court Jesters: Some Great Comics of the Silent Screen*, Kalton C. Lahue and Sam Gill merely reiterate Sennett's identification of Langdon with his screen persona.

Each of the following authors credits Capra with the development of the Langdon screen characterization and/or credits Capra with an understanding of that screen characterization that Langdon did not possess: David Robinson in *The Great Funnies: A History of Film Comedy*, Donald W. McCaffrey in *Four Great Comedians: Chaplin, Lloyd, Keaton, Langdon*, and Kevin Brownlow in *The Parade's Gone By*. . . . Langdon's artistic and commercial decline is directly linked to Capra's departure from the Langdon company in McCaffrey's book, Schonert's *Films in Review* article, and Kalton C. Lahue's *World of Laughter: The Motion Picture Comedy Short, 1910–1930*. These observations are all made with little or no substantiation and are obviously based on Sennett's personal account.

Authors of more recent commentaries on Langdon and on the Langdon films present the Capra account while expressing reservations concerning its credibility. Among these are Gerald Mast's *The Comic Mind: Comedy and the Movies,* Walter Kerr's *The Silent Clowns,* Leland A. Poague's *The Cinema of Frank Capra: An Approach to Film Comedy,* Richard Leary's article "Capra and Langdon" in the November–December 1972 issue of *Film Comment,* and Elliott Stein's Summer 1972 *Sight and Sound* article "Capra Counts His Oscars." These authors specifically address themselves to the question of authorship with respect to the Langdon comedies. However, their considerations remain inconclusive, and in every case the authors decline from making a definite commitment in favor of either Capra or Langdon.

Langdon's origination of his own comic persona and the style of performance by which it is elaborated are assumptions implicit in the notion of Harry Langdon as author and metteur-en-scène presented in this study. The facts of this matter, culled for the first time from documentary sources such as reviews and advertisements in variety artists' trade publications and other relevant biographical information, call into question the accuracy of the widely accepted notion of Harry Langdon and his role in the creation of the film comedies in which he appears.

According to this information, the distinctive comic impersonation and style of performance that Langdon exhibited in the silent film comedies in which he appears were actually created by Langdon at least as early as 1906 in a vaudeville sketch he originated and which he continued to play on the vaudeville stage in one form or another for nearly twenty years before he entered films.

Analysis of the Langdon comedies reveals a thoroughly unified comic conception whereby filmic style is closely integrated with Langdon's persona and performance style. There is also a clear continuity between Langdon's work in films and his prefilm work as a comic performer on the vaudeville stage. And among the films in which Langdon appears as featured performer there is a clear continuity at the levels of comic and formal stylistics even though Langdon's films are credited to a number of writers and directors (including Langdon himself).

The recent discussion of the authorship of the Langdon comedies has been almost exclusively concerned with narrative values. That is, arguments for or against Capra or Langdon as author of the Langdon films are based on such considerations as gag and plot construction; the necessity to accommodate narrative structure to Langdon's passive characterization; character development and consistency of characterization; the fact that Capra's insistence on the character's innocence is contradicted by the amorality exhibited by the character in the films; and Capraesque thematic motifs, narrative structures, and character types that are disclosed in the Langdon-Capra films by comparison with later Capra-directed films.

One intention of the present study is to shift the focus of this discussion. Narrative values are not elements of primary significance in Langdon's comedy. Characterization is significant insofar as it is organically unified with Langdon's mime and mise-en-scène. Sennett's observation that Langdon "seldom had the mistiest notion of what his screen stories were about" is probably correct. Whatever subtlety or sophistication in terms of plot and character development or the development of thematic motifs there may be in Langdon's films is most likely attributable to Capra or Arthur Ripley. However, the Langdon comedies do not exhibit strong narrative continuity. The individual comic situation or episode is the significant narrative unit of these films.

In this study, Harry Langdon is considered to be author as a performer to whose performance filmic structure conforms as a kind of idealized proscenium. The spectator is provided at any moment with the optimum vantage point on the mimed performance. Langdon is also considered author here as metteur-en-scène. This designation is intended as it pertains to Langdon in its original theatrical sense as one who directs placement on stage, and as it is currently applied in French as the designation "film director" is applied in English. An examination of Langdon's films suggests that Langdon had an intuitive understanding of the nature of filmic space and time. As performer under the direction of others and as performer-director, he employed specific properties of film in his creation of comedy and pathos. The notion of Harry Langdon as author is, however, a by-product of this study, which seeks primarily to examine characterization and performance as expressed in Langdon's mise-en-scène.

Langdon's comic characterization is unique. It is that of one who is chronically, pathologically semiconscious. His relation to the external circumstances that confront him is therefore only tenuous and tentative.

Though Langdon's film comedies were based on written scenarios, his comic persona is only minimally developed in dramatic and narrative terms. Langdon's comic performance also lacks mimetic and psychological specificity and is nonvirtuosic. Langdon's performance lacks not only displays of physical grace and technical skill but also the broadly expressive stock gestures and exaggerated movements of burlesque (as in a Sennett comedy) and the expressive subtlety of an acting performance by a comedian such as Charles Chaplin.

Langdon's comic persona is defined rather in and through the mise-en-scène: that is, by means of the comedian's physical relationship with respect to his external circumstances. Langdon's mime is one of physical disorientation. It is at once a demonstration of the impaired condition of the character's cognitive faculties and motor functions, and a metaphoric index to his psychological disorientation with waking life.

Langdon's rather peculiar comic character, called Harry, is described by and inspires his specialized pantomimic style. This persona and performance together prescribe a specialized mise-en-scène: from an overall adherence to preserving the continuity of filmic space and time to the formal specifications of individual shots. Thus the films are characterized formally by the use of: the long take (a single shot of relatively long duration without interruption by cutting); long-take tracking shots in depth; long-take two- and three-shots in shallow screen space; and long-take two-, three-, four-, and five-shots (shots in which from two to five principal characters are seen) in the deep space of a stationary frame.

All of these ideas and observations are based on the presumption of Langdon's responsibility for the development of the comic character and performance that is seen on the screen. This matter of responsibility is therefore taken up in chapter 2 prior to any further discussion of the relationship of Langdon's character, mime, and mise-en-scène.

Notes

1. Mack Sennett with Cameron Shipp, *King of Comedy* (Garden City, N.Y.: Doubleday, 1954), p. 142.
2. Frank Capra, *The Name above the Title* (New York: Macmillan Co., 1971), p. 64.

2
Background

Contrary to the misconceptions generated by the Sennett and Capra accounts, the evidence indicates that the distinctive comic character and style seen in the Langdon films with which Mack Sennett, Frank Capra, and Arthur Ripley have at various times been associated were created by Langdon long before the collaborative contributions of these men were made to Langdon's films. As already noted, Langdon's comic character and style were probably created in a vaudeville sketch he originated in about 1906. He continued to play in one form or other of this sketch with his first wife, Rose Frances, for the next seventeen years.

In his vaudeville act, Langdon drove onstage in a new roadster with his wife in the back seat. The couple was dressed in motoring costumes. Harry played a young man taking his sweetheart for a drive to show off his new car. The prop auto promptly broke down in front of a café or hospital, and the comic situation generally consisted of Harry's efforts to repair the car and start it up again.

The prop car (the number of cars in the act was at times increased by Langdon to two and three) was ingeniously contrived and provided Langdon with a noisy and persistent antagonist to which to respond in his own inimitable fashion. As Harry drove the car on- and offstage, it bucked and backfired loudly and visibly with flames shooting out of the exhaust as if from a blowtorch. When Harry lifted the hood in an effort to repair the car, the radiator expelled a geyserlike jet of steam and the gas tank spit fire at Harry whenever he turned his back to it. Langdon had also contrived some sort of "electrical effect," according to *Variety*,[1] to simulate the engine exploding. As a result of the explosion, engine parts and the steering wheel were fired into the air and landed all over the stage. The car was designed and constructed by Langdon to fall apart, piece by piece, either at the touch of his hand or of its own volition as the act progressed.

The act was soon joined by Langdon's younger brother, James (who was billed as Tully Langdon). Langdon's wife, Rose, and Tully were Harry's human antagonists. Both Rose, who scolded and screamed at Harry from the back seat of the car, and the noisy vehicle provided a contrast to Harry's quiet industry as he worked to repair the car. Langdon's brother played a waiter when the comic business with the car took place in front of the café set. Tully also played a cop who demands that Harry get the noisy car out of a hospital zone and harasses Harry as he attempts to do so.

Though Langdon was continuously adding new material and varying aspects of this basic comic situation, there were three versions of the act during those seventeen years in vaudeville. The first version, which Langdon played from 1906 to 1915, was called "A Night on the Boulevard." In the earliest performances of this sketch, Harry was the chauffeur of a society belle, played by Rose. This act included jokes and "snappy talk" from all three performers, gags, pantomime, a solo sung by Rose, and a finale in which the stage is darkened and the principals ride offstage into the wings as a spotlight plays over the audience.

"Johnny's New Car" was the title of the second version of Langdon's sketch. It differed from the first principally in the addition by Langdon of new and more sophisticated "mechanical effects" and of other special mechanical properties, such as a "disappearing drinking stream." Langdon also created a sophisticated lighting effect for "Johnny's New Car," which he added to the quite elaborately designed, electrically illuminated stage setting used in and retained from "A Night on the Boulevard." Both of these effects are described in greater detail elsewhere in this chapter. James Langdon entered the service during World War I at the time that Harry Langdon was touring "Johnny's New Car." He was replaced in the act by a second young woman who was billed as Cecil Langdon (though she was not actually related to Harry). She continued as a member of the act until 1923, when Langdon left vaudeville to enter films.

Langdon first presented "After the Ball," yet another variation of his old comedy sketch, at the Palace Theater in New York in 1921. "After the Ball" consisted of three "scenes," or comic episodes. The first is set on a golf course and features Harry as the quiet caddy for two chattering woman golfers. In the second scene, the comic business is carried on in front of the clubhouse. The third episode is actually a condensed version of Langdon's automobile routine of the two earlier acts.

Langdon wrote his own sketches, all of his own material, including dialogue and gags, and designed and constructed the ingenious prop cars and the elaborate, illuminated drops used in his act. He was also one of an

Langdon in costume for "A Night on the Boulevard" in a 1914 photo in the *New York Star*. (Courtesy of New York Public Library)

uncommon few vaudeville comedians who were prolific enough to write material for other vaudeville comedians.

The comic persona that Langdon decided upon at the time of his graduation to vaudeville from a ten-year apprenticeship in various forms of popular entertainments was inspired by Langdon's own physical appearance. Langdon naturally resembled a baby somewhat in facial features, stature, and physique. He enhanced this resemblance by his makeup and costume. The outward appearance Langdon bore throughout his career as a comic was essentially the same as that in which he first presented himself in vaudeville in "A Night on the Boulevard." This is indicated by a comparison of the makeup and costume that Langdon wore in films with that in which Langdon is seen in professional portraits taken during Langdon's career as a vaudeville performer.

In these photographs, Langdon is pictured in whiteface makeup, with his eyes, eyebrows, and lips outlined in dark makeup that reduces his own facial features to a cartoonlike caricature. He also wears a smudge of darker makeup on the tip of his nose as he does in many of his silent comedies.[2] In a 1910 photograph in *Variety* of "The Langdons" in costume for the motoring sketch, "A Night on the Boulevard," Langdon is wearing a car coat that is much too large.[3] In such films as *His Marriage Wow, Boobs in the Wood, Lucky Stars, Fiddlesticks,* and *The Strong Man,* Langdon wears a similar oversized overcoat, with a shirt and conventional necktie visible beneath, as in the *Variety* photograph.

Langdon is, however, best known for the costume he wore most often in his feature-length comedies: baggy, too-large trousers, which presumably had been "handed-down" to him; a short, snugly fitting jacket, which presumably he was "growing out of," with large, round buttons that barely fastened; a necktie formed in a large, full bow; and a round, small-brimmed hat with a punched-in crown. All of these articles of the comic attire Langdon wore in films, although perhaps not all assembled at one time by him as a vaudeville comic into a single costume, were worn by Langdon in his act at various times during his vaudeville career.

Langdon is sketched in the *New York Dramatic Mirror* as he appeared in 1910 on the stage of the Riverside Theater in New York in "Johnny's New Car" wearing an oversized coat with the same baggy pants and punched-in hat in which he appears most often in his films. This cartooned caricature offers a perfect likeness of Langdon's facial expression as he appears made-up in his later films.[4] Capra, in *The Name above the Title,* describes the makeup and costume that Langdon wore in a film of his earlier vaudeville sketch, which Capra says was presented to Sennett's staff of writers and directors when Langdon was engaged as a contract comedian, as being identical to that in which Langdon appears in his films.[5]

Reviews, advertisements, and articles in the variety artists' trade papers—*Variety, Billboard,* and the *New York Dramatic Mirror*—and in newspapers of the time also confirm the prefilm origins of Langdon's screen persona and the style of performance by which Langdon was later known in film. In reviews of Langdon's act that appear in these publications throughout the period of Langdon's stage career, Langdon's "simp," "boob," or "delightful dumbbell" impersonation is spoken of as a familiar favorite with vaudeville audiences. A *Variety* reviewer noted in 1922, near the end of Langdon's vaudeville career, "His 'boob' character is one of the classics."[6]

Langdon's comedy was invariably described as "dry" or "droll," and his style of performance was frequently recognized for its novelty as compared to the knockabout farce and broad burlesque that, quantitatively speaking, were the dominant forms of vaudeville comedy during most of the time Langdon was a participant. Langdon presented "comedy of a different nature,"[7] was "a comedian with a rare sense of humor,"[8] had his own "inimitable way,"[9] and, as yet another reviewer noted, was "a comedian

A cartoon by Ed Randall of the vaudeville bill at New York's Riverside Theater in the *New York Dramatic Mirror*, 14 February 1920. (Courtesy of New York Public Library)

with a style all his own."[10] In a review of "Johnny's New Car," as performed by Langdon in 1920 in a musical comedy review entitled *Jim Jam Jems,* a New York newspaper critic mentions Langdon's performance, observing that "Harry Langdon . . . provided some excellent comedy which depended more on skillful pantomime than upon dialogue to achieve its effects."[11]

Other distinguishing features by which Harry Langdon's comedy is known in film were noted by vaudeville reviewers to be the distinguishing features of Langdon's earlier work on the stage. These include the stylistic trait of making much of a minimum of gag material and Langdon's physically subdued performance. In a 1921 *Billboard* review of "Johnny's New Car," the author declares, "There is only one Harry Langdon, and each season he makes better with less effort."[12] As early as 1911, a reviewer commented in *Variety* that "the man and woman do very well with the comedy props and get a great deal from the material."[13] In a *Billboard* review of 1920, Harry's prop auto is cited as "the source of a lot of good comedy," and Langdon is commended because "he got every bit out of it that was possible."[14] During his next-to-last year in vaudeville, Langdon was recognized by a *Variety* reviewer as "an artist" who "can get laughs by the turn of a hand."[15]

Langdon and his comedy were commonly classed as "the quiet type." His act is described as having many quiet moments, and his manner of working onstage is described as "slow" and "unaffected." The only exaggeration of which Langdon was ever accused in any of the reviews of his work onstage was that of further retarding the already slow pace of his performance. When Langdon presented "After the Ball," the final version of his vaudeville routine, he was criticized by a *Variety* writer because, "in his new vehicle . . . he humors his slow personality a bit too much." The writer continues, "It is a unique and laughable technique, but it does slow up business."[16]

Capra affirms that the style of performance displayed in Langdon's films is the same as that which characterized Langdon's work on stage. In his book, Capra identifies a number of the hallmarks of Langdon's later screen performances in his own description of Langdon's mime as he recalls the film of Langdon's vaudeville act referred to previously. Capra notes that Langdon carried out his actions "in very slow pantomime," and cites Langdon's "helpless little smile;" his gestures of gently patting the inanimate automobile in an effort to calm it and impatiently wagging his finger at it, which Capra describes as childlike; and the mannerism whereby Harry holds his hat on his head by the brim as he runs.[17]

The similarity between Langdon's vaudeville routine and his performances in film is also suggested in an observation made by a *Billboard* critic that Langdon's act, "After the Ball," "has to do with the awkward idiosyncrasies of Harry" as a simpleminded caddy.[18]

Capra also concedes that Langdon came to film as a master of the extended "take 'em," or comic reaction. This hallmark of Langdon's style as a

"The Langdons" in a 1906 photo in *Billboard*. (Courtesy of New York Public Library)

film comedian was an important feature of Langdon's stage performances from as early as 1906, probably his first year in vaudeville. Langdon is pictured in a photograph that appears in a 1906 issue of *Billboard*, seated, with Rose beside him, "in their trick automobile."[19] He is gripping the steering wheel with a wide-eyed frightened stare fixed upon his face that is familiar to anyone who has seen Langdon's films. In 1920, a *Variety* reviewer proclaimed, "Harry Langdon's vapid expression is a classic."[20] Shortly thereafter, a critic reporting on *Jim Jam Jems* in the *New York Tribune* remarked, "Harry Langdon, with his trick automobile and his 'vacant stare,' brings a bit of vaudeville's very best into a new realm."[21]

Sennett's and Capra's descriptions of Langdon's vaudeville background and his stature as a professional comedian at the time he entered films are the sources of another misconception concerning Langdon. These descriptions are examples of the patronizing attitude toward Langdon adopted in the autobiographies of Sennett and Capra. However, their descriptions are contradicted by the vaudeville trade papers and newspaper reviews of Langdon's act.

In *King of Comedy*, Sennett maintains that Langdon came to the Keystone studio "from the knockabout stage with no money and no fame," and in the next sentence, that he "came from a small-town vaudeville act."[22] Capra says that Langdon "knocked about for years in the small vaudeville circuits" and "played in tank towns all his life," and alleges that the year before he signed his contract with First National for feature comedies, Langdon was playing the honky-tonks.[23]

As have other elements of Sennett and Capra's accounts, these comments have been accepted uncritically and repeated. This is hearsay perpetuated as fact. Richard Leary, in his article "Capra and Langdon," professes to be aware of this pitfall to which, he suggests, other commentators on Capra and Langdon have succumbed. It is nevertheless apparent in his article that Leary has taken Capra's word insofar as Langdon's vaudeville career is concerned. Walter Kerr has obviously taken Sennett's word as the basis of his declaration in *The Silent Clowns* that "Sennett did indeed discover Langdon, plucking him from a second-rate vaudeville act."[24]

Information in primary sources indicates not only that the comic persona and the style of performance that characterize Langdon's work in films were conceived and developed in vaudeville by Langdon himself, but also that Langdon was highly successful as a vaudeville comedian. The stages of success in vaudeville are conveniently and explicitly demarcated by its own vernacular: the "small-," "medium-," and "big-time." "Small-time" vaudeville is defined as the small-town houses of small chains like the Gus Sun Ohio circuit and houses that presented more than two shows a day and charged low or "popular" admission prices. Sullivan and Considine, and Pantages, the largest small-time chains of higher-class vaudeville houses in the small cities of the West and Midwest were often classed as "medium-time" vaudeville. The "big-time" was the Keith circuit in the East and the Orpheum circuit in the West. Langdon worked his way up through each of these stages, perfecting, polishing, and continuously adding material to the act, originally called "A Night on the Boulevard," which he continued to refine for seventeen years.

Langdon began his vaudeville career touring his act in small-time Gus Sun and Western Vaudeville Managers' Association bookings. The Gus Sun circuit and the W.V.M.A., a circuit of small-town midwestern houses, were included in a kind of farm-club system conducted by the Orpheum interests for the development of new acts with big-time potential. Harry Langdon can be counted among the many famous names who, according to Joe Laurie, Jr., in *Vaudeville: From the Honky-Tonks to the Palace*, began their careers playing the Western Time as beginners, then graduated to the Orpheum circuit, and eventually played the New York Palace.

Nearly all of the scores of reviews of Langdon's vaudeville act that appear from 1906 to 1923 are good ones; most are enthusiastic. *Billboard* reported in 1906 that the Langdons "are booked solid for the season," and "the act is making a hit everywhere."[25] The *New York Telegraph* reported and predicted in 1911 that the Langdons' "skit has been a riotous laugh from its first presentation and bids fair to obtain for itself a special niche in the hall of vaudeville comedy fame."[26] "Johnny's New Car" is described in a *Variety* review of July 1916, as "a comedy act that will stand out in any company,"[27] and, in the same month, in a *Billboard* review of the bill at the

New York Palace, as "one of the funniest acts in present-day vaudeville."[28] In 1920, "Johnny's New Car" was still being considered by *Variety* "the strongest little comedy offering in vaudeville,"[29] and, in fulfillment of the *Telegraph* prophecy, was called a "vaudeville classic" in another *Variety* review of that year.[30] In 1922, "Johnny's New Car" was cited by *Variety* as "one of vaudeville's best comedy acts."[31]

Contrary to the allegations of Sennett and Capra, the Langdons had attained the status of a top "standard act" on the big-time Keith and Orpheum circuits at least as early as 1911, and were booked regularly thereafter into the largest and most prestigious Keith and Orpheum houses, east and west: the Palace in New York, the Majestic in Chicago, and the Orpheums in Los Angeles and San Francisco, to name the top few houses. The Majestic in Chicago, the first million-dollar vaudeville theater, was the beautiful showcase theater of the Orpheum circuit. Keith's New York Palace was, in the words of Douglas Gilbert in *American Vaudeville: Its Life and Times,* "the premier vaudeville house of America." The Palace's bill was published weekly in the center columns in *Billboard* with each act listed in order of appearance and reviewed under the heading "The Topmost Rung. The Palace. Here Genius not Birth your Rank insures," or "B. F. Keith's Palace Theater. When you have played the Palace, you have 'made Broadway'."

The "standard act" in vaudeville was an act that had proven itself to be "surefire" in fulfilling whatever function, in terms of entertaining an audience, it was designed by its creators to serve and whatever purpose it was obliged to serve by its place in the rigidly formalized hierarchy of a vaudeville bill. The Langdons immediately established themselves at third on a standard vaudeville bill of eight acts. Bills occasionally contained more than eight acts, in which case the Langdons would go on fourth of nine, fifth of ten, or sixth of eleven. An act that occupied "Number Three" was usually a comedy act which could be depended upon to place the audience in a good humor early and warm up the house for the acts to come.

The reviews testify that Langdon's sketch served its purpose well. It was said of the Langdons in "A Night on the Boulevard" that they "are well nigh perpetual laugh-makers,"[32] and of the sketch in another review, that it "is always sure of enough laughs."[33] "Johnny's New Car" was called "a guaranteed laugh producer,"[34] and "one of the surest skits of years."[35]

The good standard acts were the second echelon of the vaudeville elite, and there were few headliners. The Langdons were a highly paid and popular act, and they were always working—the true sign of success among vaudevillians themselves. At the time Langdon left vaudeville to enter films, his act was earning fifteen hundred dollars a week.[36] By comparison, as noted by Douglas Gilbert, "the highest salaries in vaudeville's golden age averaged $2,500 to $4,000 a week for two shows a day. These were paid only to the great box office draws."[37] So much for Sennett's claim that Langdon came to him with no money.

Majestic Theatre
CHICAGO

FIRE NOTICE
Look around now, choose the nearest exit to your seat, and in case of disturbance of any kind, to avoid the dangers of panic, WALK (do not run) to that exit)

WEEK BEGINNING MONDAY MATINEE
JUNE 2, 1919

A
KINOGRAMS
The "Newest News" Weekly

B
BRENGK'S BRONZE STATUE HORSE
Art in Bronze
SUBJECTS
1—The Golden Steed
2—Separation
3—The Golden Horse in Its Famous Camelstretch
4—Idyll
5—At the Fountain
6—Awakening
7—The Horse of Liberty

C
"THE GIRL FROM MILWAUKEE"
A Remarkable Vocalist

D
HARRY LANGDON
With Rose and Cecil
in
"JOHNNY'S NEW CAR"

E
Geo. ROCKWELL & FOX—Al
Two Noble Nuts
The Ocean of Nonsense

Program Continued on Second Page Following

The first page of the program of the vaudeville bill at the Orpheum circuit's famous Majestic Theatre in Chicago, 2 June 1919. (Courtesy of New York Public Library)

Sennett's claim that Langdon came to the Sennett studio with no fame is equally inaccurate. It was said quite early of the Langdons in a *Billboard* review of a show at Chicago's Majestic Theater in 1913, "This team of fun makers is well and favorably known wherever there is good vaudevil [*sic*]."[38] As early as 1907, the *Elkhart,* Indiana, *Truth* referred to the Langdons' "Famous Automobile Specialty" in an announcement of their appearance in a musical comedy review called *The Show Girl*.[39] When, in 1920, Langdon took his act to Broadway and on tour in the musical comedy review, *Jim Jam Jems, Billboard* featured an article headlined, "Langdon to Leave Vaudeville," in which Langdon is referred to as "one of vaudeville's best-known performers."[40] References to Langdon's automobile act in the reviews of that show are invariably preceded by the adjective "well-known." In fact, in 1923, the year in which Langdon signed his contract with Mack Sennett, Harry Langdon was, according to a *Billboard* writer, "Harry Langdon, the famous comedian."[41] It is also either suggested or stated in a number of other reviews in *Billboard* and *Variety* that Harry Langdon was a particular favorite of the sophisticated and discriminating vaudeville audiences at the top two houses in the country: the Palace in New York, where he was always greeted with a warm welcome by a regular group of fans, and the Majestic in Chicago.[42]

Many big-time standard acts, including Langdon's, regularly played the smaller cities of the small- and medium-time circuits as headliners. For instance, in 1912, the Langdons headlined at the Orpheum in Reading, Pennsylvania, one of a chain of eastern small-time "Family Theaters" booked by the Keith-Albee United Booking Office that Langdon played at this time. He played the 1917–1918 season as a headliner on the Pantages west coast circuit in such cities as Seattle, Spokane, and Vancouver, British Columbia. However, before Langdon ended his career in vaudeville, he had reached the pinnacle of success as a vaudeville performer—appearing as a headliner at a big-city house of a big-time circuit. Langdon was co-billed with several other acts as the headline attraction at the Palace in New York in 1921 and at the Orpheum in San Francisco in 1923.

Thus, a year or so before he signed a contract for feature films with First National and just prior to signing a contract with Mack Sennett in fall of 1923, Langdon was headlining in big-time vaudeville, not playing the honky-tonks. The Sennett contract provided that Langdon was "to be cast as the Principal Comedian . . . and that no other Comic will be permitted to play a principal part," that Langdon's name would be "featured individually in large type in all billing," and that Langdon would eventually be paid two thousand dollars a week.[43] The terms of this contract confirm the other evidence cited of Langdon's true stature as a comic artist at the time of his entry into motion picture comedies.

Some critics have referred to Langdon's almost exclusive devotion to a single act during his seventeen-year vaudeville career and to the very specialized nature of Langdon's performance in films as evidence of the

Notes for Harry Langdon's original contract with Mack Sennett Comedies, written by J. A. Waldron, Sennett's general manager. (Courtesy of Academy of Motion Picture Arts and Sciences)

limited range of his skill and imagination. As a graduate of a ten-year apprenticeship in very nearly every other form of American popular entertainment, which proliferated in greatest number and variety during the period of Langdon's participation, Harry Langdon was indeed possessed of the technical virtuosity and extraordinary versatility that is almost never displayed in his films.

Between the ages of twelve and twenty-one (the age at which Langdon entered vaudeville), Harry Langdon was a performer in medicine shows, circus, minstrel shows, traveling stock, "rep" and tent shows (including "ten-twent'-thirt'" melodrama, a genre of cheap popular theater), and burlesque (or "variety" as burlesque was also known during this period).

Versatility was a standard qualification for a performer in any American popular entertainment. This requirement was dictated by the very nature of each of these various forms. Each form of popular entertainment was defined by its own set of conventions that govern its overall structure and component parts. In practice, these conventions served to provide a format for great diversity within a more or less rigidly formalized structure.

Thus, the format of most popular entertainments at around the turn of the century, the period of Langdon's apprenticeship, required the performer to "double." This meant that the circus clown, who, like every performer who worked in the ring, was an acrobat, must also "double in brass" in the band. In the smaller companies, especially in traveling medicine and tent shows, "doubling" actually meant "tripling" or even "quadrupling." The hero, or "blue-shirt lead," of a tent-show melodrama might also perform a song and dance specialty number in the entr'acte between the second and third acts, design and construct props and scenery, and play an instrument in the preshow and aftershow concerts by the orchestra (otherwise known as the cast).

The conditions of presentation that were typical of these popular entertainments also demanded remarkable versatility of the individual performer. Some companies in some forms of popular entertainment sometimes played one-night stands, though generally, most traveling shows played no less than a week in a single small town to a single audience. Sometimes, in medicine shows, for example, the performer played two or three different shows a night for a week. Whatever "business" he did, he had to be able to "change for a week," or "change strong for ten nights." Early "variety" entertainment was a "grind show," or ten to fifteen shows a night. Considering the number of skills that were required of a performer in a single show in any one of those popular entertainments in which Harry Langdon participated, and the number of shows presented in a week, it may be assumed that, as a popular entertainer, Langdon must have had a very large repertoire.

Langdon never had formal training in any of his several talents. His education was gained on the road, and each of the many kinds of companies with which he played was a school in some new "business" or skill. By the time Langdon began his vaudeville career, he had cultivated an extensive and diversified repertoire as comedian, musician, singer, dancer, acrobat, equilibrist, and "lightning sketch artist." Much of what Langdon could do, he had learned to do in his first experience as a professional entertainer—in medicine shows.

As a medicine-show entertainer, Langdon sang comic songs; danced the soft-shoe and jigs; played the banjo; did the currently popular comic impersonations of Dutchman and rube and played the stock roles of melodrama; joked and wisecracked; performed in all the traditional comic sketches that were known by heart and passed on by word of mouth by comics in medicine shows, minstrel shows, burlesque, and vaudeville alike; did acrobatic specialties of all kinds; and did a "lightning sketch artist" routine in which he cartooned caricatures of people in the crowd as the rest of the audience watched, and then distributed them to the delighted subjects. Blackface entertainment prevailed in medicine-show performances and Langdon, therefore, performed originally in blackface. The blackface specialty was common at the time to most of the popular entertainment forms in which Langdon participated—circus, minstrel shows, burlesque, and vaudeville—and predominated in most of these.

Cartoons by Harry Langdon from publicity material for Hal Roach Comedies.

As a burlesque comedian, Langdon's earliest routines were blackface musical and balancing specialties. In one of these, he performed while sitting in a chair that he balanced on two beer bottles which supported the chair's rear legs. Langdon, the chair, and the two beer bottles were supported by a column of two more chairs and two tables, each of which rested upon four beer bottles. Another of Langdon's equilibristic stunts was called a "leaning act." With his feet planted firmly, Langdon swayed his body from side to side, leaning so far to each side that it appeared to the audience as if he were defying gravity, at which point he bobbed back upright and leaned to the other side.

Langdon's musical specialties included songs and dances. He could also play nearly every musical instrument proficiently by ear. As a burlesque comic from approximately 1903 to 1905, Langdon can be counted among the hundreds of single men in blackface doing acrobatic or musical specialties who populated variety and vaudeville stages at that time.

Langdon later sublimated the diversity and technical expertise as a performer that he had attained during his extensive early experience as a popular entertainer in order to devote himself to a new and different comic conception. This clearly represents a deliberate artistic decision on

Langdon's part. Langdon abandoned technical virtuosity for a type of performance that can best be described as reductive in nature. Not only is it a type of performance that is without "attractions," but also the style of mime he adopted was one distinguished by a lack of mimetic specificity. (Within the context of this study, the term "attraction" is intended as it originated in circus: as a display of technical expertise.)

Sometime in 1905, Langdon abandoned the blackface persona of his specialty act for the whiteface mask of the new mime characterization by which he would become known in vaudeville and film. At the same time, Langdon abandoned the space of the specialty, or working "in one," to work "in four," or full stage. Working "in one" refers to performing in the shallowest stage space before a set or drop in the first entrance behind the

Harry takes a shower and, instead, showers himself with soot from a makeshift chimney in *Three's a Crowd*. (Courtesy of Gladys McConnell)

proscenium. Working "in two" is performing in a somewhat less shallow stage space that is demarcated by the second entrance behind the proscenium. Working "in three" is performing at a stage depth equivalent to the third entrance. This adoption by Langdon of a new kind of space in which to work in conjunction with his adoption of a new comic persona and style of performance suggests that Langdon conceived of a direct relation between his new comic persona and style of performance, and the space in which this persona and performance were to be presented.

The significance to Langdon of the space in which he worked onstage is also evident in all the documentary information available on Langdon's vaudeville sketch. Landon utilized the entire available stage space, working now "in four" or "in full," in which to perform his extended comic "take 'ems" in response to his human antagonists and the ever more aggressive trick auto. He also employed the illusion of a deeply recessive space, created by a painted drop, as a background for his performance. Rather than use the utility drops with which every vaudeville theater was equipped, as most touring comedy sketch artists did, Langdon carried his own set, which he designed himself to the particular specifications his act required.

This was a most elaborate set, not only according to the standards of the comedy sketch but according to the standards of any act in vaudeville. It was a feature of Langdon's act as distinctive, well known, and appreciated by vaudeville audiences as were his "inimitable" comic impersonation and pantomime style. "A Night on the Boulevard," the first version of Langdon's sketch, is named for the set.

The act opened prior to Langdon's entrance when the curtain was raised to reveal a painted drop dominated by a wide boulevard that was lined on both sides with rows of town houses, uniformly arranged trees, and street lamps. The street lamps glowed by electrical illumination from behind the drop. The boulevard scene was painted by Langdon according to classical Renaissance perspective. It created the illusion, as one impressed reviewer described it in *Billboard* in 1916, of "the boulevard lights disappearing in the distance."[44]

The staging of Langdon's vaudeville act was commented upon by reviewers as often as they remarked on his comic characterization and the style of his performance. According to these reviews, mise-en-scène—in this context, placement of actors and props onstage and scenic design; lighting and mechanical effects; timing of action, of curtain, and of action and curtain together—was an important and effective feature of Langdon's act. Langdon's vaudeville performances, as they are described in those reviews, not only demonstrate Langdon's interest in mise-en-scène but also display ingenuity and expertise in stagecraft on Langdon's part as metteur-en-scène.

The reviews indicate, for example, that Langdon's boulevard drop and his clever use of it provided a most effective opening to his act. The audience was given sufficient opportunity to appreciate the setting and to express its appreciation. According to the reviews, the set itself "was applauded as soon as the rising curtain disclosed it to view,"[45] and reliably got the Langdons a hand before the act even started.[46] When, after several moments, Langdon made his entrance on stage in the sputtering, bucking, backfiring car, he was received with a "big laugh," for which, as one observer noted in *Billboard,* "the boulevard setting and impressive opening paved the way."[47] Advertisements for Langdon's act in the trade papers guaranteed, "Always a Reception at the Start."

Perhaps owing to the popular and critical success of his "artistic" opening, Langdon conceived a yet more sophisticated visual effect that was added as the finale to Langdon's act by the time the sketch was called "Johnny's New Car." A second drop was now used by Langdon in a curtain call in which Langdon was sent offstage to an enthusiastic expression of appreciation by the audience equal to that which greeted the act when the curtain rose on the boulevard set.

After the finish of Langdon's sketch, the stage was made dim and the curtain raised again to reveal what appeared to be a road winding toward the horizon. Through a clever manipulation of lighting effects from behind the translucent drop, Langdon created the illusion of the roadster slowly making its way along the winding highway and eventually disappearing into the distance. The vehicle's path was traced by a final explosive backfire with which the car has the last word, and by its two glowing taillights, which gradually grow smaller and dimmer, and finally vanish, leaving a darkened stage.

This combination of lighting and scenic effects to simulate the slow movement of the auto into a recessive space much greater than the actual depth of the full stage was employed by Langdon as a rhythmic device. It was contrived by Langdon to enhance the audience's impression of the slow rhythm of his mime and movement (with which Langdon's comic style had, by this time, already become identified) through manipulation of spatial and temporal properties specific to theatrical mise-en-scène.

The way in which these particular theatrical effects are combined in Langdon's curtain call to serve a rhythmic function is not unlike the way in which certain elements specific to filmic mise-en-scène—the long take and the slow fade-out—often function in the films in which Langdon appears. The rhythmic structure of these films conforms to the rhythm of Langdon's performance. This notion, and the notion of a relation between the spatial proportions of individual shots and the rhythm of Langdon's performance, are the subjects of chapter 7. Langdon's film comedies all display a basic cinematic style that preserves the same conditions of spatial and temporal unity under which Langdon worked on stage.

The film style that characterizes all of Langdon's silent comedies emerged shortly after Langdon's entry into films at Mack Sennett's studio. In the Sennett films in which he is featured, Langdon influenced, in fact significantly altered, the Sennett comedy style of broad farce, fast-paced

A Sennett publicity photo captioned: "Harry Langdon is a disciple of tradition. He insists upon occupying the old dressing room at the Mack Sennett Studio which served Charlie Chaplin, Harold Lloyd, Gloria Swanson, and many other screen celebrities who began their careers on the old comedy lot." (Courtesy of Academy of Motion Picture Arts and Sciences)

action, and slapstick violence and the cinematic style that has become identified with Keystone comedies. In Langdon's films, cinematic treatment conforms to the style of performance that Langdon brought with him when he entered film after a twenty-year career as a comic performer on the vaudeville stage.

Although the accuracy of some of Mack Sennett's later comments concerning Langdon is questionable, Sennett is not to be denied full credit for recognizing Langdon's talent and the certainty of Langdon's success in motion pictures. From the start, Sennett had "picked him for a sure thing," according to an August 1928 interview with Sennett by Theodore Dreiser in *Photoplay*. Langdon was actually first "discovered" by producer Sol Lesser, from whom Sennett purchased Langdon's contract as well as several short comedy films featuring Langdon that had already been produced. At least two of these films produced by Lesser's Principal Pictures Corporation prior to Langdon's association with the Sennett studio, *Horace Greeley, Jr.* and *The White Wing's Bride,* were eventually released by Sennett through Pathé in 1925. The Lesser films may also have included the previously mentioned film of Langdon's vaudeville act that Frank Capra describes in his autobiography as one which was shown to Sennett's staff of writers and directors on Langdon's acquisition as a contract comedian. The Lesser films would have been made at some time from May to September 1923.

Sennett respected Langdon as an artist as he had no other performer, except Chaplin, who came to work at his studio. In his *Photoplay* interview, Sennett told Dreiser that he thought Langdon was a greater artist than Chaplin. Elsewhere in the interview, Sennett is quoted as saying that of all of the stars who worked for him, Langdon was "the greatest of them all." Sennett also says in that interview that he realized that, like Chaplin, Langdon had to work alone. As a result, Langdon bore the distinction, shared at Sennett's studio with Chaplin alone, of having been given free rein by Sennett. The Langdon unit at the Sennett studio operated on the basis of relative artistic autonomy. Sennett was so convinced of Langdon's talent and skill that Langdon was granted this autonomy upon entry, whereas Chaplin earned his during the first half of his first year at Sennett's studio.

Langdon's first two two-reelers at Sennett's, *Smile Please* and *Picking Peaches*, were provided for by Langdon's first, probationary contract and shot as a trial run for expediency from scenarios that had already been prepared. *Smile Please* was written for Harry Gribbon, and *Picking Peaches* was an already prepared story with the role of "the Comic" yet to be assigned. Except in these first two films, Langdon's material was specially prepared for him with story lines and gags tailored to his own comic style.

By the time of Langdon's eighth two-reeler, *The Luck of the Foolish,* the team of Harry Edwards as director and Frank Capra and Arthur Ripley as gag writers had solidified and was assigned by Sennett to the Langdon comedies. It is clear from the films that followed that both Capra and Ripley had a certain affinity for Langdon's, certainly by Sennett standards, rather eccentric comedy style. They effectively screened out of the scenarios the sort of violent and fast-paced action that seems so inappropriate in the earliest Langdon comedies for Sennett. Soon they began inventing story lines with a special regard for Langdon's unique comic persona

Langdon with Alberta Vaughn in *Picking Peaches*, his first Sennett release.

and began to include situations that, obviously, were specifically designed as opportunities in which Langdon might display his peculiar brand of pantomime to best advantage. Some examples from the scenarios are given in the following pages. Others are the frequently used gag situations in which Harry is dazed by a blow or a kiss or is drunk or drugged, which provided a premise for Langdon to present the pantomimed transitions between being conscious and being unconscious in which he specialized.

Sennett not only recognized, respected, and encouraged Langdon's individual style, but as a true showman, he exploited the "different" nature of Langdon's comedy and made much of Langdon's physically restrained and slow-paced comic style as compared to the more familiar Sennett slapstick style in publicity releases for forthcoming Langdon films. The draft of a press sheet publicizing *Picking Peaches,* Langdon's second Sennett production and the first to be released, is headed, "Chaplin Competitor Discovered." The press sheet for Langdon's third production, *Shanghaied Lovers,* claims,

> Mack Sennett, always on the alert for new types and faces, was immediately impressed with Harry Langdon's appearance while he was

Langdon out of costume in a Mack Sennett publicity portrait. (Courtesy of Academy of Motion Picture Arts and Sciences)

playing the Orpheum Circuit in their Los Angeles theatre. What most attracted the Comedy King was the positive comedy type possessed by Langdon. His easy manner in saying things with his eyes, or a mere shrug of the shoulders or tilting of his head. His walk is even something to laugh at. . . .

Under his present contract with Mack Sennett, Langdon will appear in a series of comedies specially written to suit his individual and inimitable personality. The pictures he will appear in will favor situations of humor rather than the broad, socalled [sic] slapstick gags.

Another press sheet for *Shanghaied Lovers* includes comments from supervising director Dick Jones, who is quoted as saying,

> In my opinion, Harry Langdon is one of the greatest exponents of pantomime the screen has introduced for a long time. He is naturalness itself, and a born comedian. He doesn't have to try to be funny in his actions nor does he resort to the usual "mugging" tactics so noticeable in the work of other actors.

A press sheet for *His New Mama,* Langdon's sixth film for Sennett, announces, "Harry Langdon is working under the personal supervision of Mack Sennett, who has had specially written stories prepared for him, stories in which his individual personality will be given ample opportunity." In it, Langdon is called "a real artist."

It is doubtful whether Mack Sennett, Frank Capra, Arthur Ripley, or Harry Edwards, if they had tried, could have imposed on Langdon, a professional performer for almost thirty years, twenty of which were spent performing and polishing a single act, any comic characterization or style that was, by then, not his own. Nor did they actually try to alter the comic persona and style of performance Langdon brought to film. In fact, no one ever succeeded in doing so (except perhaps in those first two Sennett films in which Langdon was given material prepared for other comedians).

In their autobiographies, both Sennett and Capra grant that Langdon arrived at the Sennett studio with a finely finished and distinctive comic style. Capra notes, "Langdon himself was a virtuoso of flitting, hesitant motions," and acknowledges that Langdon was a "great artist—whose art was the very essence of slow, slow pantomime."[48] Sennett describes Langdon's work in the Sennett films as though those performances were reflex actions to the veteran performer: "He had his routines well learned in vaudeville, and he could do them on demand."[49]

Once Langdon was onstage or in front of a camera, his slow-witted, slow-moving comic persona became, in effect, a second nature to him. Hal Roach was one who tried as producer and in one film as director in the somewhat different medium and milieu of early sound comedy shorts to alter Langdon's manner of performing before the camera. He discovered to his great frustration what Sennett must have understood—that it was useless to do otherwise than grant Langdon his freedom as performer. Roach recalled in a 1974 interview:

> everybody, at least in my studio, everybody did everything they could to get him to move faster. He would rehearse a scene exactly the way you wanted him to play it. Great! And as soon as you started the camera it was like slow motion. He slowed right down to a walk in the thing. . . .
> . . . I directed a picture myself because I thought it was the director's fault, and I couldn't move him any faster than they could. . . . The

Langdon as Pierrot in a Mack Sennett publicity portrait. (Courtesy of Academy of Motion Picture Arts and Sciences)

picture I directed was no better than anybody else directed because you finally get discouraged. . . . The hell of it was you could argue and it didn't do him any good. No matter what you said, he agreed with everything you said and he'd go right back and do it over again."[50]

Even in Langdon's last years when he was making comedy shorts for Columbia in which he had little interest other than that of earning a living, he still imposed his own style on these films. Edward Bernds, who was a writer on some of Langdon's last two-reel comedies at Columbia, has commented, "the moment you tried to speed him up and make an ordinary two-reel comic out of him, you were dead. He wasn't funny unless he could pace himself."[51]

The primary qualities of Langdon's vaudeville performance—physical subtlety and very slow pace—were practically antithetical to the Sennett style of broad farce and fast-paced slapstick, a style that was also firmly established at the time of Langdon's first Sennett comedy in 1924. Comparing Langdon's comedies with those of other Sennett comedians is ample indication of the freedom granted to Langdon as featured comedian and is evidence of the consequent subordination of the Mack Sennett comic tradition to the actually longer-standing personal comic tradition of Harry Langdon. Langdon's films are comedies of an entirely different nature in nearly every respect—comic situations and construction, gags, pace, and filmic treatment—from contemporary Sennett comedies with other comedians. Langdon's comedies by no means excluded the staple situations of broad farce and physical comedy that fortified all the Sennett scenarios. However, their elaboration by Langdon amounts to an outright reversal of many of those conventions that collectively constitute the Keystone comedy tradition.

Good examples of this are Langdon's unconventional responses in conventional comic situations of aggression and violence. As aggressor, Harry is merely ineffectual and does not instigate the customary boisterous imbroglio. Langdon's responses as the object of aggression are also atypical. There is, for instance, no such thing as a chase in Langdon's films, perhaps the single best-known trademark of Keystone comedy, because Harry doesn't pursue and doesn't know enough to run away when he is threatened or pursued.

The comic reaction or "take 'em" is another staple feature of the slapstick tradition as practiced and perfected at Sennett's studio. This includes a variety of exaggerated reactions to physical assault and other forms of aggression such as sexual advances. A common gag situation in Sennett two-reelers as it might appear in the scenario is: "Vamp plants a hot smacker. Comic takes it," or "Comic takes it big." The comic might extend the direction to "take it big" to the extremes of rolling his eyeballs around in their sockets as his bow tie spins and steam shoots out of his ears, photographed, of course, in close-up and undercranked. Or, directed to "take" a blow "big," the comic might extend the take 'em to the extreme of the "hundred-and-eight," the ultimate pratfall. In this stunt, the comic flips over backward and lands on the nape of his neck. His body thus articulates an arc of a hundred and eighty degrees.

All the customary provocations are to be found in Langdon's Sennett comedies and in later Langdon films. However, Langdon's answer to the comic take 'em in these stock situations takes the form of what has been called his "vacant stare" and "slow take 'em." The slow take 'em is Langdon's trademark, and the vacant stare is Langdon's slow take 'em in its most refined form. Very much unlike the "big" comic take described previously, Langdon's slow take 'em in its several forms involves the temporal extenuation of a blank expression or a wide-eyed stare. This may or may not be

From *The Cat's Meow*, a Sennett two-reeler. (Courtesy of Edward Finney)

punctuated at some point in its duration by a single blink of the eyes, which may be followed after a discernible pause by a second blink.

Some of Harry's atypical reactions to typical provocations that can be seen in Langdon's Sennett comedies are the following. When the sultry vamp beckons from her balcony to Harry to come to her in *Lucky Stars*, Harry's reaction is to look away from her toward the camera, stick his index finger into his mouth and blink. Harry, the simple soldier in *Soldier Man*, gazes placidly into the camera while the beautiful queen kisses him in her sumptuous boudoir and while her hand, holding a knife with which she intended to stab him, falls limp at her side. In *Saturday Afternoon*, his wife moves toward him and Harry finally realizes that she has been listening to him pretending to tell her off. He reacts by staring wide-eyed toward the camera, shifting his glance once in his wife's direction, and then quickly realigning his eyeballs straight ahead.

As a waiter in *Boobs in the Wood*, Harry spills a lampful of kerosene into the soup. The heavy, a big, mean-looking lumberjack, orders a bowl of soup. Harry looks at him and blinks, then looks toward the camera and blinks, then looks back at the heavy. Harry's cabin-mate aboard ship in *The Sea Squawk* is scrawling a note and asks Harry, "How do you spell 'murder'?" Harry replies by looking at him wide-eyed and then nodding, barely, that he doesn't know either. In *Saturday Afternoon,* Harry plops down into the rumble seat of his pal's car, then opens his eyes wide and blinks once as he reaches beneath him and extracts an oil applicator can with a long, pointy spout. Harry blinks once more as he holds up the can to look at it, then blinks again while he sets it down gently onto the rear fender. He continues looking at the offending object as the car pulls away out of the frame.

Harry's unconventional response to a blow on the head and other conventional kinds of direct physical assault, hostile or sexual, may be a moment of total immobility after which he slowly and gently lowers himself from standing to sitting position or else curls up comfortably into fetal position, as in a brawl between Harry, his pal Vernon, their dates, and the girls' two jealous boyfriends in *Saturday Afternoon.* In this most atypical Mack Sennett free-for-all, Harry is blasted in the ear with an automobile horn, punches himself in the nose, is punched in the nose by one of the girls' boyfriends, is hit squarely on the head with the head of a hammer, is punched squarely on the jaw by one of the surly boyfriends, and never takes a pratfall. In *Feet of Mud,* Harry is hit on the head with a brick that is tossed out an overhead window during one of those bothersome tong wars that plagued film comedians in the 1920s. He blinks, sways a bit as his eyelids fluctuate between open and closed, and rests himself against a column in a Chinatown facade. After the queen in *Soldier Man* kisses Harry a second time and then collapses to the floor at his feet, Harry curls up on her bed for a nap.

Other times, instead of the pratfall that is customary in such situations, Harry's body stiffens momentarily and he simply stands still. This is usually accompanied by some form of his vacant facial expression. This is the case in *The Sea Squawk* when Harry is bitten by a little monkey that gets inside his dress while he dances disguised in drag in the ship's ballroom. Another occurs in *Remember When* when Harry gets a swift kick in the pants from a husky roustabout and stands suddenly upright, blinks, and walks on.

The most significant and obvious distinction between Langdon's films and other Sennett comedies of the same period is that of pace. By the purely quantitative measure of gags-per-minute, Langdon can be seen to have dragged out less material longer than any other comedian of the time, commonly milking a gag far beyond what was then and is generally considered to be acceptably balanced comic timing. In *Feet of Mud,* there is a comic situation in which Harry tries to escape from hostile Chinese by hiding behind a table and leaning his chin on the table in order to disguise himself as one of a number of idol masks lined up there. The gag is based on the necessity for Harry to remain as still as one of the ceremonial heads in order not to be detected after a smoldering pot of narcotic incense is placed under his nose. This single, simple gag situation is sustained for a long time while Harry is seen in a single medium close-up, blinking and moving his eyes first down to the table, then right, then left, then twitching his nose, then twitching his mouth, without ever moving his head. Then Harry's eyelids droop as he starts to succumb to the effects of the drug, and pop open again as he looks around him wide-eyed.

There is a long and slow-paced routine in *Fiddlesticks,* a Sennett two-reeler, of Harry washing in the morning after waking that contains no gags whatever. In two shots of relatively long duration, Harry stands at the washstand pouring water over his hands, gently dabbing water under his chin, and cleaning his ear with his little finger. Then he looks around for a towel and can't find one. In the next shot he goes to the window and stands there while the breeze dries first his hands, then behind his ears, and then his neck. Harry then wipes under his chin with his hands, pulls back his ears again, then stands awhile holding his jacket open—first the front and then the sides—to ventilate his underarms.

In *Remember When,* after carrying around an active beehive on the end of his hobo stick for a while, Harry sits down on a stump and sees that he's picked up something along his way. In several long takes, punctuated with one insert close-up of Harry's hand reaching into the hive, Harry holds the hive and rolls it around in his hands as he casually examines it. Not until one of the bees gets inside Harry's coat is the beehive anything more than a minor annoyance to him. This comic situation, measured in terms of screen time, concerns Harry's ignorance and gradual discovery that what he's been carrying around and is holding in his lap is a live beehive, much more so than it is concerned with Harry's reactions when he is finally stung. This type of gag is very common in the films of other comedians of this period, but the priorities are normally reversed in other films to emphasize the comic's reaction rather than his naiveté.

Sennett and the staff and crew assigned by him to Langdon realized that the slow pace of Langdon's performance was an essential feature of his comic style and persona. Not only was Langdon not hurried, to which fact the films, Mack Sennett, and Frank Capra attest, but the inimitable rhythm of Keystone comedy was abandoned almost immediately in Langdon's Sennett comedies in favor of the very different rhythm of Langdon's own performance. Rather than the delirious cutting and undercranking that was customarily employed to accentuate the frantic activity of other Sennett comedians, one finds in the Sennett two- and three-reelers featuring Langdon, long takes that conform to Langdon's slow take 'em. On at least one occasion, the sequence of Harry's dazed response to a French girl's kiss in *All Night Long,* Langdon's performance is photographed redundantly in slow motion.

Both Sennett and Capra claim in their autobiographies that Langdon was not qualified emotionally or intellectually to have participated in originating and sustaining the comic characterization that Capra and Ripley had created for him. Yet both contradict themselves by also conceding that Langdon's screen character was somehow derived by Capra from, or based upon, the unique pantomimic abilities in which Langdon had specialized in vaudeville, and that Langdon freely demonstrated his art in film vehicles specifically designed for that purpose. Though inconsistent with other statements by them, these concessions by Sennett and Capra provide a plausible explanation of the exceptional nature of the Langdon comedies for Mack Sennett.

Concerning his experience as the producer of those films, Sennett says of Langdon in *King of Comedy*:

> Like Charlie Chaplin, you had to let him take his time and go through his motions. His twitters and hesitations built up a ridiculous but sympathetic little character. It was difficult at first for us to know how to use Langdon, accustomed as we were to firing the gags and the falls at the audience as fast as possible, but as new talent arrived, we found ways to screen it and cope with it. . . .
>
> Like Charlie, Harry was a slow starter. Even after we learned how to use him—I mean, saw what his essential character was for screen purposes—we had to give him a hundred feet of film or so to play around in, do little bits of business, and introduce himself.[52]

Despite the inconsistencies in the accounts of Sennett and Capra, it is not the intention of this study to disregard the considerable contributions of Capra and Ripley. Their influence on Langdon's two- and three-reelers at Sennett's after their appointment as his chief writers can be easily recognized and appreciated. However, examination of those scenarios wherein Langdon's comic persona is supposed to have been "invented" by Capra and Ripley confirms precisely what Sennett has said about providing Langdon the opportunity to go through his own routines. Each of these written continuities is punched full of holes to be filled in by Langdon on the set or on location. In fact, most of Langdon's most extenuated routines in the Sennett films must have been improvised, as they are not worked out in the scenarios or synopses.

In the scenario of *Shanghaied Lovers,* Harry is discovered "unconscious in a bunk" after being knocked out and shanghaied. The scenario continues, "Langdon comes to and gets over that he is feeling pretty rocky." The continuity for *His New Mama* outlines the following situation: "Inside the house Harry's father introduces him to the woman who is to be his stepmother and Madeline [Hurlock] gives Harry a kiss. It is not the kiss of a mother and both Harry and the old man notice this. Harry takes it in his own way." In the next scene, Harry's father gives a Christmas Eve party to introduce his future wife to the neighbors. It is described in the scenario as, "a typical small town party, designed to give Harry a chance to do a funny

A Mack Sennett publicity shot. (Courtesy of Academy of Motion Picture Arts and Sciences)

little dance with Madeline." In *The Hansom Cabman* synopsis, Harry shares a jail cell with a fellow who thinks he's Napoleon and sees imaginary reptiles. In this scene, according to the synopsis, "Harry plays around with him awhile, pretending to catch bigger and bigger reptiles than Napoleon catches."

The *Sea Squawk* scenario calls for a shipboard engagement party in which "the women all gather about Langdon to kiss him and Harry has a chance for some funny shots as the different homely looking women insist on kissing him." There is also written into the original scenario of *The Sea Squawk*, although this does not appear in the film, an opportunity for Langdon to do some of the business he used in the golfing sketch from "After the Ball."

One of several opportunities for Langdon to improvise that are found in the initial version of the *Remember When* story occurs when the sheriff catches up with Harry, who has stolen some chickens. "There is business here with chickens cackling and moving about under Harry's coat, with Harry trying to pass it off by various means." Then Harry meets the owner of a circus. "Harry does his various little tricks to convince [Vernon] Dent that he has the ability to become a clown or a performer with the circus." Harry gets a job as a stake driver and the scenario provides for "a short routine of business with this crew and Harry." The next scene calls for Harry to lead the circus parade with "a short routine of business here with the baton."

It is very likely, as Sennett and Capra have said of Langdon, that he usually didn't have the vaguest notion of what his screen stories were about, or awareness of or interest in such things as narrative continuity or integrity of characterization. Yet this seeming disregard on Langdon's part for narrative values may also be interpreted as further evidence of the extent to which Langdon's own comic style was the formative influence on his comedies for Mack Sennett and his subsequent silent films. Though Langdon's vaudeville act was, as a comedy sketch, based upon a narrative format, Langdon was accustomed to working within the standard twenty minutes allotted each act on a vaudeville bill. This twenty minutes or less included at least one song by Langdon's wife and the specially staged curtain call. This left only enough time for Langdon to establish a single, simple situation as the premise for his performance.

Several reviews of "Johnny's New Car" suggest that, even within the limited time period, narrative construction was not one of Langdon's strong points. One reviewer described "Johnny's New Car" in *Billboard* as follows: "The car containing Johnny and his lady friend rolls out on the stage and very conveniently breaks down in front of a cafe. This furnishes the plot for the comedy."[53] Another said of it in *Variety*, "It runs along to semi-situations without any particular plot, but the collection is well-pieced and makes a fine comedy vehicle."[54] In the final version of the act, "After the Ball," Langdon actually broke up his sketch into three "scenes" with individual titles that were set in different locations, employed different stage settings, and the curtain rose and fell on each of these.

Even Langdon's feature-length comedies are essentially nothing more than a loosely linked succession of simple, though sometimes greatly extenuated situations. *The Strong Man* is a film in which this certainly is the case. It is also the film upon which Capra's influence should have been the greatest of any of the Langdon comedies because this is the only one of Langdon's films that Capra, in addition to contributing to the story, also directed in its entirety. It is also a film that may justifiably be construed, at the level of narrative and dramatic construction, to be prototypical of Capra's later work as director. "Cloverdale," the small, peaceful country town in *The Strong Man* that is overrun by bootleggers, and the struggle between the good people of the town, led by Parson Brown, and the wicked city people are story elements that have much in common with certain story elements in Capra's 1946 film, *It's a Wonderful Life*. The same moral polarization differentiates the two versions of George Bailey's small home town that are presented in this later film. The first version is the town as it is; the second is the same town corrupted and transformed by evil influences as it is seen in George Bailey's fantasy visit to the town as it would have been had he never been born.

Yet the running time of *The Strong Man* is overwhelmingly devoted to four episodes, simple in terms of narrative content, that provide Langdon the opportunity to manifest Harry's indecision, innocence, physical ineptitude, and general lack of orientation to objective reality. These are the long routines with Lily in the taxi, with Lily on the sidewalk in front of her apartment building and then inside her apartment, with his annoyed fellow passenger on the bus, and with Mary Brown in the garden. Capra says of this film in *The Name above the Title*, "We had cooked up a fine Langdon 'story-line' with superb routines and gags tailor-made to suit his unique pantomimic talents."[55]

Capra's contribution to the Langdon comedies can be traced by comparing them, as *The Strong Man* has been compared, with later Capra-directed films on the basis of common character types, plot devices, and thematic motifs. In *Tramp, Tramp, Tramp*, a Langdon feature of 1926 on which Capra worked as the principal writer, Harry's old father is an artisan who is trying to keep the small family business of handmaking quality shoes alive in a losing battle against a large company that mass-produces shoes and is systematically wiping out its competition. The Burton Shoe Company represents in *Tramp, Tramp, Tramp* the sort of impersonal, avaricious, and corrupt capitalism that Edward Arnold personifies in Capra's films of the 1930s and 1940s: *You Can't Take It with You, Mr. Smith Goes to Washington*, and *Meet John Doe*.

In *Tramp, Tramp, Tramp*, this conflict is not developed at all, whereas, in those later films, the same kind of conflict is a fully developed struggle and, at least in *Mr. Smith Goes to Washington* and *Meet John Doe*, is the central issue and is elevated to the status of a morality play. In the Langdon comedies, plot devices, themes, and other elements of narrative construction were, as Capra's comment on *The Strong Man* confirms, always subordinate to Langdon's performance. Narrative values were never significant in Langdon's comedies because of the barely coherent comic character that Langdon's performance defined.

At one point in Capra's book, he recites a list of principles as the formula according to which the Langdon screen persona was "invented" by him and Arthur Ripley.[56] He then hypothetically subtracts these from the films and gets "Langdon the vaudevillian" as a remainder. The error in Capra's accounting of the creation of the Langdon comedies is that one cannot subtract Langdon the vaudevillian from those films and get as a remainder a comic formula that is suitable for any purpose other than as a vehicle for Harry Langdon. It is on this basis that Langdon can be considered author

A production still from *Sky Boy*, 1929, Langdon's second talking comedy short for Hal Roach. (Courtesy of Academy of Motion Picture Arts and Sciences)

of the Langdon comedies—not on a basis of narrative values, but as a performer whose performance is the basis of the comic and cinematic style of the films in which he appears. This is, of course, not unique, and among his peers Langdon shares this distinction with Charles Chaplin. When one considers the particular relationship between Langdon's performance and the formal design of Langdon's films, as discussed in chapter 6, the designation "author" takes on the more specific significance of "metteur-en-scène," or one who also employs properties of filmic form as a constituent of his comedy.

Though Langdon appeared in forty-two short sound comedies and sixteen sound feature films from 1929 to 1944 (the year of his death), the critical consideration of Langdon's work in film that is undertaken in the following chapters is limited to the available silent comedies, although reference is occasionally made to silent comedies featuring Langdon that are unavailable except in scenario form.

The reason for such a discrimination is that this consideration is concerned with the proposal of Harry Langdon as metteur-en-scène. The sound comedies in which Langdon appears, by and large, do not represent

Langdon as the radical rubbish collector in *Hallelujah, I'm a Bum*, 1933.

the work of Harry Langdon as metteur-en-scène. The great majority of roles he obtained in feature-length sound films were merely character or "bit" parts, and the typical conditions and methods of production of Langdon's short sound comedies differed greatly from those of his silent feature films. The Hal Roach, Educational, Paramount, and Columbia sound two-reel films in which Langdon appears as comedian were made in much less time for much less money. In fact, so were Langdon's two-reelers for Mack Sennett.

However, the significant difference between the short sound comedies and Langdon's films for Sennett is that Mack Sennett recognized great promise in Langdon's peculiar talents and, for that reason, invested a special interest in him. He also respected Langdon as an artist. Sennett therefore saw to it that special attention and every possible encouragement be given to Langdon in order that he might exercise his peculiar talents in Keystone comedies.

At the time Langdon entered sound comedies he was universally considered a "has-been." First National Pictures had dropped the option for more films as specified in Langdon's contractual arrangement with that studio because of the executives' dissatisfaction, publicly expressed, with

A publicity shot of Langdon with Madge Evans and an unidentified crew member on the set of *Hallelujah, I'm a Bum.*

the box-office receipts from Langdon's *Three's a Crowd* and *The Chaser*. Langdon subsequently had difficulty finding work in films and returned to vaudeville in 1929, though he played for a week at the Palace Theater in New York, which, in itself, was no disgrace. Langdon was forced to declare bankruptcy in 1931.

Throughout this period of the transition to sound, the film industry's and Langdon's, Langdon was plagued by legal action that had been brought against him to obtain unpaid alimony by one or both of his former wives and by other petty lawsuits, all of which were widely publicized. The fact that Langdon's financial situation remained precarious throughout the rest of his life was in some degree the result of the fact that his second wife never abandoned this pursuit and brought suit against Langdon whenever she learned he had obtained work.

Langdon was never able to overcome the has-been tag and never regained the authority or financial freedom he had previously had as producer and as producer-director of his own films. He was also no longer given the respect and special treatment that Sennett had given him. Nor was Langdon encouraged by the producers or directors of the sound comedies in which he appeared to do anything more than repeat, sometimes

A news photo in the *Los Angeles Examiner*, 25 March 1938, captioned: "With the exception of $15. Harry Langdon is 'flat broke.' The once famous comedian of the screen told the court yesterday the reason he was unable to pay Helen Walton Langdon [Langdon's second wife] $25. a week, as ordered when they were divorced in 1935. She says he is in arrears $2920. Langdon's present wife (pictured with him above) told the court 'we have nothing but $15.00.'"

verbatim, routines he had already done in his silent comedies. The most blatant remakes of earlier Langdon routines appear in *The Hitchhiker* (Educational, 1933), in which Langdon repeats the extended head-cold routine from the 1926 feature, *The Strong Man; Sue My Lawyer* (Columbia, 1938), which includes another routine from *The Strong Man* in which Langdon struggles up a flight of stairs with an unconscious woman in his arms; and *Counsel on de Fence* (Columbia, 1934), in which Langdon repeats the extended routine of trying to arouse a dummy cop that originally appeared in the 1927 silent feature *Long Pants*. *The Leather Necker* (Columbia, 1935) is a remake in its entirety of the Sennett two-reeler *All Night Long*. In fact, according to Leonard Maltin's book, *The Great Movie Shorts*, Langdon's name was being used by Columbia in the 1940s to boost lesser-known contract players in films that were intended to showcase the talents of those players rather than feature Langdon's.

More significantly perhaps, Langdon was himself, from all indications, no longer inspired or motivated by any ambition beyond merely fending off his creditors and, following his third marriage in 1934, providing for himself, his new wife, and his young son some degree of comfort and security by the only means that afforded itself to him.

Notes

1. *Variety*, 28 January 1921, p. 8.
2. *Billboard* (Cincinnati), 15 September 1906, p. 5; *New York Star*, 14 February 1914, photograph in "Harry Langdon" clipping file in the Theatre Collection of the Library and Museum of the Performing Arts of the New York Public Library at Lincoln Center, New York, New York; photograph in unidentified newspaper, dated 12 October 1919, in "Harry Langdon" clipping file in the Theatre Collection of the Library and Museum of the Performing Arts of the New York Public Library at Lincoln Center.
3. *Variety*, 5 November 1910, p. 4.
4. *New York Dramatic Mirror*, 14 February 1920, p. 266.
5. Frank Capra, *The Name above the Title* (New York: Macmillan Co., 1971), p. 58.
6. *Variety*, 13 January 1922, p. 23.
7. Ibid., 26 May 1922, p. 19.
8. *Billboard*, 18 November 1916, p. 7.
9. *Variety*, 25 November 1921, p. 22.
10. *New York Dramatic Mirror*, 26 November 1921, p. 776.
11. Review of *Jim Jam Jems* at the Cort Theatre, New York, October 1920, in unidentified, undated newspaper in "*Jim Jam Jems*" clipping file in the Theatre Collection of the Library and Museum of the Performing Arts of the New York Public Library at Lincoln Center.
12. *Billboard*, 3 September 1921, p. 9.
13. *Variety*, 11 November 1911, p. 24.
14. *Billboard*, 27 March 1920, p. 17.
15. *Variety*, 13 January 1922, p. 23.
16. Ibid., 5 May 1922, p. 17.
17. Capra, *The Name above the Title*, p. 58.
18. *Billboard*, 28 April 1923, p. 16.
19. Ibid., 15 September 1906, p. 5.

20. *Variety*, 2 July 1920, p. 7.

21. *New York Tribune*, 5 October 1920, p. 8, review of *Jim Jam Jems* in "*Jim Jam Jems*" clipping file.

22. Mack Sennett with Cameron Shipp, *King of Comedy* (Garden City, N. Y.: Doubleday, 1954), p. 140.

23. Capra, *The Name above the Title*, pp. 58–59, 63.

24. Walter Kerr, *The Silent Clowns* (New York: Alfred A. Knopf, 1975), p. 270.

25. *Billboard*, 15 September 1906, p. 5.

26. *New York Telegraph*, 11 November 1911, review of "A Night on the Boulevard" in "Harry Landgon" clipping file in the Theatre Collection of the Library and Museum of the Performing Arts of the New York Public Library at Lincoln Center.

27. *Variety*, 14 July 1916, p. 11.

28. *Billboard*, 22 July 1916, p. 7.

29. *Variety*, 19 March 1920, p. 26.

30. Ibid., 5 March 1920, p. 28.

31. Ibid., 13 January 1922, p. 23.

32. *Billboard*, 12 September 1914, p. 7.

33. *Variety*, 25 June 1915, p. 22.

34. Ibid., 31 January 1919, p. 24.

35. Ibid., 5 May 1922, p. 17.

36. J. H. Keene, "Harry Langdon," *Philadelphia Daily News*, 15 September 1930, p. 24.

37. Douglas Gilbert, *American Vaudeville: Its Life and Times* (New York: Dover, 1968), p. 6.

38. *Billboard*, 28 June 1913, p. 14.

39. *Elkhart* (Ind.) *Truth*, 7 September 1907, caption of photograph in the Locke Collection in the Theatre Collection of the Library and Museum of the Performing Arts of the New York Public Library at Lincoln Center.

40. *Billboard*, 22 May 1920, p. 16.

41. Ibid., 17 February 1923, p. 15.

42. Ibid., 28 June 1913, p. 14; 5 October 1918, p. 7; 1 February 1919, p. 7; and 29 July 1922, p. 14; *Variety*, 25 November 1921, p. 22.

43. Langdon's contract with Mack Sennett Comedies, 5 November 1923, and scenarios, synopses, and press sheets of Langdon's Sennett films referred to in this work are in the Mack Sennett Collection of the Margaret Herrick Library of the Academy of Motion Picture Arts and Sciences, Los Angeles, California.

44. *Billboard*, 13 May 1916, p. 7.

45. Ibid, 12 September 1914, p. 7; and 18 December 1918, p. 57.

46. *Variety*, 11 October 1912, p. 30; *Billboard*, 5 October 1918, p. 7.

47. *Billboard*, 3 May 1919, p. 7.

48. Capra, *The Name above the Title*, pp. 62, 72.

49. Sennett, *King of Comedy*, p. 140.

50. Hal Roach to author, Bel Air, California, 17 June 1974.

51. Edward Bernds to author, Van Nuys, California, 18 June 1974.

52. Sennett, *King of Comedy*, pp. 140–41.

53. *Billboard*, 13 May 1916, p. 7.

54. *Variety*, 14 July 1916, p. 11.

55. Capra, *The Name above the Title*, p. 67.

56. Ibid., pp. 62–63.

3
The Character

One of the traditional critical interpretations of Langdon's screen persona is that of Harry as an overgrown infant. The other traditional critical approach to identifying Langdon's screen persona is specifically and admittedly grounded in the surrealist aesthetic. Nearly every commentator considers Langdon's outward appearance and mime to be an impersonation of a baby. There are two variations on the notion of Harry as an overgrown infant.

According to one of these variations, the most common critical approach to Langdon's work, Langdon's comedy derives from the predicament of a child who is placed by gag writers into a hostile, adult world. This view is shared by such commentators as Gerald Mast in *The Comic Mind: Comedy and the Movies;* Donald W. McCaffrey in *Four Great Comedians: Chaplin, Lloyd, Keaton, Langdon;* David Robinson in *The Great Funnies: A History of Film Comedy;* Penelope Gilliatt in her 24 April 1971 column, "The Current Cinema," on Langdon in *The New Yorker* magazine; and Georges Goldfayn in his article, "L'art de Harry Langdon" in the French film journal *L'Age du Cinéma.*

The other variation of the interpretation of Langdon's screen persona as an overgrown infant is that of Harry as a child-man whose actual identity—whether infant, adolescent, or adult—cannot be specifically determined. According to this interpretation, ambiguity is the key to Langdon's comic style. This view is offered by James Agee in his essay "Comedy's Greatest Era" and by Jean-Pierre Coursodon in the chapter on Langdon in his book, *Keaton et Cie, les burlesques américains du "muet."*

The surrealist critics consider Harry to be a model of one who has attained the surrealist ambition of reconciling the states of sleeping and waking. Ado Kyrou may be considered a spokesman for this group of French critics, who have always been Langdon's most ardent champions. In his book, *Le Surréalisme au Cinéma,* Kyrou describes Harry as "the man who did not want to wake up," and maintains that "only a public sensitive to the brilliance of surrealism could penetrate into the sleep of the poet, Harry Langdon." Kyrou continues, "The restrictions, the prohibitions, the logical distinctions slide past him; he is coated with sleep and dreams. Therein resides his total revolt; he definitively rejects the real world and its laws; he sees the world around him through dreams." Speaking of *The Strong Man,* Kyrou observes: "The dreamer will emerge as the conquerer of everyday reality. In the same way that he refuses all love which does not conform to his wonderful dream, he tramples underfoot every sordid aspect of life."[1]

This interest in Langdon on the part of surrealist-oriented French critics was initially expressed in the late 1920s by a group of regular contributors to the journal *La Revue du Cinéma,* including Paul Gilson, Jean-George Auriol, André Delons, Chavance, and J.-B. Brunius. The view of Harry the dreamer that they shared is expressed by Gilson in a May 1929 article on *Three's a Crowd* entitled "Harry Langdon ou la Maladie du Sommeil":

> I salute Langdon as a privileged victim of sleeping sickness. In spite of himself he benumbs objects, people in the neighborhood, the street, the whole decor. Sleep grabs him by the hair, envelops him, bathes him in its fluid. Harry opens his eyes wide: he doesn't recognize his bicycle, the daisy which blossoms in its pot, the bricks that set the crease in his trousers. He falls asleep again. Will he get up? He sleeps standing up. . . . He passes among the living, sleepwalking.[2]

Andre G. Brunelin, in an article entitled "Harry Langdon" that appears in the August–September 1960 issue of *Cinéma 60,* offers a similar description of Harry as a character "perpetually asleep, all the time, a real sleepwalker."[3]

Freudian psychoanalysis is employed as a critical tool in these two most common approaches to analysis of Langdon's work. In several other articles, the authors discover in Freudian psychology the common core of these two interpretations—Harry as child and Harry as dreamer. Langdon's screen persona is identified by these authors as a child at the "fetal," "embryonic," or "larval" stage of development.

Richard Leary, in his *Film Comment* article "Capra and Langdon," notes how easily Harry assumes a fetal position and comments: "This regression towards subconscious behavioral levels often gave his work a surrealistic tinge—an aura the movie dream-machine was ideally suited to capture. . . . Sometimes it even seems as if Harry had been plucked from the womb, to the security of which he longed to return."[4]

In the chapter on Langdon in his book *The Crazy Mirror: Hollywood and the American Image,* Raymond Durgnat contends that Harry "retained an embryo's immunity from the outside world," while echoing the previously quoted remarks of Ado Kyrou in a reference to "the swathes of dreaming sleep through which he has to perceive the world."[5]

The French critic André Tournes in the *Jeune Cinéma* article "Harry Langdon," claims that Harry "is an age of man: an age in which one still dreams of a larval stage, of the cradle, of sleeping." Tournes cites an instance in the following reference to scenes from *Three's a Crowd* in which Harry actually embodies the characterization Leary has merely hypothesized:

> And yet, how is it possible not to recognize in the giant cradle where Harry rocks himself to sleep while holding the baby in his arms, in this Harry clinging to his sheet and hanging outside the trap-door, the child who, rather than jumping into the snow, preferred to reclimb the cord in order to live warmly in the hollow of the room?[6]

Jacques Chevallier, in his article "Tramp, Tramp, Tramp" in *Image et Son,* agrees with Tournes on the nature of Langdon's comic persona.

Walter Kerr's book *The Silent Clowns* includes the most recent, but by no means novel, critical interpretation of Langdon's comic characterization. Kerr begins his consideration of Harry Langdon by explaining why 1920s audiences responded to Langdon as a comedian and why contemporary audiences do not. According to Kerr, when Langdon entered films in 1924, he studied the work of the other silent comedians and then fashioned his comedy as a twist on the already well-known styles and forms of film comedy. Thus only audiences of the 1920s and those archivists and aficionados who have steeped themselves in silent comedy can appreciate Langdon's esoteric variation on the genre.

Kerr's theory, however, is based on the assumption that Langdon's comic style came into being on the screen in 1924 as a self-consciously contrived comment on the already well-known structures of silent film comedy. However, as we have seen, Langdon's distinctive comic persona and style of performance were conceived and well practiced by Langdon long before the work of other screen comedians who were popular in 1924 was known and before the structures of silent film comedy were even established.

This explanation by Kerr of Langdon's comic style is prefaced by a rejection of the "Harry-as-baby" notion, in which Kerr implies that he will have something new to say in the three chapters devoted to Langdon in his book. However, after one dismisses Kerr's hypothesis of "Langdon-as-comma" within the preexistent syntax of American silent comedy (which Kerr admits is relevant only for archivists and audiences of the 1920s), there remains merely the familiar notion that ambiguity is the key to Langdon's comedy. As have a number of others before him, Kerr maintains that

Langdon's art rests in the contradiction inherent in a character that is simultaneously infant, adolescent, and adult. Kerr does, however, offer the further observation that when, in Langdon's later silent films, a specific identity is defined, this ambiguity, and with it the integrity of Langdon's art, dissolved.

Langdon's mime and comedy are generally considered to be grounded in an impersonation by Langdon of a baby because many of the mannerisms, movements, and gestures that Langdon employs in his performance are imitations of infantile behavior. At times in his films, Langdon does present an excellent infant impersonation. The best example of Langdon's infant impersonation is seen in the final episode of *Tramp, Tramp, Tramp*. In this sequence, Langdon is dressed in baby clothes and bonnet and is seen in an oversized baby carriage. He does an extended pantomime routine as "Harry, Junior," while the mother and Harry, as the father, look on in doting delight. This sequence is actually a remake of a routine that Langdon initially presented in the feature-length version of the 1925 Mack Sennett comedy *His First Flame*. Langdon's mime is a demonstration of physical and intellectual deficiency and of the lack of coordination of those deficient physical functions and intellectual faculties. Langdon's mime is an imitation of infantile behavior insofar as an infant's physical and intellectual faculties are deficient because they are underdeveloped.

At other times, Harry's behavior is more accurately described as that of someone who is in a catatonic state or comatose condition, or of someone who is drunk or drugged or who has been dazed or stunned by a powerful physical blow. Harry's involuntary reflexes are normally either retarded or inoperative. One would expect Harry's leg not to budge when his knee is tapped by a doctor's percussion hammer. Harry's typical reaction to physical blows is total immobility for a moment, after which he slowly and gently lowers himself from a standing to a sitting position. Or else, he merely curls up comfortably into fetal position on the spot and placidly passes out.

Thus, an alternative to the Harry-as-overgrown-infant and surrealist approaches is offered, according to which Langdon's comic impersonation is of one who is effectively incapacitated by a pathological impairment of his rational and physical functions. This condition is attributable to the character's failure to resolve the states of sleeping and waking—a resolution that the surrealist critics claim the character has successfully accomplished.

As the character is only barely developed in dramatic or narrative terms, this alternative definition of Langdon's comic characterization is based on a close observation of Harry's outward behavior. The following analysis of Harry's abnormal behavior may be read as a cataloging of comic reactions in particular situations (though that behavior often represents the lack of traditional comic reactions), or as a cataloging of symptoms. In accordance with this alternative view of the character, descriptions of Harry's behavior are organized by symptom rather than by the familiar terminology of comic reactions and theoretical categories of traditional silent comedy criticism.

The faulty operation of Harry's involuntary reflexes can be observed in the brawl in *Saturday Afternoon*. As he gets up from his seat on the running board of his pal's roadster, Harry is punched in the nose by one of the jealous boyfriends. Harry stiffens, stands upright for a moment, and stares wide-eyed toward the camera. He then blinks once, sneezes, fumbles awkwardly around his face with his fingers, and gently eases himself back down onto the running board. Harry responds to the punch as to a chill. Instead of falling over unconscious, he sneezes and, after he is seated again, pulls his jacket up around him and folds his arms tightly around his body. Soon after, Harry is hit on the head by a loose hammerhead. He blinks and stands in place a moment, again staring straight ahead. He then slowly puts down the jack he had taken up as a weapon in order to put his hand up to his ear preparatory to assuming a position of repose. Harry then simply lets himself down gently into a sitting position on the running board—his head resting upon his hand and his elbow sliding into place against the rear wheel of the car—as he stares absently ahead and then down.

When he is punched again, Harry's response is, again, momentary immobility, followed by a blink and a check to see that his teeth are still in place. Harry stiffens again and his eyes open wide at a second punch, after which he firmly adjusts his hat, and then his head, into their former positions. Harry then turns his knees in toward each other until they meet, and, with eyes nearly closed, he begins to sink slowly toward the ground. As he continues to slide downward, his hands emerge at his sides and touch down on the ground just before he sets his body down upon his knees.

In *The Chaser,* Harry is hit in the head by a crockery pitcher flung at him by his mother-in-law. Here too, Harry stands immobile and stares wide-eyed for a moment, then blinks and looks off passively. After a cut to a close-up of a twittering canary, Harry is seen in full-shot, sinking slowly and slightly toward the floor as his knees begin to give way. He then rises slowly to a standing position again, blinks, stares passively, and begins to sink back down. Following another blink, he is up again with half-closed eyes and, finally, sinks all the way to the floor.

Another example is seen in *Tramp, Tramp, Tramp,* during a sequence in which Harry is at work on a rock pile with other prisoners on a chain gang. Harry is sitting on a rock and is struck squarely on the head with a sledgehammer by another prisoner who, working with his back to Harry, did not see Harry when he raised his hammer over his head. Harry merely looks up from his work toward the camera, scratches his hat, stands up, and sways as his knees buckle under him. Harry sits again and is hit again. Again he looks up toward the camera and blinks as he lets his own hammer slip out of his hand. Harry stands up again and bounces gently up and down at the knees in stages until he comes back to rest upon the rock.

When Lily smashes a bottle over Harry's head while he is carrying the supposedly unconscious woman to her bed in *The Strong Man,* Harry straightens, standing in his tracks, then curls up on the bed he had prepared for her and nestles up to the pillow to sleep. In Harry's dream of a boxing match with his rival in *Three's a Crowd,* Harry is knocked down by his opponent's first punch, whereupon he curls up into the fetal position on the canvas and sleeps, comfortably pillowing his head on his oversized glove.

At other times, on sustaining some physical impact or assault, Harry's body simply stiffens in momentary paralysis and does nothing else, as when he is bitten by the monkey in *The Sea Squawk,* when he is kicked by the tough roustabout in *Remember When,* and when he punches himself in the nose during the fistfight in *Saturday Afternoon.*

In *Three's a Crowd,* Harry discovers the hard way that he has left a sewing needle in the back pocket of his trousers when he leans back against a wall. The needle's entry is illustrated in close-up and is followed by a shot of Harry, in a frozen pose, staring straight ahead while holding onto his hat. This is followed by a wider shot in which Harry's full figure is seen as he continues merely to stand there, leaning flush against the wall with a completely indifferent expression on his face. In *The Chaser,* Harry, along with the entire contents of a kitchen, is blown a foot off the floor when the oven explodes. When Harry and the contents come back down, Harry stands where he lands and remains absolutely still.

Harry's voluntary actions appear to be governed by a disjunction between his perceptual and cognitive faculties and his motor responses. Those voluntary actions are delayed, misdirected, inadequate, inefficient, diverted, aborted, and otherwise inappropriate to the circumstances in which he is found. For instance, in *The Strong Man,* Harry is given directions by a doorman to the place where he can find Mary Brown, the war-

Because of Harry's uncoordinated voluntary actions, he cannot shake hands with the doorman in *The Strong Man.*

time pen pal whom Harry has been seeking. Harry is standing several feet from the doorman and has already extended one leg in that direction when he extends his arms in the opposite direction toward the doorman to thank him. The doorman, who is actually only kidding Harry, does not extend his arms toward Harry, and, because Harry does not take a step in the doorman's direction, Harry is not able to shake his hand. In the same film, Harry leans down to pet a tigerskin rug, apparently oblivious not only to the fact that it is a tiger, or indeed that it is a dead tiger, but to the distance between him and the rug, which is lying on the floor across the room. In *The Strong Man,* Harry extends his arm toward a building for support after being publicly reprimanded by a woman for making what she mistakenly believed to be improper advances; and in *Long Pants,* he reaches toward the vamp's car to lean against it after collapsing, dazed, from her kiss. In both cases Harry is short of his target by a margin of several feet.

Harry's inappropriate voluntary actions also include those in which his motor responses are more extravagant than are called for under the circumstances. To examine something slightly above or below his eyelevel, Harry shifts his whole body up or down instead of merely tilting his head at the neck. To look closely at something, Harry must move closer to it, even though he may already be no more than a foot or so away. In *Boobs in the Wood, Remember When,* and *Tramp, Tramp, Tramp,* Harry kneels down to look up and stare into the faces of the girls whom he is already directly confronting. In *Saturday Afternoon,* Harry stands up on tiptoes to look down at the kiss between his pal and his pal's girl friend, which Harry has already observed closely and for some time from a point of view just short of actually intervening into the kiss itself. To point at something, Harry extends his whole arm, as can be seen in the sequence in which Harry tries to provoke a dummy cop in *Long Pants;* or in *Saturday Afternoon,* in which he bends his whole body at the knees while pointing at some money he's hidden under the living-room carpet. When thrusting a hand out for emphasis, as in the sequence in *Long Pants* in which Harry refuses to marry Priscilla during a prewedding talk with his father, Harry thrusts forward his entire body.

To put something down, Harry bends at the knees to the ground instead of merely leaning over at the waist. This is the way Harry puts down a pen in *Soldier Man,* a phone receiver in *Saturday Afternoon,* and a bouquet of flowers in *Long Pants.* When someone picks up and hands him the pen again in *Soldier Man,* Harry reaches several inches to the side of it. In *Saturday Afternoon,* Harry stops midway as he bends over to put the telephone receiver down and never does reach the ground with it. To wink at the picture of his dream girl, Betty Burton, on the billboard in *Tramp, Tramp, Tramp,* Harry exercises every muscle in his face. When Harry raises his arms to lift off his hat, which has been pushed down over his eyes during his unsuccessful attempt to murder Priscilla in *Long Pants,* he lifts his entire body off the ground. When a Good Samaritan pours a cup of water in Harry's face to revive him after Harry feigns unconsciousness in order to rouse the dummy cop in *Long Pants*, Harry reacts as if he were drowning.

In some cases, Harry's actions may be considered inappropriate in terms of his timing. These include delayed reactions such as in *Boobs in the Wood*, when Harry runs for safety from a falling tree after it hits the ground, and Harry's delayed reaction to his fiancée's kiss in *His Marriage Wow*. In the latter example, she gives Harry a kiss on the cheek while he explains to her why he was late for the wedding. After a barely perceptible twitch, Harry continues talking, and only after a second kiss on the lips does he cease relating his story to blink and smile blissfully toward the camera.

Sometimes, Harry persists in an action longer than is necessary. In *Soldier Man*, Harry closes one eye and squints with the other in order to take aim through the sight of his rifle. He continues to do so after lowering the rifle from his shoulder and while he realigns the gun's loose barrel. Likewise, after throwing a horseshoe in *Long Pants* (which he does by extending his arm to full length instead of cocking it at the elbow, which would have been more energy-efficient), Harry continues to stand with his arm fully extended for some time after the horseshoe has left his hand.

Harry's motor functions are not only delayed or overdrawn in time, they are also sometimes premature. In *Saturday Afternooon, Tramp, Tramp, Tramp,* and *The Strong Man*, Harry assumes a sitting position in midair before he is near enough a running board in *Saturday Afternoon*, a park bench in *Tramp, Tramp, Tramp*, and a building ledge in *The Strong Man* to actually seat himself.

Harry obviously has difficulty attending, and intention is virtually absent

In *The Strong Man,* Harry assumes a sitting position in midair before he is near enough the ledge to actually seat himself.

in this character. This is indicated by his gestures and localized movements and in locomotion. Both localized movements and locomotion are, characteristically, without the direction or structure that motivation provides. Harry's inability to coordinate his movement with respect to a specified goal or objective is apparent in the films on occasions in which he overshoots his logical objective.

At least three of these occasions are seen in *Saturday Afternoon*. During his attempt to evade his wife and go with his pal, Vernon, to pick up their dates for the afternoon, Harry runs along the sidewalk away from the house and on past Vernon's waiting car. Harry has to turn around and backtrack to get into the car. Harry does the same thing when he attempts to flee the scene after accidentally throwing a brick through a storefront window. In this case, he just keeps on running past the getaway car. During the fistfight with the jealous boyfriends that follows, Harry rushes into the frame at Vernon's call for help and continues right on past Vernon and the two boyfriends.

When the girl whose face he has worshiped on billboards actually appears before him in *Tramp, Tramp, Tramp*, Harry turns from her to walk toward her picture on the billboard with one hand extended as if to touch it in order to compare the two and perhaps determine which one, if either, is flesh and blood. In his excitement, he walks right on past the billboard and into the background of the shot. In *The Strong Man*, Harry is also very excited at finally finding his pen pal, Mary Brown. He rushes toward a backstage door that opens onto the garden where Mary is drawing water from a pump. Harry starts out to enter the garden with the excuse of fetching water. He stops in his tracks when he realizes that he has forgotten his pail. He turns and rushes back toward the camera, bypassing the pail and halting abruptly again to retrace his steps and pick up the pail.

When Harry's objective is not in sight, his progress, which is aimless when a logical objective is in sight, is hopeless. In *The Strong Man,* for instance, Harry has been picked up by Lily, who tells him that she is the Mary Brown he has been looking for. She leads him, hand in hand, through the street toward her apartment. When Harry lets go of her hand for a moment to take out and look at his photo of Mary, Lily continues walking and soon passes out of the frame. When Harry looks up, Lily is gone. He stands with his finger stuck apprehensively in his mouth for a moment in the midst of the busy pedestrian traffic along the crowded sidewalk and then he starts off to the right, in the direction Lily had been leading him before he stopped. However, the crowd is moving against Harry in the opposite direction. As Harry encounters the crowd, he holds onto his hat, turns around, and is carried along with them toward screen left.

When Lily reappears at screen right after rushing back to retrieve Harry (who unknowingly possesses a stolen bankroll), Harry turns back around and starts to move against the crowd again. Lily, now moving toward screen left, is carried on past Harry, who is now moving toward screen right. At this point, Harry stops and teeters from side to side on one foot, staring straight ahead toward the camera. After watching Lily pass in the foreground, Harry starts off again to the left, stops, and takes a step forward out of the stream of traffic into the foreground, where he stands with his arms extended in a gesture of hopeless confusion at not finding her there. He then turns away from the camera and moves into background left, where Lily actually is and where they finally make contact again as Harry grabs her hand and they continue on their way.

The misdirected, diverted, and only partially executed movements and gestures that are typical of Harry's behavior are obviously the results of his inability to concentrate his attention on even a single objective or to entertain more than a single, simple thought at a time. Such a conditioned reflex as saluting a superior officer is, in Harry's case as the enlisted man, diverted midway into a tentative wave of the hand in *All Night Long*. In the same film, Harry greets the girl when they meet with a silly wave of the hand that becomes a tentative salute.

He also does not usually succeed in fully executing the conditioned reflex of tipping his hat to greet a lady or gentleman. This is seen in *Tramp, Tramp, Tramp* when Betty Burton first appears before Harry in the flesh. By the time Harry's tipping hand reaches his hat, it is joined by the other hand and becomes a gesture of holding onto his hat. He then extends his arms to clap his hands together in apparent delight, but before his hands meet, they are again diverted upward to his hat brim. In *The Strong Man*, Harry feebly raises his hand to tip his hat in a gesture of apology to the woman who reprimanded him (who has walked away by this time). In this case, he merely fails to follow through, dropping his hand back down at midmotion and bringing both hands together in front of him. In the same film, when Harry introduces himself to Mary Brown in the garden, he lifts his hat slightly with his right hand, bows, and raises his left hand as he brings his right hand down. His left hand passes by his hat brim without touching it as he begins to bring his right hand back up to his hat and lets it drop again before it touches the hat.

In *Remember When*, Harry is unable to carry out the simple movement of bringing a hand with food to his mouth in order to satisfy even such an elemental biological need as hunger. Harry has come upon a food-laden picnic table and each time he is about to put something into his mouth, he sees something else to eat and puts down what he has to pick it up. By the time the family whose picnic this is arrives to chase Harry away, he hasn't eaten a single bite. Harry's psychomotor functions are so uncoordinated that he cannot think and eat at the same time. As hungry as Harry is in *Soldier Man*, the moment he lifts his head up from the chicken leg his hand is conveying to his mouth to look around at the palace to which he has been abducted, the movement of his hand slows and then stops short of its destination. Harry is then led off to be presented to court without so much as a taste of chicken. Nor can he reach a pitcher of water in order to quench his thirst in *Tramp, Tramp, Tramp.*

Harry is also unable to make love and eat at the same time. In *Soldier Man,* the queen throws herself at Harry's feet in her boudoir while Harry concentrates strictly on feeding himself from a fruit bowl. And when Harry is looking at and/or thinking of an object of his affection, he cannot do or think of anything else. For instance, when Betty encourages him to sign an application to enter the walking race in *Tramp, Tramp, Tramp,* Harry pokes a pencil into his mouth while attempting to wet the lead and sign at the same time he is staring at her. In *Three's a Crowd,* while he gazes at his new-found "wife and child," Harry prepares a pie from start to finish without realizing that the dough he has been using is actually a diaper. Harry is so impressed at his first sight of Bebe, the vamp in *Long Pants,* that he cannot take his eyes off of her. Consequently, he mounts his bike and tries to ride over to her without noticing that a porch pillar intervenes between him and the handlebars. Harry is eventually called away from Bebe to answer a phone call from Priscilla, but his thoughts are only on Bebe as Priscilla talks. Harry tries to hang up the receiver after finishing the call and fails to accomplish this simple operation in several tries. He finally just lets the receiver drop and rushes back outside to Bebe.

Harry's locomotion is actually impaired to the degree that he rarely proceeds straightforwardly or takes even so much as a step without hesitating, halting, or changing direction. When the noon whistle finally sounds at the factory where Harry works in *Saturday Afternoon,* Harry dashes out the front entance into the street, jumping over a gutter and then taking two steps forward toward the camera. There he bounces sideways—first on his right foot, then on his left. Harry then totters in place, extending one foot at a time, from side to side while facing the camera. Finally he dashes forward toward the camera and out of the frame.

Harry cannot make a clean getaway even in cases of dire emergency. After he smashes the storefront window in *Saturday Afternoon,* Harry takes two or three steps toward the camera, then completely reverses his course, moving away from the camera toward the getaway car in the background. After taking only two hasty steps, Harry stops in his tracks and looks back in the direction of the camera at the broken window (now offscreen). He takes a single stride back toward the camera while Vernon runs away into the background of the shot, calling to Harry to follow him. Harry then reverses direction again, pivoting on the outstretched foot. He makes a complete revolution and runs toward Vernon and the car and keeps on running past Vernon and the car.

In another emergency, in *Long Pants,* Harry, perhaps with some vague notion about rescuing Bebe, comes into view from behind a massive prison wall, stops, takes a step forward toward the camera, looks around, takes a step backward to look back in the direction he has just come from, turns back toward the camera, and comes forward a bit. He then goes back to look around the corner again, turns again, and begins to walk toward the camera. He responds to the siren signaling a jailbreak by stopping, staring, and running back and forth toward and away from the camera along the prison wall. In *His First Flame,* Harry responds to a fire alarm by running back and forth inside the firehouse. As the soldier in *Soldier Man,* Harry responds to an explosion by holding onto this hat and starting out in several directions, bobbing in place from one side to another before he actually runs off out of the frame. When a bottle of doctored patent medicine explodes at his feet in *Lucky Stars,* he runs forward, following another man who flees out of the frame in the right foreground. Harry, however, halts abruptly after taking a few steps, holds onto his hat, and then turns to run out of the frame in the opposite direction.

Harry's body often succumbs to the force of inertia as he moves back and forth or totters from side to side in 'one place, hovering between two spatially differentiated alternatives. For instance, in *All Night Long,* when the sergeant finally gives in to Harry's pestering and invites him to his girl friend's home for dinner, Harry moves back and forth within a range of a few feet between the barracks entrance and the sergeant, vacillating between shaking the sergeant's hand and dressing for the occasion.

In *Saturday Afternoon,* Harry hovers between a stranger on the street who has asked him for a light and a waiting streetcar that is rapidly filling. Later, Harry is overcome and nearly incapacitated by inertia in the sequence in which he attempts to evade his wife and embark with Vernon upon an afternoon's adventure. As Harry and Vernon stand beside Vernon's car, discreetly parked some distance up the street from Harry's house, and laugh over Harry's getaway, they are interrupted when Harry's wife shouts from the house for him to come home. Harry and Vernon both turn their heads toward the house, which is out of camera range deep in the background of the shot. Harry turns back toward Vernon with his arms helplessly outstretched, brings his hands back together, and looks off into the background while extending his hindmost foot a step in that direction. He then looks back at Vernon and points in his wife's direction, turns again, and runs about three or four steps along the sidewalk back toward the house. Midway between foreground and background, Harry looks back again at his pal and faces the camera while his feet continue to carry him further into the background. Vernon gestures to Harry to "come back here," while Harry, at a momentary standstill, responds from the background by pointing in the direction of his house. He totters briefly in place between the alternatives of fidelity and fun (as, respectively, wife and home in the background, and his pal and the getaway car in the foreground), and then turns away from the camera again and takes several more steps into the background.

When Vernon calls him back, the pace of Harry's retreat slows to a stop, at which point Harry turns around to face Vernon, who again demands that he "come here." Harry then turns his head abruptly backward, then forward, and points toward the house. Vernon demands once more that Harry come to him. At this, Harry takes a few tentative steps forward and, after glancing behind him, comes forward the rest of the way in a crouch, as if hiding beneath a hedge, glancing backward one more time as he does so. As he nears Vernon and the car, Harry stands upright and begins to run at full speed. Harry runs right past them and has to stop in his tracks and turn back to finally get in the car and embark upon the adventure.

A case in which Harry is reduced to a state of complete paralysis somewhere between spatially differentiated alternatives is seen in *Lucky Stars* when Harry is momentarily immobilized by having to choose between acquiescing to the advances of the vamp, who beckons him enticingly from her balcony, and his responsibilities on the medicine-show platform in the town square below. He deserts the platform and climbs up the stairway to her balcony. After taking several halting steps in her direction, Harry runs back downstairs, then comes back up. He finally stands perched at the head of the stairs between the vamp, seen in the right background of the shot, and the medicine show, which is offscreen left. The top of Harry's body leans over in her direction while his feet remain firmly planted on the stairs.

A variation of the same scheme, now on the vertical axis, is the way in which Harry bobs up and down several times before sitting or standing and sometimes assumes a squatting position midway between sitting and standing, as when he bends down at the knees to examine something. In *Tramp, Tramp, Tramp,* he bobs vertically to a standing position from his seat on a park bench while he looks back and forth from Betty to Betty's picture on the billboard before him. Similarly, Harry bobs up from his seat on the running board of a car after the horn is blown in his ear in *Saturday Afternoon*. After Harry is told off in the street by the indignant girl whom he has unintentionally annoyed in *The Strong Man,* Harry bobs up and down unsteadily from a squatting position as the crowd begins to disperse. In the same film, Harry hovers in midair above the window ledge upon which he had been seated after standing to greet the doorman, who turns his back to Harry indifferently.

Instances in which Harry succumbs to inertia also include occasions in which he moves frantically within the bounds of a single, static frame and gets absolutely nowhere. He runs either in circles or traces a completely erratic trajectory, usually as an outward expression of erotic excitement in the form of a release of kinetic energy. A good example is seen in *Long Pants* during Harry's first encounter with Bebe. Harry casually circles her car on his bike, showing off the tricks he can do. When she finally acknowledges him with a barely perceptible smile, Harry takes off at top speed, furiously peddling his bike in circles around her car. Harry also runs around his shack in circles helplessly in *Three's a Crowd* after carrying in a beautiful girl he had discovered lying unconscious on the street, who, he also discovers during this sequence, is about to become a mother.

At his first sight of Mary Brown through the backstage door in *The Strong Man,* Harry dashes frantically around the backstage area in his excitement with no clear course—tripping, retracing his steps, bypassing the door, stalling, circling a pail on the floor in bouncing strides, and abruptly changing pace. When he sees his dream girl from the billboard for the first time in *Tramp, Tramp, Tramp,* Harry bounces up and down off of a park bench and runs back and forth to and from the billboard, the bench, and the girl. Occasionally Harry stops in midmotion to examine one or the other more closely, bends down, stands up, flaps his arms up and down at his sides, and runs around behind the bench.

At other times, after setting himself into motion, Harry is stopped dead in his tracks when different parts of his body simultaneously set out in different directions. This occurs in *The Strong Man* when Harry first spots Mary Brown through the backstage door. His feet move forward while the top of his body lurches backward. Harry grabs onto his hat as he comes to an abrupt standstill. This also happens in *Saturday Afternoon* as Harry dashes out of a phone booth after talking to his wife, who does not take well the news that he will be home two minutes late. With his second step forward, the upper part of Harry's body lurches backward. Facing the camera, he then moves his left foot one step to the right and his right foot a step to the left. The rest of his body follows his right foot to the left, which brings him to a halt.

Harry also dispays in his behavior an indifference to his surroundings that must be judged pathological and that may even be compared to the condition of autism. He is introduced in the film *Soldier Man* as "the soldier who was not accounted for—he didn't know the war was over," emerging as a lone figure silhouetted against a bare horizon. Harry's communication with the world of objective reality is severely impaired in that it is generally only one-sided. He talks to a cow and then continues that conversation with a sirloin steak as if it were the same animal in *Soldier Man.* He also converses with a headless mannequin in the same film. He engages in a heated verbal confrontation with a telephone pole in *His Marriage Wow,* and in an extended battle of wits with a dummy cop and some chatter and flirtation with a crocodile in *Long Pants.*

Harry becomes involved in a violent physical confrontation with a vacant suit of armor in *Soldier Man,* wrestles with a Chinese ceremonial statue in *Feet of Mud,* and does battle with a cyclone in *Tramp, Tramp, Tramp.* He reaches over to pat a tigerskin rug each time he passes it in *The Strong Man* and affectionately pats the front tire of his bicycle in *Long Pants.* In *His First Flame,* Harry rushes into a house he thinks is burning and rescues a ragged old fitting dummy. He is still comforting it when he is halfway down the escape ladder as if it were the girl he thinks he is saving. In *Tramp, Tramp, Tramp,* Harry falls in love with a woman on a billboard and winks, smiles, throws kisses at, and sleeps with the picture, even after meeting the flesh-and-blood model for the billboard picture.

The animate human antagonists to whom Harry addresses himself are, as often as not, either preoccupied and completely indifferent to Harry or are themselves unconscious and/or inert. This is the case in the one-sided exchange between Harry and the doorman in *The Strong Man*. Standing right beside the doorman, Harry salutes, waves, smiles, starts to tip his hat, and still fails to get even the slightest acknowledgment even though the doorman is facing Harry directly. The doorman then ignores Harry's hand, which Harry extends to thank him for his directions to where Mary Brown can be found. Earlier in the film, Harry extends his hand to an immigration officer to whom he is introduced at Ellis Island who likewise ignores it. Later, a passenger who is sitting beside Harry on a bus resumes reading his newspaper after punching Harry in the nose, completely oblivious to Harry's retaliatory glares and fist wielding.

In *Long Pants*, Bebe sits impassively in the back seat of her car staring blankly straight ahead before finally acknowledging Harry with a barely perceptible smile in his general direction while Harry circles her car on his bicycle, showing off some truly spectacular stunts. It is easy to understand why Harry has a hard time differentiating between the girl on the billboard and the living girl in *Tramp, Tramp, Tramp*. Throughout the long sequence in which Harry races frantically about in the space between the billboard (which faces the camera in the background) and the living model for the billboard (who faces Harry in the foreground), neither moves.

When Harry comes home late in *Saturday Afternoon*, he is met as he enters

Bebe (Alma Bennett) is indifferent to Harry's attentions in *Long Pants*.

the front door by a glaring wife who remains literally unmoved throughout his friendly greetings, his busy gestures, and the apologetic offering of his outstretched hand. When Harry apologizes to the girl he has unintentionally annoyed in *The Strong Man,* she has already turned her back to him and is walking away. In *Three's a Crowd,* Harry tries unsuccessfully to communicate with the unconscious girl whom he discovers lying in the snow at the foot of the stairway to his shack.

When addressed by others, Harry is often indifferent to them and does not respond, usually because he is completely unaware that he is being addressed at all. This applies to the occasions when Harry is drunk, dazed, drugged, falling asleep, or waking up. Such occasions are frequent in Langdon's films. One of these may be observed in *Tramp, Tramp, Tramp* when a cab driver tries to collect his fare from Harry, who is still under the influence of the liquor and sleeping pills he had taken to fall asleep the night before. Another occurs in *His First Flame* when Harry dozes off in a chair while his uncle tries to pursue a serious man-to-man talk with him. In *Long Pants,* Harry is still somewhat dazed by Bebe's kiss when he ignores his mother as she calls him to the phone.

When he is awake, Harry's attention is frequently and easily distracted—further evidence of Harry's one-sided communication. In *Tramp, Tramp, Tramp,* Harry gazes distractedly out the door of his father's store at Betty's picture on a billboard while his father explains to Harry in desperation that the mortgage on the family shoe store is about to be foreclosed upon.

At other times, Harry's attention becomes fixated on a single object to the extent that he is oblivious and therefore unresponsive to changes in his circumstances or situation. In *Soldier Man,* the scheming minister who has abducted Harry in order to have him impersonate the king coaches Harry on how to present himself to court. Meanwhile, Harry turns away from the minister to keep an eye on the suit of armor that he has just "subdued" in a difficult struggle. In *Long Pants,* Harry turns back twice in Bebe's direction as his mother escorts him home to answer the phone call from Priscilla. In *Tramp, Tramp, Tramp,* Harry is wakened on the morning of the race from the same position on the floor into which he had collapsed the night before while on his way across the room to get a drink from a water pitcher. When Harry, still very much under the influence of the liquor and pills, is finally dressed and dragged to the door, he grabs the pitcher on the way out as if a night's sleep had never intervened.

Generally, Harry's indifference to his surroundings is obvious in his lack of responsiveness to changes in his physical circumstances or situation. For instance, Harry tries vainly for some time to hail a cab after being knocked out and robbed in *His First Flame.* He cannot understand why no one will stop to pick him up because he is unaware that the woman who has stolen his clothes has dressed him in hers. During his sojourn on the chain gang in *Tramp, Tramp, Tramp,* Harry is handed a pistol by one of the other prisoners, who are all escaping. Harry, who is busy pounding away at a rock, merely substitutes the butt of the pistol for his small, inadequate hammer and continues pounding. He is also unaware when a railroad car runs over the chain attached to his leg and cuts off the heavy iron ball. He continues to carry the ball around with him for some time thereafter. Harry eventually meets up with his competitor in the walking race, who takes the ball and throws it over the edge of the cliff on which they are standing. The other racer did not know that his own foot was entangled in the loose end of the chain and he is carried over the cliff along with the ball. Harry, meanwhile, points back in the direction from which he has come, looking away for a moment as he explains what has happened to him. When Harry turns back to face the other racer and continue his story, he cannot figure out where the man has gone. He shrugs his shoulders and walks on.

The fact that Harry's voluntary actions are always somehow inappropriate to his circumstances clearly indicates that when Harry does respond to a particular situation or change in his situation, he has not properly perceived or comprehended its nature and significance.

Qualities beyond the range of the lowest threshold of consciousness, such as motivation, initiative, ambition, insight, foresight, and the capacity for premeditation are virtually absent in the comic character impersonated by Harry Langdon. Intellectual curiosity on Harry's part is aroused only under the condition of a confrontation at point-blank range with a material manifestation of some highly provocative fact of life. However, even at that, Harry usually comprehends the significance of such a fact only after a very long time, or not at all.

Such a confrontation occurs when Harry suddenly finds himself facing a bearded lady in *Remember When*. He stares at her and skips a few steps backward in order, perhaps, to get a better vantage point. From there, Harry kneels down practically to the ground to look up and stare at her. Harry obviously is not able to figure out who or what she is as he tips his hat to her, then offers her a cigar. Before taking his leave, Harry looks back at her once more in a sideways glance and, still curious, reaches out to compare her hairy face with his own soft cheeks.

In *The Chaser*, Harry holds a chicken over a frying pan for some time, waiting for it to lay an egg for his wife's breakfast. He finally gives up on the chicken but discovers an egg that another chicken had laid in the meantime on the ground in the spot where he had been squatting. Harry stares at the egg, blinks, puts his finger into his mouth, and then kicks it under a bush. He covers the spot by scratching in the dirt with his feet like a chicken, after looking around to make sure that no one was watching. Harry continues to stand there in the same long take, looking down and scratching his head thoughtfully for a while, then suddenly jumps up and away from the offending evidence.

The fact that Harry rarely initiates action also indicates that he lacks the capacity for premeditation. Action on Harry's part is customarily the action of some involuntary or conditioned reflex, or an action that is solely motivated by the instinct of self-preservation—to satisfy some urgent biological need or when Harry is the object of some overt aggression.

Even so, the operation of Harry's involuntary and conditioned reflexes is faulty, and he is usually incapable of responding effectively even to the impulse of his instincts. Harry often cannot run away when he is pursued to satisfy the instinct to preserve himself against aggression. In *Lucky Stars*, the citizens of San Tabasco, "a town of hot hate, hot love and hot tamales," are rioting over the poisoned patent medicine the "doctor" and Harry, as his assistant, have sold them. At one point during the riot, Harry finds himself alone on an empty street. He totters from side to side; turns around, looking for the doctor; takes a few steps into the background; halts; walks around there in a circle; and then runs a few steps forward as the doctor appears in the background, rounding the corner in great haste. As the doctor passes Harry and runs off out of the frame, Harry stops to watch him with a finger stuck into his mouth. Harry then turns around and takes a few steps backward to look back at where the doctor has come from. Harry stops again when he sees the angry mob come rushing around the corner, and then runs forward as if he were merely joining in with them. After taking only a few steps, Harry stops once more. Only at this point does he finally grab onto his hat, turn to face the camera, and run into the foreground away from his pursuers, who now follow closely on his heels.

As an unwelcome cellist in a group of street musicians in *Fiddlesticks*, Harry has similar difficulty in evading the criticism cast down upon him from above by his unwilling audience when the group is narrowly missed by a crockery pitcher. Harry is still standing in the street, looking down at the shattered remains of the pitcher after his companions have disappeared, and *then* Harry runs off to follow them.

Aggression as exhibited in Harry's behavior derives from the same instinctual impulse for self-preservation and is almost always self-defensive or retaliatory. Otherwise it is purely accidental, as when Harry inadvertently drops a boulder on the head of the fellow prisoner who has accidentally beaned him twice with a sledgehammer in *Tramp, Tramp, Tramp,* or when Harry throws a brick that strikes a cop and knocks him down in *Long Pants*. In the latter case, Harry is unaware when he throws the brick that a real cop has taken the place of the dummy cop at which Harry was aiming.

Or else, in cases of aggression on Harry's part, Harry is merely imitating the actions of someone else. When Harry belligerently bawls out the telephone pole for getting in the way of the car in which he was riding in *His Marriage Wow,* he is mimicking the actions of his lunatic companion, the driver. When he scolds the bully in *Boobs in the Wood,* Harry is merely imitating the gestures of the petite heroine as she stamps her foot and snaps her fingers to chase the bully away. In *Remember When,* Harry stands behind the sheriff and copies his threatening gestures toward a group of hoboes, to which Harry himself belongs, as the sheriff chases them across the state line.

As aggressor, Harry is ineffectual. His attempts at aggression are hindered, diverted, or aborted by the disjunction between volition and motor response that seems to govern all his voluntary actions and which is manifested in instances of indecision, hesitation, or distraction. As a soldier at the front in *The Strong Man*, for example, Harry fires when he is fired upon by the enemy, but not before first assuming a pointerlike stance, then turning toward his weapon and back again toward his target, and then retreating again to fetch the ammunition. During the fistfight in *Saturday Afternoon*, Harry is revived and emboldened with a swig of gasoline and rushes to the aid of his greatly outnumbered pal. First, Harry runs past everyone and stands in place practicing his hand- and footwork. He then takes a stand between Vernon, who has been knocked to the ground, and the two jealous boyfriends who are advancing on him. Harry merely looks back and forth from one to the others, assuring Vernon and wagging a warning finger at one of the antagonists, who then punches Harry on the jaw and knocks him silly.

In *Three's a Crowd*, Harry resolves to retaliate for getting an untrue fortune from a palm reader, but as often as he tries, he cannot carry it out. He walks deliberately to the large storefront window of the astrologer's establishment, which boasts, "Consult me and you will not go wrong," with a brick in his hand, and looks around to see if anyone is watching. He then lifts the brick into the air, stops, looks around again, then down at his palm. This inspires Harry and again he raises the hand with the brick, which, by this time, has slowly dropped to his side. He stops, however, with his arm in midair and puts the brick down on the ground. While dusting off his hands, Harry again notices his palm and again takes up the brick, poising to throw. Now he winds up repeatedly, begins a throwing motion, and then repeatedly interrupts that motion before he can actually follow through. Harry then moves closer to his target, then backs off as many steps, shrugs his shoulders, and finally tosses the brick away over his shoulder. The window is actually smashed, but it occurs through an accidental chain of events and not by any deliberate action on Harry's part.

Harry attempts to exact a similar revenge on the marriage-license bureau in *His Marriage Wow* by tossing a brick through its storefront window and again is incapable of acting upon his own resolution. Both Harry and the lunatic companion who has just driven them into a telephone pole approach the window with bricks in hand, but after the lunatic breaks the window with his brick, Harry merely puts his down and walks off instead of throwing in his two cents' worth. Harry's drawn-out altercation with the cab driver in *Tramp, Tramp, Tramp* eventually comes to violence when Harry picks up a brick and the cabbie, in turn, picks up another and throws it at Harry. It misses Harry and sails through the rear window of the cab. The altercation ends when, rather than defend himself by throwing his brick at the cabbie, Harry puts it back down and runs away.

In *The Strong Man*, Harry is completely ineffectual in his attempt at retaliation against the threats and assaults of a fellow bus passenger who becomes annoyed when Harry sneezes, coughs, and spills cough medicine on him. After the passenger warns Harry, "One more germ out of you and the Smith Brothers lose a good customer!" Harry's half-shut eyes shift in the man's direction. Harry merely glances, blinks once, continues to glare, and finally raises a tiny fist and holds it up, tentatively suspended in the vicinity of the passenger's nose.

While Harry dawdles, the man punches Harry, knocking him off his seat, then scolds him once more as Harry resumes his place. When the man returns to his newspaper, Harry reverts to his previous tactic of glaring at his antagonist, then blinks and looks ahead toward the camera impassively for a moment as if blinking had caused him to forget the offense. However, a second blink seems to restore Harry to his previous train of thought and he resumes glaring at the passenger as if he had never interrupted himself. Harry then raises his fist again and it hovers about his antagonist's face. Harry's antagonist, meanwhile, ignores Harry's ineffectual threats and continues to read his newspaper.

Harry now undertakes a feeble punching action, but his fist never comes into actual physical contact with his antagonist. It appears as if some invisible barrier comes between Harry and the man, stopping Harry's fist abruptly in midaction. Harry brings his fist unsteadily back down to his lap, looks ahead, and then looks back at the man. At this, Harry's fist abruptly jerks up again and he takes aim again as if to punch him. Again Harry pulls his hand away, and pounds it up and down on his knee as if in frustration, again facing the camera. Harry blinks, looks toward his indifferent antagonist, looks ahead and blinks, and then turns again toward the man. Harry waves his fist meekly around in the air and then brings it back down into his lap again. Once more, Harry looks at the man, raises his fist, aims it, and slowly advances it closer and closer toward the man's face. Without even looking up from his paper, the man brushes Harry's fist aside as he would a pesky housefly, and thus decisively thwarts Harry's advances.

The agonizingly prolonged sequence in which Harry attempts to murder Priscilla in *Long Pants* is an elaborate demonstration of Harry's total physical ineptitude and is also an extended metaphor for his sexual impotence. Harry has great difficulty, first, in extricating a pistol from his trousers; once it has been extracted, he is not able to fire it. By the end of the sequence, Harry is physically immobilized. He presents a ridiculous picture, sitting on a log with one foot in a bear trap, his top hat pushed down over his face to the shoulders, and his dress shirt hanging, disheveled, outside of his pants. After rescuing Harry from the bear trap and tidying up his appearance, Priscilla picks up the pistol and playfully takes target practice using Bebe's photograph in the newspaper as her target. She not only succeeds in firing the pistol, but hits her mark between the eyes.

Harry is not only unable to shoot Priscilla, a character who is easily as naive as Harry, but, as seen in *The Chaser,* he is also incapable of carrying out a similar act of aggression even against himself. In one of his attempts at suicide in the film, Harry places a gun first at his head, then sticks it into his side, holds it against his foot, then puts it into his shirt and holds it against his chest. Harry gives up when he feels the unpleasant touch of the cold metal against his skin.

As Harry is incapable of acting effectively, even in self-defense to satisfy the instinct of self-preservation, he is also incapable of acting effectively to satisfy the instinct of preservation of species. Harry is equally inept in the role of sexual aggressor. In *Boobs in the Wood,* Harry, a lumberjack, is wooed by a girl who is too impatient to wait for Harry to initiate a relationship. Harry does not seem to know what to make of her advances, but he does seem to be afraid of her. She starts to follow Harry through the woods as he wanders around looking for a tree small enough to chop down. When she starts running after him, Harry runs away. When he stops, she catches up and flirtatiously offers him something to eat. As Harry innocently accepts and starts to eat it, she puckers her lips, closes her eyes, leans toward Harry, and waits for him to kiss her.

However, only Harry's curiosity is aroused, and he stares at the girl for some time. He extends a tentative hand toward her face, but draws it back and diverts it to his hat before actually touching her and backs away at the same time. The girl is undaunted and now tries teasing him and then skipping away in order to get Harry to chase her. Harry merely watches, so the girl stops and runs in place to give Harry a better idea of what he is supposed to do. Harry obviously still has not caught on, since, instead of pursuing her, he merely imitates her and runs in place. She approaches Harry once more, "tags" him, and runs back to her former position, where

Harry has difficulty establishing physical contact with Mary (Priscilla Bonner) in *The Strong Man.*

she stops and again puckers up. This time, Harry follows, but stops short, finger in mouth, when she stops. Harry retreats to his former position while keeping an eye on her. When she follows and confronts him again, Harry raises an ax in self-defense. The girl now apparently gives up and walks dejectedly away. As she does, Harry drops his defenses and starts to follow her with apologetically outstretched arms, to which she promptly responds by turning around eagerly. Harry responds to her just as promptly by running away, and the two disappear as she chases him out of the frame.

Sometimes, the roles of hostile and amorous aggressor are related, as in the metaphorical attempted murder in *Long Pants*. In any case, Harry has the same difficulty in establishing physical contact with the objects of his affection in *The Strong Man* and *Tramp, Tramp, Tramp* as he does with the man on the bus during the head-cold routine in *The Strong Man*. In each film, there is an occasion on which Harry sits beside the girl of his dreams on a bench with ample opportunity to try to win her through amorous advances. In *The Strong Man*, Harry smiles at the blind heroine, laughs with his palm bashfully pressed against his mouth, chews on his hat, and then covers his face with it. Next, Harry just gazes at Mary for a while, blinking occasionally, and then finally nestles up to her to whisper in her ear.

As Harry gazes at Mary's profile, he tentatively fondles her cheek, chin, and hair. He does not actually touch her; his hand merely plays about her face in the air. He starts to touch her arm, but diverts his hand to his hat before actually doing so and then continues to look and play with his hand about her hair. After all this, Harry does take her hand, presses and pats it,

Harry and his sleeping sweetheart, Doris Dawson, on a park bench in *Heart Trouble*.

and then shyly covers both their hands with his hat. When Mary smiles, Harry brings her hand up to his lips but hesitates, looking back and forth at her before administering a quick peck on the back of her hand. After doing so, he abruptly brings her hand back down, glances at her once more, and then sighs and sinks back in his seat.

Harry sits on a bench with Betty in *Tramp, Tramp, Tramp* and for a long time merely looks at or glances back and forth at her. When Betty eventually returns his glance, looking directly at Harry for the first time, he suddenly averts his gaze and stares straight ahead with his hands folded in his lap, blinking occasionally. As she encourages him to register for the walking race, Harry stabs himself in the mouth with a pencil, and when she wishes him well, Harry merely stares ahead, wide-eyed, and blinks twice. Harry is encouraged further when Betty places her hand on his and promises to meet him at the end of the race. Harry reciprocates by patting her hand, though he hesitates after raising his hand to pat her cheek. He withdraws his hand before any physical contact is made and shakes her hand instead. As she starts to leave, Harry brings her hand up to his lips, but lets it slip out of his hands before he can kiss it and instead kisses his own two hands.

Such romantic tactics are hardly the sort supposed to sweep women off their feet, although Harry does do just that, once at least. This occurs in *The Chaser* when Harry stealthily approaches an unsuspecting woman who is a total stranger to him. Harry takes her in his arms and literally fells her with his kiss. In this case, however, as in those instances in which Harry initiates a hostile advance, Harry is merely imitating the actions of another. Harry's model for this amorous advance has been provided by a woman, also a total stranger, who has just tried to seduce Harry in exactly the same fashion, except for the fact that sexual roles and places in the mise-en-scène are reversed here.

Thus, Langdon's comic impersonation as it is defined by Langdon's mime may be identified as that of a person whose physical and intellectual faculties have been either pathologically impaired or impaired temporarily by some intoxicating influence or physical blow. This definition is just as defensible as identifying the character as an infant. Langdon's mime describes his comic character as one who is perpetually hovering between consciousness and unconsciousness. (The terms *consciousness* and *unconsciousness* are intended here and throughout this study, not as in Freudian terminology, but in a strictly clinical sense of either having or not having command of one's physical and mental faculties.)

The fact that slow transitions between sleeping and waking and between being conscious and being unconscious represent the single most common theme of Langdon's pantomime performance would seem to support this definition of Langdon's character. Sleeping or waking are often the subjects of extended pantomime routines in Langdon's films. *Three's a Crowd* begins with a very long sequence in which Langdon presents a skillfully

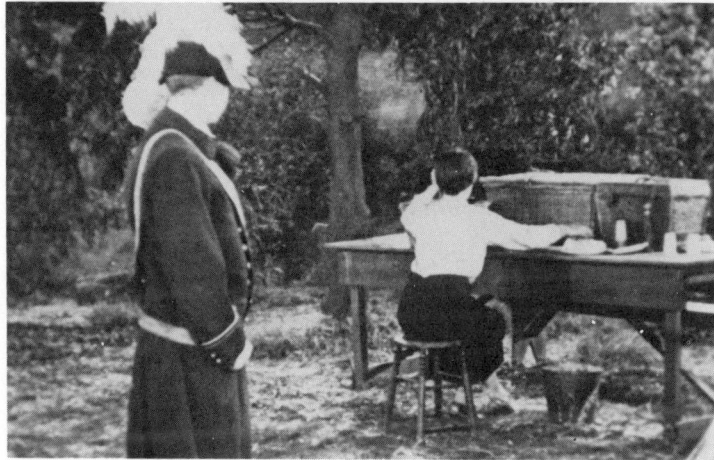

After a strange woman approaches Harry in order to seduce him *(above)*, Harry imitates her actions when he approaches another woman in a reversal of sexual roles and mise-en-scène *(below). The Chaser.* (Courtesy of Gladys McConnell)

pantomimed impression of Harry awakening in the morning. Harry visibly hovers between sleeping and waking as he repeatedly sits up in bed, then tips back over into a prone position, surrendering again to the irresistible influence of sleep. While sitting, Harry opens his eyes wide, appearing startled or staring vacantly. He blinks, yawns, and looks around his room until his eyelids again slide gradually closed. A companion to this routine is another long pantomime by Langdon in *Three's a Crowd* in which Harry falls asleep while rocking a baby to sleep as he sits and rocks with the baby in his arms in the baby's makeshift cradle.

The two-reeler *His Marriage Wow* includes a long sequence in which

Harry gradually succumbs to sleep as the result of having drunk too much wine (although Harry believes that he has been poisoned). As Harry sits at the table during his wedding dinner, talking and sipping the supposedly poisoned coffee, his eyelids drowsily slide into a half-closed position and his movements and gestures decelerate to the pace of slow motion. Harry, by now convinced that his coffee was poisoned by his bride in a family plot to get his life insurance, stumbles away from the table and into a chair. Harry gets up out of the chair when he finds himself surrounded by his bride, his newly acquired in-laws, and other members of the wedding party. When he then finds himself facing his bride, Harry changes direction and staggers toward another chair in the foreground of the shot. As he nears the chair, he starts to wobble at the knees and finally lets himself down into the chair. Apparently still insecure, Harry moves rather quickly into an adjoining room where he slows to a halt and starts to collapse to the floor on his way to a chair in the middle of this room, bouncing up and down a few times at the knees. He manages to make his way forward, haltingly, a few more steps before sinking down onto his hands and knees, then curls up in the middle of the floor into fetal position to sleep it off.

This routine is also followed by a briefer companion routine of Harry being awakened from his nap on the floor. Here, Harry is pulled to his feet and sinks back down, crawls around the floor on his hands and knees, and falls into and is pulled back out of a chair while staggering aimlessly around the room more or less upright until he is finally led out the door.

Tramp, Tramp, Tramp features another long pantomime routine in which Harry slowly succumbs to the sleep-inducing influence of a handful of sleeping tablets washed down with liquor. This transition from waking to sleeping, presented in several stationary long takes and mostly in medium shot, may be considered a companion piece to the equally lengthy transition from sleeping to waking with which *Three's a Crowd* begins. This transition is introduced by a prelude in which Harry is caught in a shower of goose down. The prelude sequence has been compared by the French critics to the dormitory sequence in Jean Vigo's *Zero for Conduct*.

In this routine, Harry remains seated, facing the camera, and insists that he cannot sleep while his eyelids fluctuate between wide open, shut, and halfway between these two positions. This goes on for some time before Harry attempts to stand up and quench his thirst with a drink from a pitcher that stands on a table across the room. From a standing position, Harry leans forward and reaches out for the pitcher as if it were at arm's length. Not reaching it, he is pulled forward a few steps by the weight of his body and, from there, begins an uncertain progress forward, which is, at the same time, a steady progress downward toward the floor. Harry touches down first on his hands, which cushion his fall, and then sets himself down gently upon his hands and knees. Then, drawing his arms around him, Harry folds up in the middle of the floor and sleeps.

Harry is capable of curling up into a fetal position and nodding off at any time in any place, even under such unlikely circumstances as in the midst of the barely settled rubble of the music hall that he has just demolished with a cannon in *The Strong Man,* while being seduced by a queen in her palatial boudoir in *Soldier Man,* on his way up a flight of stairs in *His First Flame,* on the canvas in the midst of a boxing match during his dream in *Three's a Crowd,* while sitting astride the running boards of two automobiles moving through city traffic in *Saturday Afternoon,* and on a bed in the apartment of the notorious "Lily of Broadway" immediately following a desperate struggle with her to defend his virtue in *The Strong Man. All Night Long* begins as Harry awakens in a dark, empty theater after falling asleep "in the middle of *Parlor, Bedroom and Bath,*" and in *Lucky Stars,* he cuddles up to sleep on the bosom of a hot-tempered South American vamp while she attempts to stab Harry in the back.

Certain gag situations, which are employed repeatedly in Langdon's films, provide Langdon ample opportunity to present his pantomimed impression of someone suspended between consciousness and unconsciousness. Harry is often dazed by a blow or a woman's kiss, or becomes intoxicated by alcohol, or drugs, or both. Examples include the instance in *Feet of Mud* in which Harry is hit on the head by a brick thrown from above and is led into an opium den where he curls up cozily to sleep off the effects of the blow; the instance in which Harry staggers out into the street, unaware that he is dressed in women's clothes after being knocked unconscious and dragged into a doorway by the female thief in *His First Flame;* and the occasions on which Harry hovers in midair after being struck in the head by an airborne pitcher in *The Chaser* and by a sledgehammer in *Tramp, Tramp, Tramp.* In *Saturday Afternoon,* Harry emerges dazed from a closed rumble seat after sustaining the physical punishment of a high-speed drive over rugged terrain. He falls out of the car onto the ground and sways tenuously to his feet on rubber legs, and then stands in one place gazing off absently as the automobile's tool kit is picked out of his clothes piece by piece.

Harry is so stunned from punches during the fistfight in *Saturday Afternoon* that after finally sinking to the ground on his hands and knees, he wanders around on all fours, head down, completely oblivious to, and consequently bumping headfirst into, every obstacle in his erratic path. He finally climbs up to sit astride the running boards of two parked cars where he lapses peacefully into unconsciousness.

When the effects of the punches begin to wear off, Harry starts to come around but he is still in such a daze that he does not notice the ground suddenly moving beneath him as the two cars drive off together into the city streets—even though he occasionally looks down, even though one foot falls repeatedly off the running board and scrapes along the road surface, and even though a traffic cop has to jump up over Harry as the two cars approach him. A telephone pole at a fork in the street, however, does not jump out of Harry's way and Harry's ride ends with Harry wrapped around the telephone pole until several bystanders arrive to unwrap him. Again, Harry bobs up and down on rubber legs, unable to stand, as his rescuers help him into his wife's waiting car.

In one sequence in *The Strong Man,* Harry falls off a stepladder while backing up a flight of stairs with Lily in his arms after failing to notice that he had already reached the landing and begun climbing the stepladder. As he sways and staggers to his feet, Harry picks up a roll of carpet, which he carries into Lily's room instead of Lily. Once both Harry and Lily are inside her apartment, she knocks him unconscious by hitting him on the head with a bottle. In *Long Pants,* Harry is dazed twice—once by a ricocheting horseshoe and, soon thereafter, by a horse that jerks Harry to the ground during his attempt to murder Priscilla, his unwanted bride-to-be.

A woman's kiss seems to have an effect on Harry similar to that of a powerful physical blow. For instance, when Bebe finally acknowledges Harry and gives him a little peck on the lips in *Long Pants,* his entire body becomes limp, his eyes close, and then, holding on to his hat with both hands, Harry slowly falls over backward out of her car. Afterwards, he becomes entangled in his bicycle. Following a second kiss, Harry slides off the running board and reels backward a few steps. He extends a hand toward the car for support and does not reach it, then teeters back and forth within a range of a few steps, and slides down and bounces back up off of the running board.

When Harry is dazed by the French girl's kiss in *All Night Long,* his reaction is filmed partially in slow motion and represents some extraordinary ecstatic condition that is wholly inaccessible to empathic identification by the viewer. When Nanette kisses Harry, his hand falls from her shoulder and hangs limp at his side. When she steps back, Harry is revealed, standing paralyzed, with eyes closed and a blissful smile upon his face. He then falls over backward through a nearby open window. Now there is a cut to a shot of Harry outside the farmhouse. He sits up and begins to crawl around on his hands and knees, trying to reenter the house by pushing his way, head first, through the stone facade. Failing to make any progress, he eventually slides up to his feet as his forward movement is diverted by the vertical wall. With his body pressed flush against the wall, Harry continues his forward motion and is now diverted sideways as he merely slides along the wall. Failing again to make any headway, Harry backs up a bit and walks into the wall repeatedly from a step or two away.

He finally pushes off from the wall and starts to walk toward the front door, first swaying backward, at which point the camera speed changes to slow motion. Harry starts off again toward the window, now taking huge, high steps, which, by the time he reaches the windowsill, have diminished to short, tiny steps as he tries and fails to reenter the house by walking in through the window. The camera speed changes back to normal as Harry lurches backward again away from the house, then tips back over forward, and finally falls into the door.

Harry's sleep in the long routines from *His Marriage Wow* and *Tramp, Tramp, Tramp* described previously is induced by the narcotic influence of too much wine in *His Marriage Wow,* and by a combination of drugs and alcohol in *Tramp, Tramp, Tramp.* There is another rather long routine in *Feet of Mud* in which Langdon pantomimes, through twitches and blinks of his eyes, nose, and mouth; a smile of pleasure; and alternately drooping and startled-open eyelids that Harry is succumbing to the influence of an opiate that is burning under his nose. In *The Sea Squawk,* the girl administers whiskey to revive Harry after he is knocked out by the heavy, and his subsequent behavior displays the effects of both the whiskey and the blow.

The Mack Sennett scenarios, synopses, and prepared reviews of other Langdon comedies, some of which are currently unavailable in film form, provide additional examples of similar gag situations. In the scenario for *Shanghaied Lovers,* Harry is hit on the head and "staggers a little bit." He is hit again, "staggers more violently . . . slides down to a sitting position almost drunk," after which, according to the scenario, "we go to a close-up of Langdon, showing him trying his best to keep his senses." After he is shanghaied, "Langdon, unconscious in a bunk, comes to and gets over that he is feeling pretty rocky," and staggers out the door of the cabin. The prepared review for *The Cat's Meow* describes, "One scene in particular" in which "an ether-soaked sponge flies back into Langdon's face." In *The Hansom Cabman,* according to the synopsis, Harry becomes dizzy when he inhales pipe smoke from his Chinese passengers. According to the synopsis of *Plain Clothes,* Harry becomes dizzy, then falls over unconscious when he inhales the gas that he has turned on to overcome the crooks and is "still dazed" after being revived.

What is most interesting and informative about these instances is that a comparison of Harry's behavior when he is under the influence of sleep or other externally induced intoxicants, to his behavior when he is not, clearly establishes the fact that there is no appreciable difference in the character's behavior or in Langdon's mime whether such a premise for his condition is provided or not. Harry can easily stand in for the chronically intoxicated king in *Soldier Man.* As the imposter, Harry is not even able to snap his fingers to punctuate a command. Harry's hand falls far short when he reaches for the doorman's hand to shake it in *The Strong Man* when he is not drugged or drunk. Harry is no less indifferent or unresponsive to his father's desperate plea to him to save the family business from imminent foreclosure when he is sober in *Tramp, Tramp, Tramp* than he is to the persistent demands of the cabbie who tries to collect his fare from Harry when he is drunk later in that film. And Harry certainly moves no more steadily, quickly, or purposefully when he is not under the influence of sleep, drink, drugs, a kiss, or a blow than he does when he is under one of these influences. Harry's reaction to Nanette's kiss in *All Night Long* is remarkable not only for the originality of the pantomimed performance itself but also because this sequence makes evident the fact that there is no appreciable difference in the pace of Langdon's mime and movement as seen here in slow motion and as recorded at normal camera speed. Filming Harry's reaction to Nanette's kiss in slow motion is redundant.

Thus, in Langdon's films, Harry is frequently either falling asleep, waking, or gaining or losing consciousness. At all these times, he is more or less indifferent to the objective reality of the situations in which he is found. He is never fully aware of the objective reality of the situations in which he is found (except in rare instances yet to be discussed in which a transition to cognition is actually accomplished) because his rational faculties are somehow otherwise impeded or impaired. The fact that a less than fully conscious condition constitutes the predominant theme of Langdon's pantomime and provides the premise for the stylistic qualities that characterize Langdon's performance as a whole leads one to think of the comic character Langdon impersonated as a pathologically acute case of comic absentmindedness. Harry is most appropriately characterized by his literal absence of mind, as opposed to the presence of mind that may also be described as being conscious. For his conception of this comic characterization and for the style of performance by which that characterization is elaborated, Langdon can be judged unique as a comic artist.

Harry's outward appearance as a strange composite of infant and adult and as one whose rational faculties are almost totally subordinated to sleep, dreams, hallucinations, alcohol- and drug-induced intoxication, and semiconscious dazes induced by physical blows or by a woman's kiss are surely the qualities in Langdon's comedy which engaged André Breton and Jean Cocteau and which have provided the basis for a consideration of Langdon's work in surrealist terms on the part of a number of French critics from the 1920s to the present.

In his 1970–71 *Jeune Cinéma* article "Harry Langdon," André Tournes discusses Harry's resolution of sleeping and dreaming with waking life and of fantasy with reality through references to examples from a number of Langdon's films. His comments are typical of the surrealist attitude toward the comedy of Harry Langdon. Tournes explains:

> Harry is not a character defined by what happens to him or by what he does, he is an age of man: an age in which one still dreams of a larval state, of the cradle, of sleeping instead of boxing, of breaking stones, of marrying a simpleton, of serving soup or of firing at the German opposite him. It is the age of hesitation between two small loaves of bread, between leaving and drinking, between the desire and fear of a kiss. It is also an age in which one dreams dreams of compensation; and since it is 1926, these dreams are nourished by the cinema. Harry in short pants becomes the good-looking young man of the city of *Metropolis;* Harry the soldier, an operetta king who decrees condemnations to death; Harry the timid lover, a boxer in giant gloves. In these successful sequences, the interpretation of dream is not relegated to the parapet ghetto of "dream" or of "memory"; rather it is immediately apparent that the man-child

completely transforms himself, firing on the enemy with caramels, fighting the cyclone with small stones and scattering the outlaws who have corrupted the village in *The Strong Man* with a volley from a trick cannon. In *Tramp, Tramp, Tramp,* Capra, undoubtedly confusing Harry with Buster . . . makes him run a marathon before giving him the woman and small child; but this is to overlook the fact that Harry does not conquer, that his victims are given to him, that the balloon falls all by itself into his kangaroo-like pocket and that like the small child, he does not need to act like the knight-errant in order to be cuddled and loved.[7]

However, this description of Harry as one who has attained the surrealist ideal of a resolution of dream and fantasy life with waking reality is not a proper identification of the comic persona elaborated in Langdon's performance. Langdon's comic impersonation is, rather, that of one who is largely incapacitated by his failure to resolve those two states. Langdon's mime describes someone who is neither completely unconscious or fully conscious, but who is perpetually in transition between consciousness and unconsciousness. Langdon's mime, furthermore, describes someone who, in this condition, is constantly confronted by the demands of what the surrealists would term "waking life," but who has not sufficient command over his physical or cognitive faculties to respond in a manner that is judged appropriate to the situation according to standards of rational behavior. Harry's responses range from demonstrations of physical and mental ineptitude to the complete debilitation of inertia and paralysis. Langdon's comic character, therefore, does not offer a model of the surrealist ambition attained, just as it is improperly identified as an impersonation of a baby.

A *dis*junction between consciousness and unconsciousness is, in fact, commonly the subject of those gags and gag situations in Langdon's films in which he pantomimes a slow transition from waking to sleeping and vice versa, and between consciousness and unconsciousness, as when dazed by a blow, or succumbing to or recovering from the intoxicating influence of alcohol, drugs, or the girl's kiss. These slow transitions appear to be difficult and sometimes painful for Harry.

A similar disjunction at the parallel level of cognition is the subject of gags and gag situations in Langdon's films in which he performs gradual and also apparently difficult and sometimes painful transitions or awakenings from blissful ignorance to intellectual awareness. In certain situations that are obviously tailored to Harry's infantile appearance and presumable inexperience, it is a transition from innocence or naiveté to an erotic or an emotional awakening and a certain degree of maturity.

Harry's gradual transitions from ignorance, innocence, or naiveté to an awareness of the objective reality of a particular situation are the counterparts to his gradual transitions between sleeping and waking or between being conscious and being unconscious. The transition to cognition is rendered as some kind of awakening on Harry's part—intellectual, emotional, or carnal. The analogous relationship between these two kinds of transitions is suggested by the similarity of Harry's behavior in both types of situations, the similarity of Langdon's mime in both types of situations, and a similar cinematic treatment of both kinds of transitions (a stationary long take of Harry that is usually equal to the time of the transition itself).

For example, Harry tries to commit suicide in *The Chaser* by poisoning himself. After drinking the poison, Harry lies down on the kitchen floor, covers himself with a tablecloth, places a farewell note on top of the tablecloth, and waits there to die. He waits, lying completely inert for nearly a minute before making the discovery that he is not dead. (This take is interrupted once by a brief insert shot of Harry from a closer camera distance.) Harry makes this discovery when nature's urgent call causes him to sit up suddenly and dash upstairs to the bathroom. The "poison" Harry took was actually castor oil, and if it were not for the castor-oil-induced somatic stimulus to his intellectual discovery of the fact that he was alive, Harry might have remained on the kitchen floor indefinitely.

In *Soldier Man* and *Saturday Afternoon*, Harry merely looks up to discover two interesting facts of life confronting him directly at point-blank range. Harry blinks, stares fixedly at, is startled by, and examines closely a cow's udder in *Soldier Man* and a prolonged kiss between Vernon and his girl friend in *Saturday Afternoon*. In *Long Pants*, a woman's bare thigh is exposed in the foreground of a close shot in which Harry is seen eating his lunch. While the woman adjusts her garter literally right before Harry's eyes, Harry continues eating his sandwich and chattering to Bebe, who is off-screen hiding inside a wooden crate. Harry finally looks directly at the woman's thigh but gives no outward indication that he recognizes its erotic implications or even that he has seen it at all until he begins to take another bite of his sandwich. His eyes suddenly pop wide open, and in the next shot, Harry jumps up as if stung and runs away.

Harry's transition from innocence to experience when Lily becomes intimate with him in the back seat of a cab in *The Strong Man* is also slow and difficult. This too is presented in a long static take. The shot is interrupted once, midway, with a cutaway to an insert of a snapshot of Mary Brown when Harry takes it out to compare it with Lily, who is posing as Mary Brown in order to recover the stolen bankroll that Lily has hidden in Harry's pocket. Harry has been sitting beside Lily in the cab, happily engaged in eating a bag of popcorn, until he feels her hand sliding in between his back pocket and the seat. Harry immediately jumps up, and then sinks back down low in his seat and remains in that position for some time, completely motionless except for his eyes.

Harry's eyes follow Lily's every movement as she nonchalantly crosses her legs and lights and smokes a cigarette. Still in the same protective crouch, Harry eventually brings a finger up to his mouth in a familiar gesture of apprehension and looks out the window on his side of the cab. He finally sits up to look at the snapshot and compare it with Lily, and then

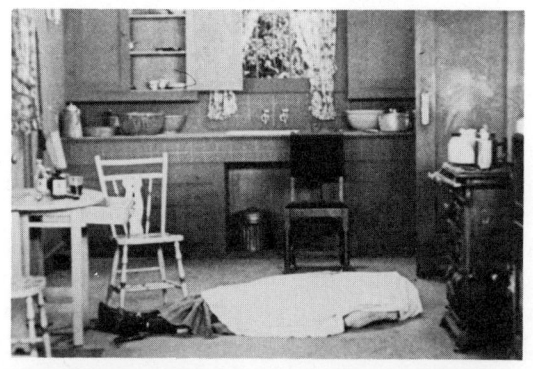
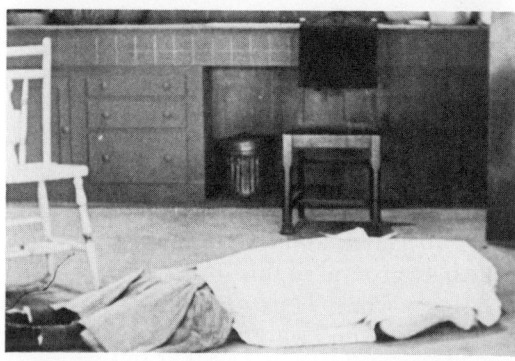

Harry lies inert on the kitchen floor waiting to die after trying to poison himself with castor oil in *The Chaser*. (Courtesy of Gladys McConnell)

starts to climb out of the cab. Lily pulls him back down into his seat and begins caressing him while Harry sits rigidly with one hand holding on to his hat, the other still clutching his bag of popcorn, with his eyes fixed upon her, except for an occasional blink. Lily tries again to get her money, but the moment she touches Harry's jacket to open it, he jumps up like a jack-in-the-box admidst a shower of popcorn, and then crings in the corner of the cab, holding his jacket tightly closed and holding on to his hat with the other hand until the end of the ride.

Harry is literally incapacitated at certain moments in which one of those imminent demands of waking life with which he is constantly confronted precipitates an intellectual, emotional, or sensual awakening. These occasions in which Harry momentarily gains presence of mind, that is, in which the transition from blissful ignorance to cognition or from innocence to experience is actually accomplished, are rare. They are rendered as moments of profound psychological impact, even as traumatic experiences by Harry's response of physical paralysis, presented in the filmic form of an extraordinarily long, static take.

One such moment occurs in *The Strong Man* when, after finally having found Mary Brown and delightedly and animatedly presenting himself to her in the garden, Harry learns that she is blind. After telling him this, Mary turns her back to Harry and moves toward a bench to sit. Harry is seen standing in the background of this shot, watching Mary with his hands behind his back. After a while, Harry tentatively extends a hand as if to assist her while she makes her way unsurely to the bench in the foreground. His hand drops back down to his side and he merely stands in place looking at Mary, who is now seated. There is a closer shot of Harry standing in exactly the same position and continuing to stare blankly in Mary's direction, followed by a return to the original camera setup as Mary, in the foreground, wipes away a tear. Harry has still not moved or even blinked an eye, and he remains motionless throughout the duration of this shot, which then slowly fades to black.

One other such moment occurs in *Three's a Crowd* when, after entering his shack, Harry stands as if paralyzed, staring vacantly at the girl whom he has taken in and her newborn child for the first time. They are seen, also motionless, asleep in the foreground in an extremely long, static take that is also concluded by a slow fade-out.

In probably the most traumatic of these incapacitating awakenings, Harry sits perfectly still throughout a long take with his back to the camera watching Bebe literally mop up the floor with a female rival in the dressing room of a seedy nightclub in *Long Pants*. Bebe, who represents to Harry the incarnation of his romantic fantasies—his "damsel in distress"—is actually an ex-convict and is currently a heroin smuggler. Previous to this rude conclusion to their relationship, Harry had accompanied Bebe on a crime spree that included two bank robberies and a score of holdups while he remained sublimely ignorant of her actual occupation and the fact that he

Harry makes the slow and difficult transition from innocence to experience in the back seat of a cab in *The Strong Man*. Langdon with Gertrude Astor.

was acting as an accomplice in her crimes. In one of those incidents, Bebe uses Harry as a lookout while she holds up a man on the street. Harry stands by, naively engaged in a reverie as he plays with the wedding ring he plans to offer Bebe. Meanwhile, Bebe strips the man of his clothes and valuables after kicking and pistol-whipping him. Harry delightedly receives what he thinks are gifts from her as she hands him the loot piece by piece. With Harry tagging along, Bebe goes on from there to fleece another victim after making sexual advances to him in order to get close enough to explore his pockets.

From the beginning of the skirmish between Bebe and Betty, her rival, to the end of the film when Harry, as the sadder-but-wiser son, returns to the security of his overprotective parents' home, Harry is subject to paralytic seizures and seems to have a wide-eyed stare permanently fixed upon his face.

When Betty first enters the dressing room, Harry smiles courteously and tips his hat. Harry's smile soon fades when Betty and Bebe immediately face off to have it out. Harry is frozen where he stands in this hat-aloft posture, except for his head, which turns from Bebe to Betty as they exchange impolite epithets. In the last frontal shot of Harry before the cut to the shot in which he observes the conclusion of the battle between the two women with his back to the camera, Harry looks back and forth between them with the same wide-eyed stare that is on his face when he finally stands up and turns to face the camera after the fight is over.

This is followed by the gag title as spoken by Harry, "Why, I'm surprised!" The gag title seems anticlimatic, to say the least, and superfluous to Langdon's pantomime. It sounds as though it was chosen at some point in

Harry stands between Bebe and Betty (Betty Francisco), paralyzed by a profound awakening, in *Long Pants*.

the postproduction of the film from one of those lists of a dozen alternative gag titles compiled by the gag writers for insertion at a particular point in the story. It does not express the sentiment that seems to have inspired Langdon's mime in this instance. (This also applies to the gag title—"Are you sure you're Mary Brown"—spoken by Harry in *The Strong Man*, which is inserted into the scene between Harry and Lily in the back seat of the taxicab.) This is not the last of Harry's eye-opening experiences in *Long Pants*. He watches with the same expression as Bebe then instigates a shoot-out with her former lover, who has entered the room, and kills him.

Harry is subsequently revealed, when the crowd of onlookers who have rushed into the dressing room clears away, sitting absolutely still on the floor holding a wounded arm with a wide-eyed, vacant stare fixed upon his face. Harry finally blinks once, at which point there is a fade-out and transition to a new sequence in which Harry is now discovered peering out from behind the bars of a jail cell that he shares with a group of hardened-looking felons. Harry is still holding on to his wounded arm, now in a sling, and still retains the wide-eyed gaze even as he is led out of jail and sent on his way home. Harry walks like a zombie at a constant pace, staring straight ahead with an unchanging, impassive expression all the way home, through the front gate, up the walk to the front door, and into the house, where he seats himself at the dinner table just as the rest of the family are saying grace.

The fact that Harry is apparently stunned by the psychological impact of an emotional or intellectual discovery as effectively as he is by a powerful knockout blow, as well as the fact that both kinds of incidents are presented in a similar filmic treatment, reinforces the analogy between the condition of being conscious in a clinical sense and cognition. These moments of profound emotional, erotic, or intellectual awakening in which Harry becomes fully aware of the world of waking reality and correctly perceives his own relation to it—that is, moments in which Harry gains presence of mind—constitute pathos in Langdon's comedies. The poignancy of these pathetic moments in Langdon's films may be compared to that of the shock of recognition of classical tragedy. Harry's shock in *Long Pants* at the revelation of Bebe's true identity and at an inkling of his own sexual identity is no less profound than that aroused by the discoveries of Oedipus or Hamlet. These moments of pathos in Langdon's films are also sometimes concluded with a gradual fade-out that functions very much like a curtain does on stage to provide a dramatic punctuation to the scene, as in the pathetic moments in *The Strong Man* and *Three's a Crowd.*

The disjunction between consciousness as waking and unconsciousness as sleep, dream, and fantasy is also a significant narrative motif in Langdon's films, from the Sennett two-reelers to the final features directed by Langdon himself. Langdon's films frequently include dream or fantasy sequences in which the dream or fantasy is always clearly demarcated from waking reality within the context of the film's narrative structure and at times, also in terms of visual treatment.

Most of the running time of the three-reel comedy *Soldier Man* represents Harry's dream of being abducted and posing as a king and of being seduced by and, in turn, seducing a queen in her palatial boudoir in a display of sexual potency when a mere kiss causes her to collapse to the floor at his feet. The dream is sharply contrasted with mundane reality when, after nonchalantly curling up in the queen's bed for a nap after devastating her with a kiss in the dream, he awakes in his own bed in the framing story to a wife who would rather wash dishes than kiss him. Nevertheless, Harry is determined to test his prowess as a lover. He prepares to

Harry dreams of being abducted and of posing as a chronically inebriated king in *Soldier Man.*

reenact the dream by carefully placing a pillow on the floor after calculating where his wife will fall, and then kisses her. When she merely stares at him, he tries giving her a little push. This has no effect either and as Harry's wife continues dressing him, he stares at her for a moment, blinks, and then rubs his eyes and scratches his head as the shot fades out, ending the film.

The sequence of Harry's fantasy in *Long Pants* in which he is seen as he imagines himself—the dashing hero of a Ruritanian romance—was photographed in Technicolor. It is the only Technicolor sequence in the film as it was originally released. Harry's dream of meeting Gladys's husband in the boxing ring and of losing the fight but winning the girl in *Three's a Crowd* is also clearly set off from the reality of the framing story by the way it is lit, as well as by the strange costumes and props and the bizarre nature of the events depicted.

Harry wakes up within the dream when Gladys's husband, grimacing and dressed as a melodrama villain, appears at the door of Harry's shack. He has come to snatch Harry's newfound family from him. A thunderstorm that is raging outside causes everything inside the shack to shake and sway violently. Gladys goes to the boxing match in her nightgown, galoshes, and a sun hat. Standing at ringside, holding her baby in her arms, Gladys

The royal wedding in Harry's Ruritanian fantasy in *Long Pants*. Langdon and Alma Bennett. Harry's fantasy originally ran a full reel and was photographed in Technicolor. This shot does not appear in the film as it was trimmed after its original release.

roots for Harry to win with a bloodthirsty passion. The sharp contrasts of highlight and shadow and the flickering lightning effects in the interior of Harry's shack, and the harshly glaring overhead lighting of the boxing ring contrast sharply with the softly illuminated, gauze-diffused look in which the rest of the film is photographed.

In *Long Pants*, Harry's fantasied murder of Priscilla and Harry's subsequent attempt to enact his fantasy in actuality are differentiated primarily by differences in content. In Harry's fantasy, the deed is smoothly and efficiently done, whereas in actuality it is hopelessly botched and is therefore, for one thing, a much longer sequence. The sequence is a torturous ordeal of frustration and humiliation for Harry, rather than a wish fulfillment as it is in his fantasy.

Both sequences begin with shots of Harry and Priscilla dressed in formal wedding attire, walking into the foreground through a corridor of eerily looming trees. The early images in the sequence of the murder attempt exhibit the same softly diffused visual quality as those of the fantasy sequence. However, as soon as the discrepancies in content begin to occur, a discrepancy in visual treatment becomes apparent. The visual style of the fantasy sequence is, at this point, no longer copied. One other stylistic distinction between the two sequences is the fact that the figures of Harry and Priscilla are superimposed and transparent in some shots in the fantasy sequence, whereas the two figures appear substantial in all of the shots of the murder attempt in actuality.

The approach to the subject of dreams exhibited in Langdon's comedies is different from the presentation of dream or fantasy sequences in the films of Buster Keaton. Dreams and fantasies are also of significant thematic interest in Keaton's comedies (which many French critics also consider surrealistic). In many of Keaton's comedies, however, the distinction between dream or hallucination and waking is deliberately confused.

The Playhouse, for instance, opens with an impossible sequence in which Buster portrays the entire cast, crew, orchestra, and audience of "Buster Keaton's Minstrels" by means of montage synthesis and a multiple-image split-screen special-effect technique. The sequence concludes with a dissolve from a two-shot of a married couple, both played by Keaton, applauding the show to a shot of Buster applauding in his sleep in what appears to be his bedroom in what appears to be a transition to waking reality as his boss awakens him. While Buster sits up drowsily on the bed and gets his hat and goes out the "bedroom" door, the "bedroom" disintegrates before our eyes. When the bedroom set in which Buster, the stagehand, has snuck a nap is struck, what was presumed to be waking reality is revealed to the viewer as a theatrical illusion. At this point, one is not sure whether the backstage set that comes into view as the walls of the bedroom set are raised into the flies is intended as waking reality either.

As a projectionist in *Sherlock Junior,* Buster literally traverses the boundaries between fantasy, dreams, filmic illusionism, and waking reality—that is, of course, within the illusionistic context of the film itself—frequently and with the greatest of ease. He falls asleep in the projection booth and the images of his dream are projected onto the theater screen. To make the transition from filmic illusion to Buster's dream, the characters in the film merely turn their backs to the camera. When they turn back again to face the camera, they are the people in Buster's dream. Buster's dreamed self, as a superimposed figure, takes leave of Buster's body in the projection booth. Then, as a substantial figure, the dreamed self walks down the center aisle of the theater, climbs up on stage, and walks into, and then falls out of his dream. Once the camera setup changes to exclude the proscenium, orchestra, and audience, which had previously framed the images on the screen, there is no longer any distinction whatever at the level of filmic treatment between waking reality (the framing story) and Buster's dream. A reverse-angle shot of Buster asleep inside the projection booth, framed by the booth window, is another element of cinematic treatment that adds to the confusion of dream, fantasy, reality, and illusion in this sequence.

Buster accomplishes the reconciliation of fantasy and reality that Harry can not. Buster adapts his fantasy to waking life, or vice versa, with apparent success at the end of *Sherlock Junior*. When the girl comes to visit him in the booth, Buster takes his cues for winning the girl directly from the characters on the screen. This can be compared to Harry's miserable failure in *Long Pants* when he tries to enact in real life his fantasy of murdering Priscilla. When Buster sees the screen lover turn the screen heroine toward him and pat her hands, Buster does likewise with his girl friend. When Buster sees the screen lover kiss the heroine's hands and then place a ring on her finger, Buster kisses the girl's hands and places a ring on her finger. When Buster sees the screen lover kiss the heroine on the lips, Buster kisses his girl friend; and when the screen heroine complies, so does Buster's girl friend. However, Buster can only scratch his head in consternation when the image on the theater screen fades out from a shot of the lovers embracing and fades in to a shot of the same two characters as the proud parents of twin babies.

Rather than accomplishing a reconciliation of these two states of being, Harry is continually bewildered, perplexed, and even shocked at the discrepancies between dreams or fantasies and waking reality—that is, when his dreams or fantasies do not "come true." This applies to the example from *Soldier Man* in which Harry's kiss fails to have the same effect on his wife after he wakes as it did upon the queen in his dream. This also applies to Harry's consternation at the great discrepancy between the murder of Priscilla as he fancied it and the actual murder attempt in which he is foiled at every turn.

Harry is introduced in the earlier Sennett comedy, *Feet of Mud*, as a football player sitting on the bench during a game, gazing longingly at a mental image of his dream girl that is superimposed on a fan's balloon. When the balloon is grazed by a peanut shell and bursts, Harry is suddenly shocked out of his reverie.

When Harry awakens in the dark, empty movie theater at the beginning of *All Night Long*, he appears completely confused and disoriented as he stares around him wide-eyed with a finger stuck apprehensively in his mouth. Before getting up from his seat, he glances nervously from side to side holding on to his hat. Harry then, typically, takes a step to the right and finally goes off left.

Harry is equally bewildered, perplexed, and shocked at the congruence of reality with his dreams and fantasies—that is, when his dreams do "come true." In both instances—when his dreams do or do not come true—Harry's response is either a frenetic inertia or physical paralysis. This applies to *The Strong Man* in which Harry frantically races around backstage when he finally just happens to find Mary Brown, his overseas wartime pen pal whose snapshot he has been carrying with him in a heretofore fruitless search. Another example is the moment in *Tramp, Tramp, Tramp* when the girl whose image Harry has worshiped on a larger-than-life-size billboard appears before him in the flesh, dressed just as she is in her picture.

One other such moment occurs in *Long Pants* when the heroine of Harry's fantasies, as portrayed in the fantasy sequence at the beginning of the film, appears to him later in real life in the person of Bebe Blair. "Then—," even as Harry is acting out the fantasy seen earlier—embracing, kissing, and caressing an imaginary heroine—"like the answer to a maiden's prayer, there came to Oak Grove Beautiful Bebe Blair," as a title informs us. When Harry sees her, he stops in his tracks. Then he takes a step backward in her direction, stops again, and stands there, staring at her and blinking his eyes occasionally. When he is given the slightest encouragement from Bebe, Harry begins to pedal his bicycle furiously in circles around her car. After being called home by his mother, Harry returns to find Bebe gone and a love note he mistakenly believes is intended for him. Harry's reaction after reading the note is the same awkward, excited dance of delight at his dream come true that he performs in the garden in *The Strong Man* when he presents himself to Mary Brown.

In *Three's a Crowd,* Harry dreams of having a family and pretends that a rag doll is his own child. When the abandoned girl, Gladys, and her child come into his life, "It sounds like some fairy tale—," as his boss's wife observes, "him longing for a wife and baby and them sent to him that way."

Langdon and Alma Bennett as the incarnation of Harry's romantic fantasies—an ex-convict who is presently smuggling heroin. *Long Pants.*

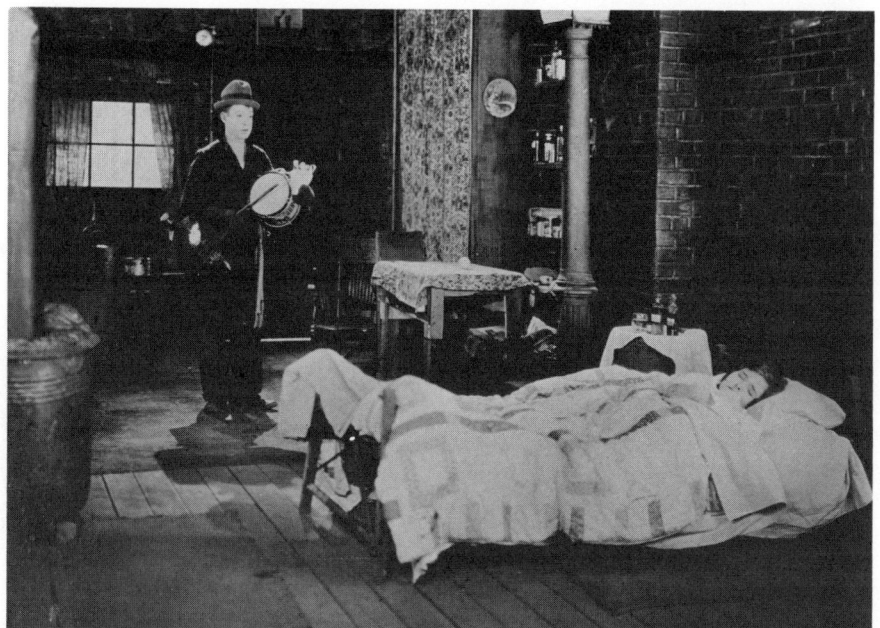

Harry is shocked when his dreams come true. Here he is stopped in his tracks by the sight of Gladys (Gladys McConnell) and her newborn child in *Three's a Crowd*. (Courtesy of Gladys McConnell)

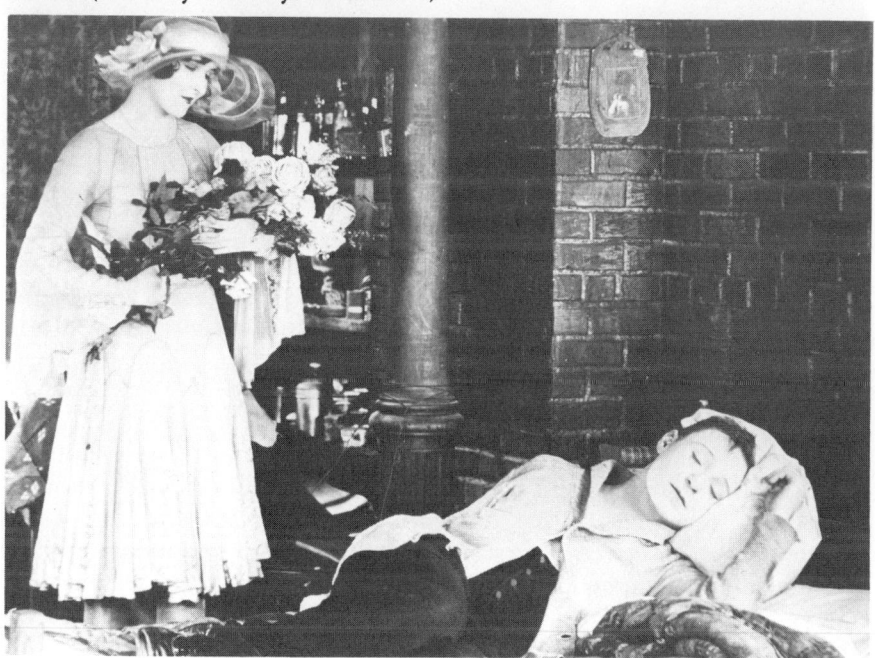

In the dream sequence cut from *Three's a Crowd* after previews, Gladys comes to Harry's room and covers him with flowers as he sleeps. (Courtesy of Gladys McConnell)

After rescuing the unconscious girl, Harry begins to feed her some soup and looks closely at her face and the baby clothes with a wide-eyed expression fixed upon his face. He then gets up and totters in place from side to side, runs around once in a circle, and resumes his original kneeling position at her bedside. Harry's momentary paralysis and then frantic inertia are typical responses to his dream—in this case for a wife and child—come true. The static tableau in which Harry maintains an arrested pose for the duration of one of the longest of Langdon's long takes when he later beholds the mother and newborn infant is another example of the paralyzing effect on Harry of a dream come true.

In another sequence cut from the beginning of *Three's a Crowd*, Harry spots Gladys through his telescope and falls in love with her. (Courtesy of Gladys McConnell)

Harry's reaction in the sequence in which he looks at the pregnant girl closely for the first time had a further significance in the original version of the film as previewed. In that version, there is a dream sequence at the beginning of the film in which Gladys appears at Harry's bedside, standing over him and looking on lovingly while he sleeps. In the sequence in which Harry stares at the girl as originally intended, he recognizes not only that these are the wife and child he has been longing for but also that this is the very girl for whom he had longed and who comes to him in his dreams.[8]

The footage cut from the beginning of *Three's a Crowd* also included a shot in which Gladys beckons Harry to her as seen from Harry's point of

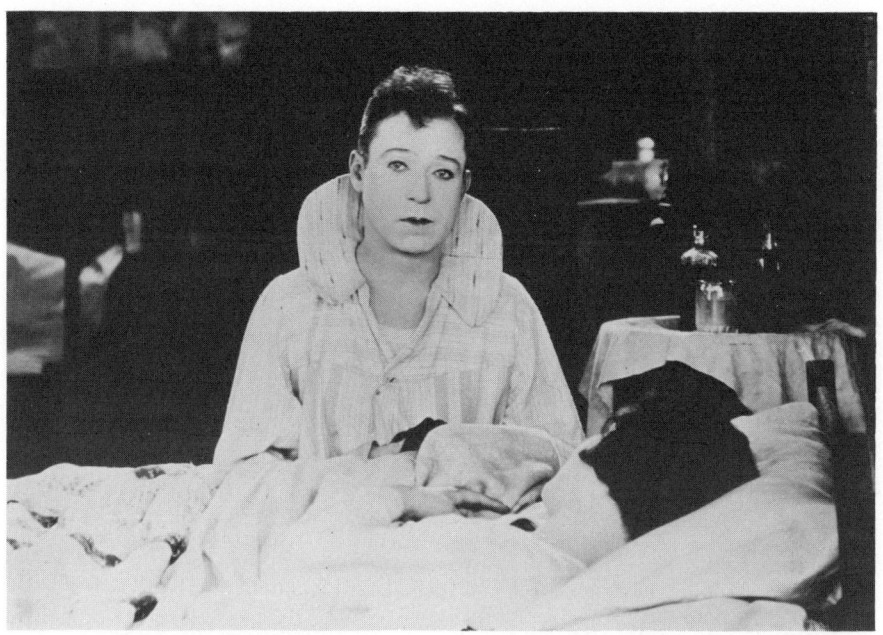

Harry and his dream come true of a family of his own in *Three's a Crowd*. (Courtesy of Gladys McConnell)

Harry is shocked when dreams do not come true. He bids his "family" farewell when Gladys's reformed husband (Cornelius Keefe) comes to take his wife and child home in *Three's a Crowd*. (Courtesy of Gladys McConnell)

Harry Von Housen, son of German parents, tries to enlist in the U.S. Army when war with Germany breaks out in *Heart Trouble*.

view through the long funnel of his telescope. (This shot may or may not have been part of the dream sequence. Gladys may also have been greeting her lover here, the man who is introduced later in the film as her husband, since there was also a sequence of exposition of Glady's story included in the footage that was cut from the film after previews. In the shot in which Gladys appears to beckon to Harry, we may be seeing her merely through Harry's wishful viewpoint.)

Harry consults a palm reader for assurance that his dream has, in fact,

Harry is declared "unfit" because he is "underweight, too short, has fallen arches, halitosis, dandruff, myopia, you-tell-'em, and what-have-you." *Heart Trouble*.

become reality. The palm reader tells Harry that he need not worry about the girl's husband taking his newfound family from him. When this does occur in *Three's a Crowd,* we are given further examples of Harry's response when dreams do not come true. He awakens from the dream in which, though he has lost the boxing match he still has the girl's love, to the

Harry, sitting in the doorway of his father's bakery, is disappointed when his dream of proving his loyalty does not come true. Langdon with Lionel Belmore in *Heart Trouble.*

Harry, as surprised as he was disappointed, when his dream comes true in *Heart Trouble*. Harry is proclaimed a hero after he unknowingly foils the plans of a group of spies and saves the life of the colonel who told him he was too small to join the army. Langdon with Doris Dawson.

complete contradiction of his wishes as expressed in the dream. From the shot of Harry curling up to sleep on the canvas as Gladys (wearing the hat in which she is seen in the first, excised dream sequence) kisses him, there is a cut to an exterior view of the shack in which the husband is seen knocking at the door in actuality. The husband is seen here as he was first seen in the opening shots of the dream sequence, though in the dream sequence he is seen from inside the cabin and in the more stylized mock-melodrama presentation previously described.

Harry then awakes, still sitting in the child's crib where he had fallen asleep, to see the reformed husband embracing his wife in a joyful reunion.

Harry brings a finger to his mouth and his eyes open wide as he watches. Then, as the husband and wife kiss and prepare to leave the shack with the child, Harry looks on from a chair, sitting still, except to blink his eyes and glance once at his palm. Harry watches from the doorway of the shack as the family enters the husband's car on the street below. Harry holds a lantern above his head, immobilized in a static tableau just as he was when he realized that his dream had come true.

Notes

1. Ado Kyrou, *Le Surréalisme au Cinéma* (Paris: Le Terrain Vague, 1963), pp. 168–69, 169, 170.

2. Paul Gilson, "Harry Langdon ou la Maladie du Sommeil," *La Revue du Cinéma*, (Paris), no. 3 (May 1929): no page number.

3. Andre G. Brunelin, "Harry Langdon," *Cinéma 60*, (Paris), no. 49 (August–September 1960): 75.

4. Richard Leary, "Capra and Langdon," *Film Comment* 8 (November–December 1972): 16.

5. Raymond Durgnat, *The Crazy Mirror: Hollywood and the American Image* (New York: Horizon Press, 1969), p. 89.

6. André Tournes, "Harry Langdon," *Jeune Cinéma*, (Paris), no. 51 (December 1970–January 1971): 18.

7. Ibid.

8. Information on the original version of *Three's a Crowd* was provided the author in an interview with Langdon's co-star in the film, Gladys McConnell, Laguna Hills, California, 5 July 1974, and from production stills in her collection.

4
The Performance

According to the methodology adopted in the previous chapter for analyzing and interpreting Langdon's comic characterization, Harry is defined by Langdon's pantomime of sleeping and waking or of gaining or losing consciousness, and by Harry's responses when he is confronted by certain imminent demands of waking life (including a lack of any apparent response whatever). These demands can be categorized as follows:
1. a materially manifest fact of life;
2. the standard comic antagonists—heavy, cop, or vamp—whose hostile or amorous advances threaten imminent physical violence, as well as those inanimate, indifferent, or inert "antagonists" who do not actually threaten violence but with whom Harry, nevertheless, becomes engaged in one-sided encounters; and
3. two or more moral, logical, or intellectual alternatives or options that are physically manifest and spatially differentiated.

Taken together, items 1 through 3 serve as a definition of objective reality within the boundaries of Langdon's comic cosmos. Most of Langdon's film comedies are largely made up of a loosely linked succession of these basic situations with little real narrative or dramatic development of plot and characterization.

Harry's responses in these situations are invariably somehow inappropriate to the circumstances that confront him, judged, that is, according to standards of rational behavior. In other words, Harry's responses are judged inappropriate by the observer who is in full possession of his or her rational faculties as compared to his or her own estimated response if he or she were in the same situation.

Category 1 includes such highly affective provocations as the prolonged kiss between Vernon and his girl friend in *Saturday Afternoon,* a woman's bare thigh in *Long Pants,* the bearded lady in *Remember When,* and the fact that Mary Brown is blind in *The Strong Man.* Harry demonstrates inappropriate responses to the kinds of comic antagonists listed in category 2 by moving too much when he is confronted with Lily's body after she pretends to faint in front of her apartment building in a scheme to lure him up to her room in *The Strong Man,* or by not moving at all after she reaches into his back pocket for the bankroll in the back seat of the taxicab. Harry may also go too far, as occurs when Harry overshoots the belligerent boyfriends during the fracas in *Saturday Afternoon,* or not go far enough, as in Harry's futile attempts to land a retaliatory punch on the nose of the passenger who is sitting beside him on the bus in *The Strong Man.* Category 3 includes the long routine in *Tramp, Tramp, Tramp* in which Harry runs back and forth between Betty on the billboard and Betty in the flesh in order to decide which one of them is real.

Each of these examples and the various categories of Harry's abnormal behavior that were considered as symptoms of a pathological absentmindedness in chapter 3 can also be considered within a theoretical framework which is a variation of Sigmund Freud's classic formula for the comedy of movement and mental functions. The Freudian formula, cursorily summarized from *Jokes and Their Relation to the Unconscious,* is that a person appears comic if, in comparison with the observer, the person makes too great an expenditure of energy on physical functions and too little on mental or intellectual functions. The Langdon variation of that formula involves either too little or too great an expenditure of physical energy, which takes the form of either inadequate or inefficient physical responses, respectively, to the various demands of waking life that confront him. Harry's inadequate and inefficient physical responses are the expression of a mental (intellectual, emotional, psychological) under- or overreaction to the particular circumstances of such a confrontation—in other words, a too little or too great expenditure of mental or psychic energy. These are under- or overreactions as compared by the rational observer to his or her own estimated reaction under the same circumstances.

For example, in *Saturday Afternoon* Harry stands literally under the noses of Vernon and his girl friend while they make eyes at each other and kiss. Harry stares at them fixedly with wide-open eyes for the duration of this romantic interchange, though he also blinks and shifts his glance between the two participants repeatedly. Each time their lips meet, Harry's head snaps abruptly back to the point of contact in a single, double, and even triple take. He subsequently climbs over and under them to examine this phenomenon more closely. Harry's excessive, inefficient expenditure of physical energy to look and comprehend is evidence of his insufficient intellectual activity. The excessive expenditure of physical energy on his astonished overreactions is an expression of a too great expenditure of

The Performance

emotional energy in response to what Harry sees and comprehends.

Harry's response to the accidental revelation of the woman's bare thigh in *Long Pants* takes the form of an unnecessary expenditure of physical energy and represents a psychological and emotional overreaction to a fleeting brush with knowledge of the flesh. On the other hand, Harry's emotional overreaction to the revelation of Mary Brown's blindness in *The Strong Man* is expressed in the form of physical paralysis. When he finds himself facing the bearded lady in *Remember When*, Harry expends too much physical energy in order to comprehend the nature of this somewhat unusual fact of life as evidence of his ignorance of such a fact.

Harry's immobile, defensive crouching in a corner of the cab after Lily reaches for the bankroll in his back pocket in *The Strong Man* is an expression of his psychological overreaction to this brief but intimate contact with Lily. Shortly thereafter, Harry's unnecessarily agitated emotional response to Lily's amorous advances takes the form of unnecessary, extravagant physical activity when she tries to coax him up to her apartment. For a long time after she pretends to faint, Harry walks, teeters, and runs toward and away from her inert body along the length of half a city block.

Harry cringes in a corner of the cab in an emotional overreaction to his brief, intimate contact with Lily in *The Strong Man*.

When Harry runs right on past the hostile antagonists during the fistfight in *Saturday Afternoon*, he is displaying a physically inefficient response to those particular circumstances. Here, Harry moves too much as an expression of an overexcited emotional reaction. During the sequence on the bus in *The Strong Man*, Harry's fist never makes contact with his target—the passenger sitting next to him—because of Harry's inadequate exertion of physical energy. This is evidence of a psychological underreac-

Harry runs back and forth over half a block in a physical and psychological overreaction to Lily's attempts to coax him up to her apartment in *The Strong Man*.

tion on Harry's part. Harry simply has not the self-defensive instincts and cannot muster the aggressive energy that would come naturally to the observer if he or she had just been knocked to the floor, as in Harry's situation.

Whenever Harry engages in a one-sided communication with some inanimate, indifferent, or inert antagonist, he exhibits an intellectual underreaction to the particular physical circumstances with which he is confronted. Harry keeps on talking to, arguing with, or fighting with an inanimate, indifferent, or inert antagonist for a long time and usually in close proximity without realizing that they do not or cannot hear him, respond to him, or suffer his blows. Generally speaking, such instances demonstrate the extent to which Harry is out of touch in psychological terms with objective reality. All of these examples involve a physically inefficient response on Harry's part—as in Harry's argument with the telephone pole in *His Marriage Wow*, his prolonged confrontation with the dummy cop in *Long Pants*, and his wrestling bouts with the dummy in *Feet of Mud* and with the vacant suit of armor in *Soldier Man*. This also pertains to Harry's animated greetings to the indifferent doorman in *The Strong Man*, and to his irate wife in *Saturday Afternoon*, who is not indifferent but does remain inert and unmoved after Harry comes home late. Harry continues to relate to the doorman and to his wife even though his greetings are not acknowledged by either of them.

Category 3 examples, in which Harry is confronted by two or more moral, logical, or intellectual alternatives, demonstrate that Harry is not capable of abstract thinking. He can only comprehend the significance of a situation of this sort and act accordingly (that is, according to the standards of rational behavior) if he is able to stand and/or move between the two or more options or alternatives that confront him. And even if all of Harry's options are in plain sight at point-blank range, he can only comprehend the significance of that situation after a long time. This is the manner in which Harry finally decides which of the two Bettys is the real one in *Tramp, Tramp, Tramp*.

This is also how Harry decides to present to his pal, Vernon, a couple of prostitutes whom he spots on the street as substitutes for their dates for the afternoon who have not shown up in *Saturday Afternoon*. First, Harry stands at center frame looking toward Vernon, who is sitting beside a storefront at Harry's right. Harry turns away, then looks back at Vernon, and then ambles back to the street corner at frame left and looks around it down the street at the floozies, who are offscreen. As Harry turns again in Vernon's direction, he hesitates and turns his glance back toward the streetwalkers. Finally, Harry goes around the corner, out of the frame, and returns with the two streetwalkers, one on each arm. Harry's responses to these category 3 situations are most inefficient. He engages in extravagant and completely unnecessary physical activity in lieu of obviously inadequate intellectual activity.

Harry must always have at least two "things" to compare in order to make a choice or arrive at a decision or conclusion. In *The Strong Man*, Harry tries to find Mary Brown by holding up her photo in one hand to refer to while he runs around on the street corner where he has been told that she can be found, looking into the faces of every girl who passes. When he is accosted by Lily in the taxicab, Harry pulls out the photo again and glances back and forth between the photo and Lily, who claims to be Mary Brown, and on the basis of that comparison, decides that she is not. When the vamp seductively beckons Harry to her in *Lucky Stars,* he takes his horoscope out of his pocket and compares her with its prediction that, "You will fall in love with a beautiful dark woman," before he ventures as much as a step off of the medicine show platform. When Nanette makes eyes at Harry across the dinner table in *All Night Long,* Harry takes out a photo of his girl back home and compares the two before making eyes back across the table at Nanette.

Instances in which Harry actually "arrives at" a decision, even after a long time, are rare. More often, Harry will stand and/or move for a long time between two or more alternatives or options, all of which are physically manifest and separated spatially, and yield to the incapacitating effect of inertia. In *Lucky Stars,* Harry hovers indecisively for some time between the medicine show platform in the square below and the seductive Latin beauty on a balcony overlooking the square who beckons him to her and then pretends to faint in order to encourage Harry to venture closer. In *His Marriage Wow,* Harry hovers indecisively for some time in the aisle of the wrong church between the two alternatives of getting to his own wedding at the right church (for which he is already late) by exiting through the door in the background of this shot, or of retrieving the money from the offering box that he has paid in advance for the ceremony to the wrong minister, who is standing in the foreground holding the box.

This same scheme is found in *Saturday Afternoon*. In one case, Harry shuttles in animated suspension between the alternatives of staying home and remaining faithful to his wife or getting into Vernon's car and going to meet their dates and cheating on his wife. Harry's wife calls to him from somewhere in the background of this shot with Vernon's car in the foreground. In another case, Harry totters in animated suspension between being courteous by complying with the request of a man on his left for a light, or getting home on time by catching the streetcar that is about to depart at Harry's right.

In *The Strong Man*, Harry hesitates between shaking the doorman's hand to thank the doorman for directing him to Mary Brown and getting to Mary Brown as fast as he possibly can. Harry is stopped dead in his tracks at a point in space between his two alternatives. In this case, Harry is reduced again to a momentary paralysis. When that occurs, he is actually expending too little physical energy to get him to either of his destinations/alternatives, and too little mental energy in resolving upon a course of action and upon coordinating the various psychomotor functions required to carry one out.

Another example of suspended animation occurs in *Saturday Afternoon*. Harry is walking home from work, having missed the streetcar, and passes Vernon and two girls with whom Vernon is chatting. Harry is already two or three steps beyond them when Vernon calls him back. Harry's legs and lower body continue on for two steps toward screen right while Harry's head and upper torso turn back toward Vernon and the girls, who are standing in background left. Here Harry is torn at the waist in a moral predicament between the two spatially differentiated alternatives of getting home as soon as possible to his impatient and already irate wife, thus remaining faithful and preserving domestic tranquillity, or of being unfaithful, at least in spirit, and having a good time.

Harry now swivels back around and resumes his homeward course and then sidesteps in the direction of Vernon and the girls, retracing the same two steps he has just taken forward. Vernon now leans forward to whisper in Harry's ear. At this point, Harry turns toward home again and takes a long and energetic stride in that direction while pointing at his offscreen obligation with an outstretched arm. The momentum of Harry's inertia is interrupted as he halts in his tracks and his head turns back again toward Vernon and the girls. Again he takes two sidesteps to meet Vernon in center frame, moving in reverse over the same space in which he has just come forward. In fact, these are the same two steps he has already retraced once before.

After Vernon tells Harry that one of the girls is interested in him, Harry wipes his hand off and extends it toward the girl, who is standing in the background at screen left, while remaining firmly anchored at a safe distance from her with one foot planted in a homeward-bound direction. When she comes forward to shake Harry's outstretched hand, he brings the hand up in a friendly wave and turns away from her to head for home again. After taking only one or two steps, Harry is pulled back by Vernon to the central point between Harry's two possible courses of action around which he hovers throughout the sequence.

When the moral, logical, or intellectual options that present themselves to Harry in a particular narrative situation are not all in plain sight, his only response to the decision or choice called for in that situation is inertia. Harry's inefficient, hyperactive physical response in such situations is evidence of an intellectual paralysis. For instance, in *Tramp, Tramp, Tramp,* the family business is about to be foreclosed upon. Harry's father informs him, "The money must be raised in three months—it's up to you!" Harry resolves, "I'll get the money in three months if it takes a year," and manages to get out the front door of the shop as far as the sidewalk. Here Harry stops, then starts off several times, first in one direction, then the other, actually pacing from side to side in front of the store. Harry finally comes to a standstill in the center of the sidewalk and scratches his head. Since Harry is not literally faced with any concrete and clearly demarcated alternatives in this situation, he cannot even figure out which way to go (let alone being able to conceptualize a plan for obtaining the money).

The instructions in the astrologer's advice to Harry in *Lucky Stars* to "Follow that star and you'll find fame and fortune," are also too abstract for Harry to comprehend and apply. Harry looks through the astrologer's telescope to locate his lucky star, then starts to go twice, stopping twice to look up at the star for direction. Harry, naturally, starts off on his pursuit of fame and fortune on the wrong foot (and then on the wrong train). As in the previous example, Harry totters from side to side getting nowhere, taking several steps in one direction and then in the other before, in this example, he finally ambles off out of the frame. When Harry is told by the conductor that he is on the wrong train, he runs up and down the aisle of the already moving train in complete confusion.

Harry gets explicit instructions from a traffic cop on how to get to the right church for his wedding in *His Marriage Wow,* but this does not seem to make any difference. Harry cannot retain or apply the cop's directions. He exits out of the frame to the left after looking back at the cop for his approval of every step. He then goes around the block in a circle and reappears on screen in the background of this same shot. Harry then makes his way along an intersecting street to the point from which he started out, passes the cop, and keeps on going. Harry eventually stops, runs back and forth a bit from side to side in the foreground of the shot, and then turns around and runs back to the cop, who sends Harry out of the frame at left again.

Harry Langdon is the only one of the major comedians of the genre of American silent film comedy whose performance in no way involves the virtuosic display. Any sort of performance other than Langdon's mime of slow transitions between sleeping and waking, consciousness and unconsciousness, and his inefficient or inadequate responses to the kinds of simple situations that have been described would be inappropriate to a character whose physical and intellectual faculties are so severely impaired and who at times is completely incapacitated by his condition. This is why Langdon abandoned the many skills he had acquired in popular entertainments when he first created this new character for vaudeville.

Langdon's performance lacks the density of allusion, articulateness, and psychological subtlety of Charles Chaplin's pantomimic acting. It also lacks the technical skill, physical grace, and agility that are displayed in the performances of all three of his most important rivals in terms of popular and critical recognition—Chaplin, Buster Keaton, and Harold Lloyd. And Langdon's performance lacks the acrobatic and athletic exhibitions of physical strength, speed, and endurance that constitute attractions in the films of Keaton and Lloyd, in particular. In fact, in Langdon's performances, comic ineptitude often extends to the complete physical debilitation of inertia or paralysis.

Even in situations in Keaton's comedies in which he is behaving like an inept boob, Keaton's performance of the inappropriate, inefficient, or inadequate response in a given circumstance customarily involves a feat of physical strength and coordination that is equal to or greater than that required by the proper response. Such is the case in Keaton's 1927 feature comedy *College*, in which he puts the shot, runs the track, high-jumps, broad-jumps, jumps the high hurdles, and pole-vaults badly, but in most cases he does so with greater strength and facility than are required when he later performs these events correctly in an all-out effort to rescue the girl.

This sequence from *College* can be compared with a sequence in *The Strong Man* in which Harry is sent out on the stage of a saloon in the drunken strong man's place to do his act. A "strong man" is just what Harry is not. In fact, *The Strong Man* is known in France by the title, *L'Athlèt Incomplet*. Harry stumbles on stage dressed in the huge strong man's oversized trunks, tripping over his own feet. He then stands at center stage amid the paraphernalia used in the act, looking out at the expectant audience with an impassive expression on his face. Harry eventually tries to lift one of the weights and cannot budge it. Failing at this and in an effort to appease the stony-faced patrons, Harry launches into a tap dance that is neither good nor spectacularly or skillfully bad; it's just bad. After first tripping over an empty bucket, Harry does manage the dubious feat of lifting it up over his head. Then he loses a barbell down a hole in the stage and nearly injures himself while attempting to execute a split in another meager effort to entertain the increasingly raucous audience.

Harry's feeble attempts at copying the strong man's stunts are all futile, so every time one of these attempts fails, he resorts to copying the only part of Zandow's act he can copy. Even though he has done nothing, Harry regularly executes an expansive bow with his arms extended at his sides and one foot placed behind the other, and flourishes a towel as he wipes the nonexistent perspiration from his hands and face.

This sequence from *The Strong Man* can also be compared to similar situations in Chaplin's *The Circus* and *Modern Times*. In *The Circus*, Charlie accidentally becomes part of a circus performance when he is chased into the ring by a cop. Chaplin, as the character Charlie is a "sensation" and becomes "the hit of the show," as the titles assure us. In comparison, Langdon, as the character Harry is merely clumsy and awkward. The same thing happens to Charlie in *Modern Times* as occurs in *The Circus* and as happens to Harry in *The Strong Man*. As a waiter who is about to make his debut as a cabaret singer, Charlie appears to be hopelessly unprepared and suffering from stage fright. However, once he is before the audience out on the nightclub floor he is completely at ease and immediately takes command. Charlie's comic song is greeted with an ovation and again he is instantly transformed into a star.

The instances in Langdon's films in which the skill and grace of which Harry Langdon was capable are rare and briefly glimpsed since Langdon adhered consistently to a style of performance that was predicated upon the absence of those qualities. The only occasion that offers any indication of Langdon's technical expertise is the sequence in *Long Pants* in which Harry circles Bebe's car performing tricks on his bicycle in order to impress her. Though Harry is never seen closer than medium-long shot distance, the stunt was actually performed by Langdon and was one of his early stage routines.

The several instances in which Langdon's pantomime, other than that of sleeping or waking or of gaining or losing consciousness, displays relative mimetic specificity or grace of movement and gesture are those occasions when Langdon is literally "out of character." An example is the first fantasy sequence in *Long Pants*. Harry imagines himself to be precisely what he is not, but would like to be—a dashing officer from a Ruritanian romance who scales the high palace wall to the heroine's balcony, where he passionately sweeps her into his arms. Another example occurs later in the film when, after donning his first pair of long trousers, Harry reenacts the fantasy embrace in pantomime. Langdon is similarly out of character in *The Strong Man* when he presents an excellent female impersonation while portraying both roles in a pantomimed reenactment of his adventure with the imposter of Mary Brown.

Unlike Chaplin's mime, Langdon's mime is not dense or articulate. The term *density* is intended here as a measure of quantity, and *articulateness* is intended as a measure of quality of denotative and connotative reference. For example, in Chaplin's clever and agile manipulation of an alarm clock in *The Pawnshop*, Charlie refers in rapid succession to a human heart, a goblet of fine crystal, a piece of fine porcelain, a machine part, a can of sardines, an article of jewelry (which he inspects through a telephone mouthpiece as if the mouthpiece were a jeweler's magnifier), a bad tooth, and a bolt of cloth.

This density of reference is not reserved in Chaplin's work merely for set pieces such as the one just described. Nearly every movement or gesture that Chaplin makes is either a mimed allusion or a demonstration of his technical skill, or both. Furthermore, Chaplin is engaged in some movement or gesture of this kind nearly every moment. One of these innumerable incidental gestures in Chaplin's films—incidental, that is, in terms of its relevance to plot—can be seen in *The Rink* when Charlie, as a waiter in a restaurant, adds up the cost of the items on the customer's dinner check. Charlie holds the check in one hand and with the other computes the total, and probably his tip, item by item, "performing" the calculation by carrying out each operation in the air. Here, Chaplin's pantomime is based on the gag that immediately precedes it. In this gag, Charlie makes out the customer's check after inspecting the man's necktie and looking behind the man's ear. Another example is seen during a dice game in *The Immigrant* when Charlie throws the dice with an exaggerated baseball pitcher's windup.

In comparison, there is a routine in Langdon's *Three's a Crowd* in which Harry struggles to defrost a frozen diaper that is at least three times longer than Chaplin's *Pawnshop* routine but does not include a single joke based on a mimed metaphor or other double meaning, although in the sequence that follows, Harry becomes distracted while making a pie and mistakenly substitutes the diaper for the pie dough. Nevertheless, it is only this single allusion that sustains a second long pantomime routine in which Harry distractedly kneads, rolls out, and shapes the diaper as if it were dough.

The articulateness of Chaplin's mime can be appreciated when one considers the seemingly infinite variety of movements, postures, gestures, and facial expressions that he employs to connote a wide range of subjective, psychological significations—from the very specific definition of some subtle emotional nuance to a provocatively ambiguous gesture that Chaplin invests with a multitude of possible, even simultaneously contradictory interpretations. One example of this is the final shot in *City Lights*. The tramp has just revealed himself to the beautiful flower girl as her benefactor. The girl then looks upon him for the first time since having her sight restored and says, "Yes, I can see now." Chaplin's expression in this long-held close-up has been interpreted as one of tragic disappointment at the recognition of his own pitiful inadequacy and just as defensibly as an apprehensive but hopeful suspense as the image slowly fades to black.

This example from *City Lights* can be compared to a similar pathetic situation in Langdon's *The Strong Man*. After Harry introduces himself to the heroine as the soldier with whom she has been corresponding, she reveals to him that she is blind. The sequence concludes with a shot of Harry standing motionless and staring at her with a blank expression fixed upon his face until the shot gradually fades out. Harry's expression is, however, neither ambiguous nor enigmatic. Nor is any subjective or psychological significance clearly implied or discernible in Harry's countenance.

As Langdon does not present the subtly expressive pantomime that Chaplin does, neither does he engage in the exaggerated gestures and expansive movements of broadly expressive physical comedy and burlesque as in the typical Sennett two-reeler.

Langdon's performance exhibits a strict adherence to a highly exclusive repertoire of movements, gestures, and facial expressions that he rarely expanded or varied once it was fully developed at some point in his vaudeville career. Judging from the reviews, this point was certainly reached by the time Langdon presented the sketch "After the Ball." The mimetic value of this very limited vocabulary ranges from minimally expressive to opaque.

Included among the actions that compose Langdon's repertoire is the performance of simple operations such as holding down his hat by the brim as he runs or hurriedly rounds a corner. Other actions are certain gestures whose significances are merely those predetermined by common usage.

One of the simple actions in Langdon's repertoire is to run while holding on to his hat brim. *Heart Trouble*.

Langdon's gestures include putting his index finger into his mouth to signify apprehension or doubt. Langdon with Doris Dawson in *Heart Trouble*.

Examples of these are Harry pressing his palm over his mouth to signify embarrassment, Harry putting his index finger into his mouth to signify apprehension, Harry scratching his head to signify confusion, Harry lifting a brick over his head and then poising to throw it as a sign of hostility, Harry brushing off one hand with the other in a gesture of finality, a clumsy pat to signify affection, a pointerlike stance to signify helpless con-

A typical Langdon facial expression is one in which his eyebrows and the corners of his mouth are raised slightly to form a smile. *Heart Trouble*.

Another expression is a shift of glance indicated by a shift in direction of Harry's eyeballs only. Langdon with Doris Dawson in *Heart Trouble*.

sternation, outstretched arms in a gesture of supplication or apology, and an awkward wave as a friendly greeting.

In order of descending referential value, the typical Langdon facial expressions include a screwing of the mouth into a minute grimace, a slight raising of the eyebrows and the corners of the mouth into a smile, a shifting of glance that is indicated by a change of direction of eyeballs only, a glare effected with momentarily knitted brows, a blink of the eyes in an otherwise blank visage, and a wide-eyed gaze which, when temporally extenuated, becomes a frozen stare.

Langdon's repetition of the same few gestures and expressions in response to the varied narrative circumstances and gag situations of a single film as well as over the course of thirty-one silent films deprives those gestures and expressions that bear some minimal signifying capacity of

Langdon's vacant stare in *The Strong Man*.

Langdon's wide-eyed stare in *Heart Trouble*.

their specificity—confounding interpretation further. For instance, Harry blinks his eyes after he is hit on the head, at moments of carnal revelation, and likewise at pathetic climaxes in which the impact is an emotional one.

Langdon's comic character is described by his performance in such a way that the sort of interpretive speculation that is often practiced on and provoked by Chaplin's films is effectively discouraged in Langdon's films. This can be observed by comparing a situation in Langdon's *Long Pants* with a similar situation in Chaplin's *The Tramp*. In *The Tramp*, Charlie suffers from unrequited love and leaves the girl a farewell note. As he turns his back to the camera to fondle the girl's hat, Charlie's shuddering shoulders subtly convey his sorrow. In *Long Pants*, Harry sits absolutely motionless with his back to the camera watching Bebe, the woman of his naive romantic fantasies, brawl and maul her rival. Langdon's posture provides no cue or clues on which to ground a reading of his impressions or reactions.

Nor does Langdon's immobile posture and his position with respect to the camera qualify as an elliptical device whereby the viewer's participation is solicited in imagining the character's subjective reaction to this incident. The sort of performance just described as typical of Langdon, consistently sustained, provides the viewer with no nucleus in terms of characterization from which to generate any such presumptions.

Another possible strategy in this particular situation from *Long Pants* might be to elicit a certain comic tension or suspense on the part of the viewer in anticipation of Harry's finally turning to the camera to disclose a reaction that somehow fulfills, exceeds, or comically reverses the viewer's expectations. However, the "reaction shot" of Harry that follows the long take in which he sits with his back to the camera is merely a shot of Harry's by now familiar and therefore by now also inexpressive wide-eyed stare.

It is Harry's physical relationship to the spectacle of his "damsel in distress" viciously maiming or murdering and the long time he remains motionless in that position that convey to the viewer some sense of Harry's naiveté, innocence, inexperience, and the affective, psychological impact of this profound disillusionment upon him. Harry's reaction is that he is literally paralyzed by the spectacle for as long as it takes place before him (and is subject to sporadic paralytic seizures for some time thereafter).

5
The Mise-en-Scène

Langdon's mime cannot be separated from the context provided by Langdon's mise-en-scène. The small vocabulary of initially inarticulate expressions and gestures, whose significances are further depreciated by their repetition under diverse narrative circumstances, presents a character that is psychologically opaque. This, combined with the tendency to "milk," or drag out in time, a minimum of gag or plot material and the lack of virtuosic attractions define Langdon's peculiar style of comic performance as reductive in nature.

Langdon's mime considered, as it should be, within the context of Harry's physical placement, in time, with respect to some highly provocative fact of life, some inanimate, indifferent, inert, hostile, or amorous antagonist, or a choice between spatially distinct alternatives, defines a comic character that is, at best, obscure. Langdon's vacant stare, blinks, simple and oft-repeated gestures, and immobile postures must be referred by the viewer to some fact, antagonist, or logical, intellectual, or moral alternative in order for the viewer to derive any sort of significance from Langdon's essentially inarticulate pantomime.

For example, in the following sequence from *The Strong Man*, the worldly "Lily of Broadway" has lured Harry as far as the entrance to her apartment building. In this sequence, Lily undertakes a scheme to get him up to her room so that she can recover a stolen bankroll that is, unbeknownst to Harry, hidden in his jacket. ("Medium long shot" is a description of the distance between camera and subject at which characters and setting are included in the shot. "Medium shot" refers to a closer camera distance at which the character is seen in the shot from the waist up.)

SHOT A. *Medium long shot.* At the entrance to Lily's apartment building, Harry hesitates, draws his hand away from hers, and retreats at an oblique angle to Lily into background left. While Lily, at the steps leading to the apartment house lobby in foreground right, tries to coax Harry back, Harry stands in the background and stares at her, scratches his head, puts his hand to his hat as if to tip it, turns away from her, and takes several steps further into the background toward the left frameline. (550 frames)

SHOT B. *Medium shot.* Lily thinks. (74 frames)

SHOT C. *Medium long shot.* In the foreground, Lily pretends to faint and falls to the sidewalk at the apartment building entrance while Harry continues into background left. As she falls, he stops, turns to watch, then stands in place and stares at her inert body. He eventually leans forward slightly in her direction. (126 frames)

SHOT D. *Medium shot.* Harry continues to stare. (54 frames)

SHOT E. *Medium long shot.* Harry, in the foreground, hesitatingly takes a few steps toward Lily, who is now seen in the background at an oblique angle to Harry. (53 frames)

SHOT F. *Medium long shot (reverse angle).* Harry, in the background, is stationary, standing midway between his previous position and Lily's body on the sidewalk in the foreground. He leans forward in her direction and back, looks at her, points to her, and eventually totters back off into the background toward the left frameline. (422 frames)

One derives from this sequence an understanding of Harry's virginal naiveté and instinctual apprehension. One does not derive this understanding from Harry's vacant stare, or from Harry's scratching his head, putting his hand to his hat, pointing, or simply tottering back and forth. All of these are movements and gestures that Langdon repeats in all kinds of situations. One does derive an understanding of Harry's virginal naiveté and instinctual apprehension from the spatial differential between Harry and Lily and the length of time he stands and stares, dawdles, and totters toward and away from the vamp as she coaxes him at the apartment building entrance or lies inert on the sidewalk.

The elements of Langdon's mise-en-scène—Harry's physical disposition, or placement, in time with respect to a manifestation of one of those demands of waking life which, as an integral feature of Langdon's conception of the character, constantly confront him—together articulate Harry's under- and overreactions as: anxiety, apprehension, ecstasy, ignorance, naiveté, bewilderment, indecision, cognition, the dawning of carnal knowledge, an emotional awakening, and so forth. Other than Langdon's extended pantomimed transitions between sleeping and waking and between being conscious and being unconscious, it is this mise-en-scène scheme that lends the only mimetic specificity to Langdon's pantomime and which provides the minimal psychological dimension of his characterization, even though Langdon's comic persona and performance are presented within a narrative format.

Langdon's mise-en-scène can therefore be defined in terms of Harry's spatial relation to some fact of life, antagonist, or alternative, and the long time it takes him to comprehend—correctly, incorrectly, or not at all—the significance of the fact or situation that confronts him; and to act—appropriately, inappropriately, or not at all.

In *Three's a Crowd*, the viewer knows that Harry is ecstatic when he beholds a fact of life that represents his dreams come true from Harry's frantic movement back and forth and in circles after his first close look at Gladys, whom he has just rescued. Or, when Harry stands and faces the newborn infant who fulfills his fondest dreams in *Three's a Crowd*, and does not move at all for a very long time, the viewer knows of the profound emotional impact of the event upon him. When Harry stands still for a long time across from Mary Brown in the garden in *The Strong Man*, the viewer knows that Harry has finally comprehended the fact that she is blind. (The fact that Harry's response of temporary paralysis to a confrontation with some highly provocative fact of life such as these is the same as his response to the physical impact of a powerful blow affirms the notion that Harry has suffered a profound psychological or emotional impact in these pathetic moments.)

The viewer knows of Harry's naiveté, sexual inexperience, and apprehension at the prospect of an erotic encounter by the distance he maintains between himself and women. This is seen in the game of tag between Harry and the girl through the woods in *Boobs in the Wood* in which the girl tries unsuccessfully for some time to arouse Harry's affections and encourage his advances, and in the extended sequence on the sidewalk in front of Lily's apartment building in *The Strong Man*.

Another demonstration of Harry's relationship with women occurs shortly afterward inside Lily's apartment. Harry hovers between the door of the apartment in the background and Lily, who lies on a sofa in the foreground holding out the key to the locked apartment door. Another example occurs in *His First Flame* in which Harry is delivering a profeminist speech to an appreciative audience of women. Becoming carried away, he ventures down from the speaker's rostrum into the center aisle, but when the audience becomes enthusiastic and stands up to cheer, Harry dashes back up the aisle to the safe distance of the speaker's platform.

Harry's encounter with the vamp in *Lucky Stars* is probably the most elaborate of Harry's encounters with aggressive women. Harry has already ventured as far as the top of the stairway to her balcony. He stands in the foreground at the beginning of this shot, looking back and forth between

Harry's naiveté is understood by observing the distance he maintains between himself and women. Here he watches as Bud (Bud Jamison) joins the girls' school picnic in *The Chaser*. (Courtesy of Gladys McConnell)

the vamp and the medicine-show stage, which is where he is supposed to be working and where he is at a safe distance from her. She is seated across the frame from Harry in background right. Harry takes a few halting steps across the balcony in her direction, holding onto his hat. The moment she starts to get up from her seat, Harry turns around, retreats back to the stairway, and starts down the stairs. As he starts down, she sits back down.

Just when Harry is almost out of sight near the bottom of the stairway at frame left, she pretends to faint. At this, Harry turns and starts back up the stairs, but stops in his tracks when he reaches the top. From this position in the foreground, Harry leans the top of his body forward to look at the vamp, who is motionless in the chair in the background, with his feet firmly planted on the top step as if to take him back down the stairs the moment she moves a muscle. Moving slowly and in stops and starts, Harry edges closer to her while she remains inert. He finally reaches her just as she starts to "come around."

The length of time Harry sits in *close* proximity beside the objects of his desire without making physical contact also informs the viewer of his apprehension, inexperience, and insecurity as a lover. This is seen when Harry sits with Mary Brown on the bench in the garden in *The Strong Man* and with Betty on the park bench in *Tramp, Tramp, Tramp*. The length of time and trouble Harry takes to examine the kiss between Vernon and his girl friend in *Saturday Afternoon* or the bearded lady in *Remember When*, both highly provocative facts of life with which Harry is confronted, informs the viewer of Harry's basic ignorance of the world and its ways.

The viewer can ascertain the measure of Harry's indifference to the world of waking reality that surrounds him by observing for how long and at what range he is confronted by various hostile or amorous antagonists before responding to them either inappropriately or not at all. Harry's pathological indifference can be appreciated in *Saturday Afternoon* through the long time Harry remains unaware of his wife's presence as she stands behind him while Harry pretends to tell her off. The extent of Harry's indifference can also be appreciated through the long time Harry remains unaware of the sheriff's presence as he practically leans over Harry's shoulder while Harry chatters blithely about the chickens he has stolen and shows them off to the other hoboes in *Remember When*. An indifference owing to his susceptibility to the effects of sleeping pills and alcohol is apparent in *Tramp, Tramp, Tramp* in the long time Harry stands, stares, blinks, and does not respond in the face of the persistent demands of the irate cabbie for his fare on the morning after.

The viewer can also ascertain the extent to which Harry is psychologically out of touch with the external world by observing for how long and at what distance Harry is confronted by some inanimate, indifferent, or inert antagonist without realizing that his "antagonist" is, in fact, inanimate, indifferent, or inert while he continues to talk to, argue, or wrestle with it. Throughout Harry's attempt to provoke the dummy cop in *Long Pants*, Harry, as a timid and inept aggressor, never ventures close enough to discover, presuming he could, that this is not a live cop. The space between Harry and the dummy cop is the distance required to sustain the illusion on Harry's part that this is a live cop, even though, regardless of Harry's persistent and prolonged agitation, the cop does not blink an eye. Rather than approach the cop, Harry keeps his distance and continues to agitate to no avail.

One is also made aware of Harry's indecisiveness, doubt, or confusion by the long time he hovers between spatially differentiated options or alternative courses of action. In *Lucky Stars,* Harry vacillates between business and pleasure—that is, between the saloon and the medicine-show stage. He hesitates between courtesy and convenience as he moves between the man who asks for a light and the departing streetcar in *Saturday Afternoon*. In the same film, Harry's animated suspension between wife and home, and Vernon and the girls, and later between wife and home, and Vernon and the car in which Harry and Vernon are to drive off to meet the girls, informs the viewer of the anxiety aroused in Harry by the conflict between preserving marital fidelity and domestic peace and indulging his instincts. When Harry runs up and down the aisle between the wrong minister, who holds the fee for Harry's wedding ceremony in an offering box, and the front door of the wrong church in *His Marriage Wow*, one is made aware of Harry's inability to resolve upon a course of economy, or expediency.

Harry hesitates between sitting and standing on those occasions when he bobs up and down a few times before sitting or standing—on a park bench, on a running board, or on a window ledge—as a manifestation of the same qualities of indecisiveness, doubt, or confusion. These are examples of animated suspension on a vertical axis. The times when Harry assumes a squatting position midway between sitting and standing are examples of suspended animation on the vertical axis.

Harry's lack of initiative, ambition, and motivation, and his inability to think abstractly can be discerned by the viewer whenever Harry's options are not physically manifest and his alternative courses of action are not clearly demarcated. Harry responds to his father's urgent plea to save the family business from foreclosure in *Tramp, Tramp, Tramp* and to the astrologer's prediction of fame and fortune in *Lucky Stars* in both instances by starting, stopping, and shuttling from side to side within an area of about four square feet.

Thus, Langdon's mise-en-scène is the complement to a pantomime style whereby gesture and movement do not refer. Instead the spectator must refer Langdon's mime to the character's immediate physical circumstances in order to derive denotative or connotative significance.

There is also a figurative dimension in Langdon's work that is evidence of a highly unified and not unsophisticated comic conception on Langdon's part. As noted previously, when confronted by a choice between spatially differentiated alternatives, Harry moves between them laterally, in depth, or vertically for so long that he succumbs to the incapacitation of inertia. Harry's physical situation of suspension in time and space between the alternatives that confront him is symbolic of his psychological situation of suspension somewhere between unconsciousness, sleeping, dreaming, and fantasy and the lowest threshold of consciousness. Harry's incapacitation by inertia and paralysis is, at the same time, a symptom of his failure to resolve these various states of being. This figurative level of Langdon's work, like the minimal specificity of Langdon's mime and the psychological dimension of Langdon's comic character, is also spelled out in and through Langdon's mise-en-scène.

This metaphoric notion applies as well to Harry's execution of certain gestures and localized movements as it does to Harry's suspended locomotion. During the routine in which Harry contends with a bad head cold on the bus in *The Strong Man,* Harry's hand, which holds a spoonful of medicine, hovers in midair between his mouth and his lap while he hesitates between taking it and being cured, or not taking it and sparing himself a distasteful experience.

Those localized movements and gestures that are truncated midway in their execution, as when Harry vacillates between eating or not eating, or between tipping or not tipping his hat, are additional examples of suspended animation that are, at once, symbolic and symptomatic of Harry's psychic condition. In *Remember When,* each time Harry takes a piece of food from the picnic table, the hand with the food stops at a point in midair between Harry's mouth and the food-laden table. In *Saturday Afternoon,* while Harry's wife scolds him over the telephone for missing his streetcar, he leans over in the phone booth to place the receiver on the floor. Harry's movement toward the floor is halted midway after which he sits up again and brings the receiver back up to his ear. Harry's arm is halted in midmotion before Harry can execute the gesture of tipping his hat to Mary Brown while he introduces himself to her in the garden and to the woman on the street whom he has offended in *The Strong Man.*

Harry's suspension between a conscious and an unconscious condition is the subject of Langdon's pantomime in those instances in which he hovers awhile in midair after sustaining a powerful physical blow, at first momentarily immobilized and then slowly and gently lowering himself from standing to sitting position. Another spatiotemporal metaphor for Harry's condition is seen in *His Marriage Wow* when Harry succumbs to a drunken stupor and bounces up and down at the knees on his way across a room to a chair. He then falls short of his objective, collapsing midway between his point of departure and his objective. The same thing happens in *Tramp, Tramp, Tramp* when Harry tries to make his way in a drunken and drug-induced stupor from one side of a room toward a pitcher of water on the other side. When Harry is later aroused in both of these instances, his transition from unconsciousness back to consciousness is represented the same way. Harry hovers between standing upright each time he is pulled to his feet, and sinking back down to the floor.

Harry's suspension between waking and falling asleep is the subject of Langdon's pantomime in the opening sequence of *Three's a Crowd.* After his alarm clock rings, Harry rocks in bed with his upper body alternating between sitting up and tipping back over into a prone position. At the same time, Harry's eyelids are alternately sliding closed and fluttering open as yet another index of Harry's psychic situation. In all the examples in which Harry is drunk, or dazed by a blow or by a kiss, or drugged, or falling asleep, or waking up, his eyelids fluctuate between wide open and shut, or else they are momentarily fixed, or suspended, in a position midway between open and closed as an indication of his semiconscious condition.

Another more general aspect of the figurative dimension in Langdon's work includes these examples of animated suspension and suspended animation and the rest of Harry's inappropriate responses—overshooting or undershooting a logical objective and otherwise moving too much or not enough, reaching too far or not far enough, moving too late or too soon; and Harry's lack of any apparent response—not moving at all. All of these are manifested as a differential in space and time between Harry and some fact of life, antagonist, or alternative. Harry's physical disorientation in space and time with respect to these facts of life; antagonists; and moral, logical and intellectual alternatives, considered as emblems of objective reality, provides an overall metaphor for Harry's psychic disorientation with respect to the world of waking life. Harry is both literally and figuratively "out of touch" with objective reality.

This overall metaphoric significance of Langdon's mise-en-scène is ideally demonstrated in the following example from *Tramp, Tramp, Tramp*. The camera tracks out in front of a group of racers in a medium high angle, medium long shot at the start of a cross-country walking race. Harry, who has actually happened into the race by chance, is initially seen bringing up the rear as he halts and hesitates. Harry, cheating, now runs a few paces, catches up, and then pulls out in front of the other racers. The camera continues to track out ahead of Harry as he veers to the right at a fork in the road. Meanwhile, the pack of racers, seen in the upper left region of the frame, continue on, veering left. As the camera, centered upon Harry, continues to precede him as he walks on, the diverging paths of Harry and the pack of racers are seen to widen until the racers disappear at the upper left edge of the frame. Harry, of course, is completely unaware of this development.

The widening divergence in distance and direction between Harry and the racers is directly related to the long time Harry remains unaware that the other racers are no longer following him. The comic content of this particular comic situation derives from Langdon's characterization of one whose relation to the external circumstances with which is he confronted is only tenuous and tentative. Langdon's comic character is defined in this example by the increasing distance between Harry and the racers and the long time Harry remains unaware that he has gone astray.

In this and all the other examples cited, Harry's behavior is governed by the fact that his mental faculties and physical functions are impaired by his chronically semiconscious condition to such a degree that he cannot concentrate his attention on a specified objective in order to motivate an appropriate action and give direction and structure to his movement—whether it be a gesture, a localized movement, or locomotion. The differential in space and time between Harry and any one of those demands of waking life, in this case the other racers, symbolizes Harry's psychologically disoriented relationship to objective reality.

Harry's disoriented relationship to the world of waking reality is the subject of Langdon's comic performance. Langdon's performance, in conjunction with Langdon's mis-en-scène, defines Langdon's comic characterization and is the source of comedy and pathos in Langdon's films as elaborated in Harry's inadequate and inefficient physical responses and his psychological under- and overreactions. The elements of Langdon's mise-en-scène—placement and timing—are therefore integral constituents of Harry Langdon's comedy and pathos, characterization and mime.

6
Film Form

If, as concluded in chapter 5, Harry's disoriented relation to the world of waking reality is the subject of Langdon's performance, defines Langdon's comic characterization, and is the source of comedy and pathos in Langdon's films, then Langdon's fimic mise-en-scène must include both Harry and the world. All the silent comedies in which Harry Langdon appears as a featured performer are consistently characterized by a film style that is based on the formal premise of spatiotemporal continuity.

This is a filmic format in which Harry and the various emblems of objective reality that confront him are most often contained within a single shot. Langdon's films are made up of long takes; long-take moving-camera shots; long-take two- and three-shots in shallow screen space; and long-take two-, three-, four-, and five-shots in the deep space of a wider camera setup.

These are formal characteristics of a film style that is now generally referred to as the "mise-en-scène style." This film style was first defined as a film-critical classification by the French critic and film theorist André Bazin. (Filmmakers such as Orson Welles, William Wyler, F. W. Murnau, Jean Renoir, and Roberto Rossellini have been identified as practitioners of this style.)

Langdon did not purposely set out in his films to adopt certain formal filmic conventions that would subsequently be labeled "mise-en-scène" and become recognized as a film style that is most closely identified with the theatrical tradition and aesthetic. Yet this film style first emerged in Langdon's first extended encounter as a veteran performer with the new medium at Mack Sennett's studio. Langdon brought to film from his career on the vaudeville stage a conception of comic persona and style of performance that invokes a filmic mise-en-scène that preserves the conditions of spatiotemporal unity. It was under these conditions that Langdon's comic conception was originally developed, and it was under these conditions that he worked onstage for twenty years.

We now consider the relationship between Langdon's comic persona and style of performance and the basic format of spatiotemporal continuity in which this relationship is presented in film. Harry is a character in whom such qualities as initiative, ambition, motivation, and the capacity for premeditation are absent. Harry does not initiate action. The persistent demands of waking life—some highly aggressive or affective stimulus or urgent biological need—serve as the only instigation of the character to action. The only action on Harry's part is seen in his inadequate and inefficient physical responses to direct confrontation by the imminent demands of a manifest fact of life, an antagonist, or a choice between alternatives.

These same stimuli are the only instigation to intellection on Harry's part. Harry is not capable of abstract thinking, and intellection is aroused in him only in response to the same situation of a direct confrontation by one of these demands of waking life. A comic persona such as this prescribes a film style that preserves the proximity and simultaneity of Harry's response and the instigation of that response.

Langdon's nonvirtuosic performance and nonreferential pantomimic style also prescribe a cinematic structure that is based on the principle of spatiotemporal continuity. The spectator must refer Langdon's performance to some point of reference. Spatiotemporal unity is required in order that the viewer can ascertain the measure of Harry's disoriented relation to the world that surrounds him—the subject of Langdon's performance. Harry's physical disorientation with objective reality is therefore measurable at any moment as a differential in space and time between Harry and one of these facts of life, antagonists, or alternatives as a point of reference. The viewer must be given the opportunity to observe that Harry is moving too much or not enough, reaching too far or not far enough, moving too late, too soon, for too long, not long enough, or not at all with regard to one of these demands of waking life.

As shown in chapter 5, these quantitative measures have a qualitative significance. They lend the only mimetic specificity to that performance as a demonstration of the faulty operation of Harry's physical and intellectual faculties. As the manifestation of Harry's psychological under- and overreactions in specific situations, these quantitative measurements also provide a psychological dimension to Langdon's comic character that is otherwise not provided in the Langdon comedies through character development in dramatic or narrative terms or, in terms of mimetic values, by Langdon's performance.

This quantitative differential in space and time between Harry and a point of reference is also a source of comedy and pathos in Langdon's films. In terms of comedy, the viewer must be given the opportunity to observe how far Harry overshoots or undershoots a logical objective, how long Harry runs back and forth between two alternative courses of action without getting anywhere, or how long Harry does nothing but stand and stare when he is confronted by the overt advances of some hostile or amorous antagonist. The viewer may then compare Harry's inappropriate physical responses and psychological under- and overreactions to his or her own estimated responses and reactions if he or she were in the same situation.

In terms of pathos, the viewer must be given the opportunity to observe how long Harry confronts some highly provocative fact of life at point-blank range before he comprehends its significance. The requirement of a filmic format of spatiotemporal continuity applies to these static tableaux in which Harry's comprehension of the nature and significance of some highly provocative fact of life precipitates a profound emotional, erotic, or intellectual awakening. The viewer must be given the opportunity to observe how long Harry stands expressionless and motionless in order to appreciate the pathetic significance of the extent of Harry's innocence or naiveté, the difficulty with which he comprehends such a fact and makes the transition to cognition or emotional maturity, and the profound psychological impact such a discovery has upon him.

To better understand how the mise-en-scène film style of Langdon's comedies derives from and conforms to Langdon's comic character and style of performance, it is helpful to consider Langdon's comedy in terms of an alternative film style that relies on montage. This comparison shows how the comic style Langdon brought to film demands a film style that is based on spatiotemporal continuity as a prerequisite and largely proscribes or precludes the use of montage.

Generally, the montage style is a film style in which meaning is created through relationships between shots. Montage is a significant feature of the film comedies of both Buster Keaton and Harold Lloyd. In the films of both, comic content and cinematic form are, to a large degree, conceived and constructed in terms of edit analysis of action through alternation of camera position (distance and angle) with respect to the subject of the shot and through intershot associations.

The mode of analysis applied here to the comedies of Harry Langdon, one concerned with the relation of persona and performance to the formal characteristics of the film style in which the comedy is presented, may also be applied to the work of comedians other than Langdon. As shown in chapter 8, not only Langdon's but also the distinctive cinematic styles of other comics such as Keaton, Lloyd, and Chaplin display a unique relationship with a distinctive comic characterization and performance style.

Montage would invariably imply certain qualities, a level of con-

Harry must confront a highly provocative fact of life at point-blank range for a long time before he can comprehend its significance. Harry comes upon Gladys in the street in *Three's a Crowd*. **(Courtesy of Gladys McConnell)**

sciousness, and a psychological and intellectual sophistication that is wholly inappropriate to the character elaborated in Langdon's performance. Harry is described by that performance as one who, much of the time, is in a drunken or drug-induced stupor, or a semiconscious daze, or is dozing, and who is perpetually hovering between consciousness and unconsciousness as a permanent pathological condition. He is fully conscious only in rare moments and his physical as well as mental functions are severely impaired by this condition. Therefore, the use of point-of-view and reaction shots and the use of shot-reverse shot sequences are minimal in Langdon's silent comedies. When, occasionally, such an edit construction does appear in a Langdon film, it is usually not significant in terms of development of characterization or plot, or in terms of comic or pathetic content.

The subjective viewpoint sequence involves a shot of a character, followed by a shot of some subject that is intended to represent what that character is seeing. The subject is photographed as seen from the position of the character. This "point-of-view shot" is followed by a return to the original camera setup for a "reaction shot" of the character that represents his reaction to what he (and the viewer) has just seen.

Such edit constructions as the subjective viewpoint sequence, as it is commonly used, explicitly define a character's psychological position and specifically orient a character in terms of his physical position with respect to a particular object of his glance. This was demonstrated in the famous "Kuleshov experiment" in which close-ups of the actor Mozhukhin were intercut with stock shots of various subjects. This led the audience to derive certain associations from the juxtaposition of images in such a way that each shot of a subject—a crying infant, a revolver, a bowl of soup—caused the viewer to assume that Mozhukhin was looking at the infant, the revolver, and the bowl of soup and to assign a specific significance—pity, fear, and hunger, respectively—to Mozhukhin's expression in each case. In fact, the implied trajectory of glance was imaginary. Mozhukhin could not have been looking at any of those subjects because Mozhukhin and the subjects of those other shots were not coexistent in spatial or temporal terms. Nor was he reacting to those "sights." He was instructed to maintain a neutral expression while the close-up of him was being filmed and was completely unaware of the subjects with which his image would be intercut.

In this way, cutting from Harry to a point-of-view shot of some person, place, or object would invariably orient too specifically in psychological terms a character that is defined by his psychological disorientation with the world of waking reality as expressed in his physical disorientation with his surroundings. Such a sequence would establish a too explicit trajectory of glance, thereby establishing a direction and concentration of attention toward a specified objective that is wholly inappropriate to a character who is indifferent to his surroundings.

Such a point-of-view sequence would also imply an intention on Harry's part toward a specified objective as the goal or motivation for subsequent movements or gestures. It might also imply premeditation of actions by the character in succeeding shots in which the order of shots suggests a correspondence to the character's train of thought. These are further implications of the point-of-view sequence that disqualify it as a possible means of presentation since the comic character created and impersonated by Harry Langdon is not capable of abstract thinking and can only entertain a single, simple thought at a time; and even at that, is easily and frequently distracted. For the same reason, there is also in Langdon's films, no significant use of offscreen space that would involve Harry in coming to terms with something not in plain sight in a space outside the frame.

Harry's dissociation with objective reality is established best through a style of cinematic presentation in which the coexistence of Harry and his immediate physical surroundings is preserved. Harry often merely gazes ahead toward the camera with an impassive expression and possibly a blink or two. In this characteristic expression, or lack of one—Harry's vacant stare—Harry's glance or attention is not directed toward any specific objective. The vacant stare requires spatiotemporal unity for its definition and precludes the point-of-view sequence since the vacant stare is defined by its duration and the fact that there is no particular object of Harry's glance. Harry's vacant stare is seen in the aftermath of the brawl and shootout in the nightclub dressing room in *Long Pants*. In one shot, Harry is sitting on the floor of the dressing room holding his wounded arm and staring straight ahead with wide-open eyes while the legs and feet of onlookers crisscross the frame as they move around in the foreground of the shot. In the next sequence, Harry, still holding his arm, which is now in a sling, gazes ahead toward the camera impassively from behind the bars of a prison cell as several of the hardened criminals with whom he is sharing the cell pass by in front of Harry in the foreground.

At other times, Harry's gaze may be fixed on something, but this does not necessarily mean that he sees it or comprehends its significance as a point-of-view shot would suggest. That something is not necessarily, or even usually, the object of his attention as the point-of-view shot would also imply. In *Long Pants,* Harry is confronted by a woman's bare thigh that is exposed right before his very eyes at point-blank range for a long time before he looks at it. Then he looks at it for a while before he finally sees it and recognizes its erotic significance. The shot ends at this moment of recognition, and in the next shot Harry jumps up and runs away.

The use of reaction shots is also incompatible with Langdon's conception of comic character and performance because Harry's reactions are not expressed in overt expressions or gestures, but as some kind of inappropriate physical response at the instigation of some usually highly aggressive or affective fact of life, antagonist, or dilemma. Harry's under- and over-reactions are defined not by montage but by the mise-en-scène. They are defined by Harry's physical relationship in space and time to one of these imminent demands of waking life. Cutting back to Harry from some person, place, or object, as in a reaction-shot sequence, would attach undue significance to an overworn and basically noncommittal expression or gesture, such as a blink or a tip of the hat and others in Langdon's limited repertoire of expressions and gestures.

To put it another way, such intercutting would not encourage the viewer's appreciation of Harry's physical disorientation with respect to his circumstances. And it would surely discourage the viewer's appreciation of the long time it takes Harry to comprehend—correctly, incorrectly, or not at all—the significance of the fact or situation that confronts him; and to act—appropriately, inappropriately, or not at all. Such intercutting would establish a too direct action/reaction connection rather than emphasize the character's somnambulistic insensitivity to the physical circumstances that confront him and his immunity to changes in those circumstances. A case in point occurs while Harry is on the chain gang in *Tramp, Tramp, Tramp*. Harry is busy trying to make little rocks out of big ones and for this reason he is unable to, at the same time, also take notice of the massive breakout that is going on around him.

The intercutting in a point-of-view and reaction shot sequence would also establish a too direct action/reaction connection rather than emphasize the difficulty with which Harry makes transitions between a conscious and an unconscious condition, or transitions to cognition or emotional maturity. Harry is seen watching the fight between Bebe and Betty in the nightclub dressing room in *Long Pants* in a medium long shot of long duration in which he sits motionless with his back to the camera in the foreground. The fight takes place in the background of the same shot. This incident could not be presented in terms of point-of-view and reaction shot and still present the character as Langdon conceived it or convey the incident's pathetic significance. Characterization and meaning are not expressed in the frozen stare that one would see if there was a cut to a reaction shot of Harry from a point-of-view shot of the battle. The character's naiveté and the significance of this incident to Harry as a profound emotional awakening can only be expressed in a long take in which the incident is presented in terms of the long time Harry must sit absolutely still before the spectacle, which unfolds in plain sight of him without any effort on his part to direct his attention to it, before its significance finally sinks in.

For the same reason, a single medium long shot of long duration is used and point-of-view and reaction shots are not used in *Three's a Crowd* when Harry comes home and is confronted with the sight of Gladys and her newborn child, a fact of life whose significance to Harry is that his fondest dreams have come true. In this shot, Harry stands absolutely still in the middle of the room, facing the camera so that the viewer can see his fixed, impassive expression throughout the duration of this very long take.

As it is not appropriate to establish a trajectory to orient Harry's glance and thereby orient his attention and subsequent actions with respect to a specified objective by the use of a point-of-view shot, neither is it appropriate to clearly establish the trajectory of Harry's locomotion by cutting away from Harry to some person, place, or object. Intercutting such as this, as it is commonly used, would confer upon that person, place, or object the significance of either "point of departure" or "destination." This, in turn, would establish a direction and lend structure to Harry's movement, thus implying motivation on Harry's part. Harry's locomotion is characteristically without the direction and structure that is provided by motivation either toward some specific logical objective as a destination or away from some specific point of departure.

This is clearly seen in the example in *Tramp, Tramp, Tramp* in which Harry starts out upon the cross-country walking race, first bringing up the rear as he halts and hesitates and then veering off away from the pack of racers after catching up, even though the family business and the girl of his dreams are at stake. A single medium high angle, medium long tracking shot that is frontally centered on Harry precedes him and traces the widening divergence in distance and direction between Harry and the other racers, who are on course.

Any notions of a point of departure, logical objective, or destination in Langdon's films are strictly those of the viewer. As far as Harry is concerned, there is no point of departure, logical objective, or destination. Harry's locomotion is characterized by running in place; running around in circles, back and forth, or in a completely erratic trajectory, often for a long time, without getting anywhere; or by undershooting (hesitating, halting, and stopping short) and overshooting something that to the viewer seems a logical objective.

Spatiotemporal continuity is, therefore, prescribed as the filmic form in which to present Harry's locomotion. In order to appreciate Harry's *dis*oriented relation to the world around him, the viewer must be given the opportunity to observe Harry's aim*less* movement in relation to his immediate physical circumstances for the duration of the long time that he moves and gets nowhere or does not move at all. Harry's aim*less*ness is seen in the single, stationary medium high angle, medium long shot in *The Strong Man* in which he is seen stranded in the midst of busy pedestrian traffic on a crowded sidewalk after letting go of Lily's hand. This cinematic treatment of Harry's predicament is one in which the viewer can plainly see that Harry has no logical objective or destination, and that with no one to lead him, he just does not know where, or whether or not, to go.

The shot-reverse shot sequence is a standard edit construction in narrative films. It consists of intercutting between characters who are engaged in an exchange of dialogue or some other dramatic interaction. The shot-reverse shot sequence is another montage construction that is, in effect, excluded from the film style of Langdon's comedies since Langdon's performance, comedy, and pathos concern a character whose communication with objective reality is generally only one-sided. Harry's response when he is addressed by others is slow or delayed, even when he is confronted by one of those highly provocative or insistent antagonists in plain sight or at point-blank range. Or he does not acknowledge the person at all, usually because he is unaware that he is being addressed. On the other hand, Harry frequently addresses himself to inanimate, indifferent, or inert "antagonists" and continues to relate to them, often for a long time and sometimes at point-blank range, without ever noticing their failure to acknowledge him. To intercut between Harry and a person addressing Harry or between Harry and an inanimate, indifferent, or inert antagonist in the form of a shot-reverse shot sequence as it is commonly used would suggest some kind of intercourse.

The shot-reverse shot sequence, therefore, is not used to present such confrontations as these. The means of presentation that is used preserves the coexistence of the noncommunicants in the space and time of a single shot. To appreciate the character's pathological indifference to the world around him, one must be given the opportunity to observe Harry's failure to acknowledge the person addressing him while that person continues to try to arouse Harry. One must also be given the opportunity to observe Harry continuing to talk to, argue, or wrestle with one of those inanimate, indifferent, or inert antagonists while they fail to acknowledge him.

When such confrontations are presented within a cinematic format of spatiotemporal unity, the viewer is aware not only of the simultaneity of provocation and lack of response but can also appreciate the duration, uninterrupted by cutting, of these one-sided encounters as evidence of the character's other than fully conscious condition. In *Tramp, Tramp, Tramp,* the cabbie who pesters Harry for his fare, and Harry, who is intoxicated and ignores his persistent demands, are seen together in two full shots, each of which is a long take. ("Full shot" refers to a full-figure shot of a character or characters.) In *His First Flame,* Harry and his uncle are seen together when Harry dozes off while his uncle tries to talk with him man-to-man. In *All Night Long,* the sergeant, who is looking around for someone to invite to dinner at his girl friend's house, remains oblivious to Harry, who is parading around under his nose, saluting and waving at him in a full shot of both. Later, the sergeant and Harry are seen together when the sergeant ignores Harry's outstretched hand as Harry embarks on a suicide mission. Harry's outstretched fist is ignored by the antagonist sitting beside him on the bus in *The Strong Man* while Harry waves it around the man's nose in a medium two-shot.

Harry's noncommunication with the telephone pole that he angrily scolds in *His Marriage Wow* is seen in a full two-shot of Harry and the pole. Harry comforts the fitting dummy he rescues from the fire in *His First Flame* in a medium close-up two-shot. ("Medium close-up" refers to a shot in which a character is seen from the shoulders up.) Harry tries to rouse the dummy cop in *Long Pants* in medium long shots in which he and the dummy cop alternate in the foreground of each of those shots. Harry is

Harry in a one-sided communication with an inanimate antagonist in *Heart Trouble*.

seen in medium close-up two-shots smiling at the perpetually smiling, slightly-larger-than-life-size billboard images of Betty Burton while he pastes them up around his room in *Tramp, Tramp, Tramp*.

Editing as it is employed in Langdon's films is not montage. Character, comedy, and pathos are not created by relationships between shots, but reside in the mise-en-scène—in Harry's relationship, in terms of placement and timing, to some fact of life, antagonist, or alternative. This relationship is the basic unit of expression in Langdon's films.

Montage is not significant in Langdon's films as a means of narrative and dramatic development. Even the sort of editing based on simple narrative logic—editing to merely establish a logical continuity between scenes of dramatic action—is not used significantly in Langdon's films. (This is not to mention the Griffithian montage employed in the construction of Harold Lloyd's comedy-melodramas to create suspense.) Langdon's film comedies, even his feature-length comedies, are essentially episodic with narratives structured around two or three extended confrontations by Harry with various demands of waking life. In the features, several of these episodes may consume as much as two-thirds of the running time of an individual film. This is the case in *The Strong Man,* in which approximately two-thirds of its eighty minutes is taken up by the confrontation between Harry and Lily in the back seat of the taxicab, the confrontation between Harry and Lily on the sidewalk in front of her apartment building, Harry's struggle with a head cold and a fellow passenger on the bus, and the scene between Harry and Mary Brown in the garden. The disparate episodes in the feature comedy *Tramp, Tramp, Tramp* (Harry's narcotic overdose, Harry's cliffhanging adventure, Harry's ill-fated attempt at poaching, Harry's sojourn on a chain gang, the jailbreak, and his encounter with a cyclone) are tied together by the thin plot thread of the cross-country walking race.

The only cutting "scheme" employed in Langdon's comedies involves cutting from a shot of Harry to another shot of Harry from a different camera setup in a way that perpetuates rather than violates the sense of spatial contiguity and temporal continuity between shots. This kind of cutting can be seen in the head-cold sequence on the bus in *The Strong Man.* Most of this sequence consists of several long-take medium two-shots of Harry and the passenger sitting beside him whom Harry is annoying. The cuts that occur during this eleven-minute sequence are primarily cuts away from this medium two-shot setup into medium close-ups (which also include several rather long takes) of Harry sneezing, sputtering, wiping his nose, and dallying with a teaspoon of cough medicine; cuts into close-up inserts for necessary information such as the mix-up of Harry's jar of salve with a jar of Limburger cheese; and cuts out to a wider shot of the interior of the bus in which Harry is seen seated at the end of a corridor formed by two rows of passengers seated along either side of the bus.

Except for several of these inserts and shots of each row of passengers looking at Harry in which Harry is not seen, and several solo medium close-ups of Harry's annoyed antagonist speaking to Harry that frame a dialogue title, the camera is centered on Harry (though the camera distance from Harry as the subject of the shots changes at times during the sequence). Establishing elliptical or metaphoric associations between shots is not an intention of the cutting in this sequence, or in Langdon's films in general.

Another sample of this cutting scheme is the long routine in *Long Pants* in which Harry tries to rouse the dummy cop. That sequence consists of intercutting between reverse-angle shots of long duration of Harry and the dummy as in a standard shot-reverse shot sequence, and cuts to closer shots of Harry as he continues to try to agitate the cop (which are also mostly long takes). Yet in those reverse-angle shots, the distance between Harry and the dummy is carefully maintained by photographing the dummy in medium long shot in the background from behind Harry, who is seen in full shot in the foreground; or by photographing Harry in medium long shot in the background from over the dummy's head and shoulder, which are seen in medium shot in the foreground. Both Harry and his inanimate antagonist are included in each of these reverse-angle shots. The semblance of temporal continuity between shots is also carefully preserved throughout this lengthy sequence by matching the action from shot to shot.

There is no significant montage manipulation of time and space as the basis of gags in Langdon's comedies as there is in the films of Buster Keaton, Harold Lloyd, Mack Sennett, and other of Langdon's contemporaries. For instance, in *The Balloonatic,* Keaton employs a temporal ellipsis between shots as the basis of a gag. Buster climbs in beside a girl in a boat that disappears into the Tunnel of Love, and the shot fades out. A second shot fades in as the boat emerges from the Tunnel of Love carrying the girl and Buster, who now has a black eye and a crushed hat.

Sometimes Keaton employed montage manipulation of time and space to create simple cause/effect relationships between shots as a structure for gags. This is used frequently in Keaton's two-reeler *The Electric House,* in cuts from Buster's rival crossing wires in the control room of the all-electric home Buster has designed, as the cause, to the various comic effects as Buster encounters each of his electronic conveniences gone haywire. Another of these is the final gag in that film in which the girl and her irate father pull in opposite directions a lever that empties and fills the swimming pool as they alternately try to save and drown Buster, who is at the bottom of the pool. After each shot of one of them pulling the lever, there is a cut to the pool with Buster in it, emptying or filling in undercranked and, when it fills, reverse-motion photography.

Nor is anything found in Langdon's films that is comparable to the more complex cause/effect structures that can be seen in Johnnie Gray's efforts to evade and waylay the pursuing enemy locomotives and reach Confederate lines in time to warn of the coming attack in Keaton's feature comedy *The General.* In that long sequence, intercutting elaborates a complex process of logical thinking on Johnnie's part as engineer of the events that take place.

One also does not see in Langdon's films gags that are effected by a change in camera distance and angle on a single subject from one shot to the next such as both Keaton and Lloyd often used for "surprise gags" in their films. In Keaton's two-reeler *Back Stage,* Buster appears to be climbing up and down a flight of stairs as he appears and disappears behind a banister. A cut to a different angle on Buster and the banister reveals to the viewer that there is no stairway and that the banister is merely a prop. Buster is not climbing up and down, but is merely kneeling down and standing up as he does some carpentry work on the floor behind the prop banister.

Another surprise gag based on the manipulation of film space by cutting to a different camera distance on the same subject is the final gag in *The Balloonatic*. Buster and his girl friend glide along in a canoe in full shot. There is a cut to an extreme long shot to inform the audience that there is a steep waterfall ahead, then a cut to another full shot of the blissful, seemingly unwary lovebirds gliding along in the canoe. There is another extreme long shot of the waterfall, and then a somewhat closer shot of the waterfall. Now there is a cut to the happy couple in the canoe in a medium shot. In the next long shot, the canoe is seen starting out over the edge of the waterfall and then continuing over the edge on a level course. At this point, there is a cut to a full shot of Buster continuing to serenade the girl inside the canoe as if nothing were happening. Here a cut to an extreme long shot in which they are maintaining their course in midair reveals that Buster has attached his hot-air balloon to the canoe.

The opening gag of Harold Lloyd's feature comedy *Safety Last* is another surprise gag that is effected by editing which alters camera angle on the subject. In the first shot, Harold bids his mother and girl friend a sad farewell from behind bars with a priest standing beside him and a noose looming ominously in the background. In the second shot, Harold is seen from the opposite side of the barred gate. In this reverse angle, the viewer can see that Harold is actually saying good-bye to his girl friend and mother at a railroad station. The priest is just another passenger and the noose is actually a mailbag loop.

Other standard silent comedy gag structures, such as the traditional edit structures of comic aggression, are also not to be found in Langdon's comedies. "Comic aggression" not only means physical aggression between comic characters but also the sort of comic aggression that is directed against the viewer in the form of suspense. Those edit structures of action/reaction in which aggression between comic characters is typically presented are virtually absent in Langdon's comedies. In Langdon's films both protagonist and antagonist, aggressive action and reaction, are seen together in a single shot. Those comic situations in which Harry is confronted by the hostile or amorous advances of some aggressive antagonist are typically presented in a stationary long or medium long shot in depth; in a tracking shot; or in a two-shot in the shallower space of a full, medium, or medium close-up shot.

For example, in *Saturday Afternoon* the camera follows Harry and a woman with whom he has just been "fixed up" by his pal, Vernon. They are walking together playfully, hand in hand, in a full shot as she teases Harry, paws him, and pulls on his clothes. When Harry's overall strap slides off of his shoulder, Harry stops and stares at her as the camera movement slows momentarily and the shot continues. The camera then moves on with the pair, who continue walking while Harry now keeps an eye on her. In *The Chaser,* a strange woman gradually advances upon Harry, whom she spots standing around in a park, and embraces and kisses him. Her advance and advances and the slight smile, slight frown, and blinks with which Harry responds to the seduction are seen in several long shots, three-quarter shots (a character seen from the knees up), and medium close-ups in which Harry and the woman alternate in foreground and background of reverse-angle shots with both seen together in each shot.

The big fistfight in *Saturday Afternoon* also involves no action/reaction editing. Harry's confrontations with hostile aggressors include a full shot in which one of the girl's boyfriends enters the frame from the right, punches Harry in the nose, and exits at left while Harry stands and stares, blinks, sneezes, and lets himself down gently to a seat in response. In another shot, five of the six parties involved in the fight are seen in a long shot in which three of them surround Harry's pal, Vernon, as Harry comes to his pal's rescue. Harry bypasses the fight scene and stops in foreground center where he practices his moves while the two jealous boyfriends advance ominously from the background. Harry eventually does make an effort to defend Vernon in a subsequent full three-shot, but while Harry is busy reassuring his pal and preparing to defend him, Harry's antagonist lands a punch squarely on Harry's jaw. Harry is still standing, however, and before the shot is over, the boyfriend lands a second punch, to which Harry responds in the same shot by readjusting everything knocked askew and then sinking slowly to the ground.

In *Tramp, Tramp, Tramp,* each time Harry is accidentally hit in the head with a sledgehammer by a fellow prisoner who is working with his back to him; Harry, the other prisoner, the blow, and Harry's typically undemonstrative response to the blow are all seen together in several three-quarter shots. When the tough circus roustabout kicks Harry in the pants in *Remember When*, both the assault and Harry's unconventional response—he blinks once, then walks away—are also contained in a single shot.

Those classic edit structures of comic aggression against the viewer, like the classic comic "chase sequence," in which editing is employed to create comic suspense, are also absent in Langdon's films. Another example is the kind of gag sequence whose construction is based on creating a rhythm of tension and relief, which is perhaps best exemplified in the "thrill comedy" of Harold Lloyd. This sort of editing is used to "build" a gag sequence that is constructed according to the kind of cumulative comic effect that was defined by James Agee in "Comedy's Greatest Era," as a "ladder of laughs" along which the viewer is carried by comic momentum from the "titter" to the "boffo." Agee illustrates this by referring to the building-climbing thrill comedy sequence in Lloyd's *Safety Last*.

None of these comic suspense sequences are found in Langdon's films, and there are no chases. Harry almost never initiates action and therefore does not pursue or run away when he is pursued. The girl who flirts with Harry in *Boobs in the Wood* cannot get him to chase her even though she skips playfully up to and away from him and runs in place to show him what he's supposed to do. Harry just imitates her by running in place himself. When the girl runs up and "tags" Harry and runs away, Harry takes a few steps forward to follow her but stops as soon as she stops as if they were playing "Simon Says." This nonchase takes place in a single shot of long duration in which the two figures are seen in various configurations and in which the action is played out in the entire depth and breadth of this long shot. Harry, naturally, fails to instigate a chase with the dummy cop that he taunts in *Long Pants*.

When he is threatened or pursued, Harry is usually not aware that he is being threatened or pursued. Action/reaction, chase, and suspense sequences do not suit this character. Harry and his potential aggressors are almost always seen together in the same shot, as in *Soldier Man* and *Lucky Stars* when Harry nonchalantly eats and sleeps while the two women lift their daggers to stab him. In one shot in *The Strong Man*, Harry walks around on a busy street corner looking for Mary Brown, unaware that he is being followed around by a strange woman who has her hand in his pocket. In *Remember When*, Harry and the sheriff occupy the foreground and background of a single shot as Harry displays his stolen chickens while the sheriff looks on over Harry's shoulder.

In other situations in which he is pursued or threatened, Harry runs back and forth from side to side, or to and fro in depth, or around in circles without getting anywhere, as when he is pursued by the angry mob in *Lucky Stars*. Or else he stops dead in his tracks or stands in place as if paralyzed. Therefore, one does not see parallel edited chase sequences in Langdon's comedies. There is no parallel edited chase sequence and no chase in *The Chaser* when the strange woman advances upon Harry in the park. Instead, Harry stands absolutely still, facing her as if he were transfixed while she makes her way toward him across a long shot and then a three-quarter shot.

There are also no thrill comedy suspense sequences in Harry Langdon's films since these depend on the comic character's acute awareness of the danger he is in and consist of his consequent desperate attempts to escape. In *Saturday Afternoon*, Harry, dazed by several punches during the fistfight, finds a place to light astride the running boards of two parked cars. He is in such a stupor that he does not notice the pavement whizzing by beneath him when the two cars start moving together through city traffic, or the cop, or the telephone pole that lies ahead directly in line with the interstice that Harry occupies between the two cars.

The fast thinking and quick reflexes required of the comic character in a successful thrill comedy sequence make such a sequence impossible in a film that features the slow-witted character created by Langdon, just as the fast-paced action required in a successful comedy chase sequence makes a chase sequence impossible in a film comedy that features a character that is as slow-moving as Langdon's. In fact, the nonchases and sequences in Langdon's films that may be called antithrill sequences assert most effectively that the rhythm of these films is not narrative-derived but, rather, derives directly from the slow rhythm of Langdon's mime and movement.

These antithrill sequences are seen in *Tramp, Tramp, Tramp* and *Three's a Crowd*. In the former, Harry is seen at long-shot range climbing over a fence in the left foreground of a shot in which the viewer sees, but Harry does not see, miles of landscape in the right background stretching out below him from an extreme high angle at extreme long-shot distance. Harry hangs suspended in midair by his sweater and his belt, which are caught on a nail. In the series of shots that follows, Harry tries to find a foothold in the fence and is then busily preoccupied with loosening his sweater from the nail and unbuckling his belt in order to free himself. Close-ups of Harry's feet and his hands unbuckling the belt are intercut with shots of Harry seen against the background of the countryside far below. Throughout all of these shots, Harry is unaware of the extreme danger of his situation.

Just as Harry finishes unbuckling his belt in the last of those close-ups, there is a cut to a medium shot of Harry in which he looks down for the first time and knows that he is in danger. The medium shot is followed by a rare point-of-view shot and a return to a medium shot in which Harry's only overt reaction is to stick his finger into his mouth. Harry starts to rebuckle his belt in a close-up as he looks down again in another point-of-view sequence. Then Harry is seen at full-shot range against the landscape in the background, attempting to cling to the fence in a clumsy kind of reflex action. In this same shot, he then grabs on to his belt and the nail and pulls a hammer out of his pocket.

Shots of Harry seen against the distant horizon are now intercut at a casual pace with close-ups and medium close-ups that detail his casual progress in removing other nails from the fence and using them to refasten his sweater and in inadvertently loosening the slab of fence to which he is attached. In the last of these shots, Harry is seen in medium shot holding onto his hat as he hangs from the piece of fence that now cuts across the frame diagonally at an angle of about forty-five degrees. In the next shot, a long shot, Harry dangles out over the abyss and then tries awkwardly rather than desperately to climb back over the fence to the other side. In the next medium shot, the slab of fence tilts some more as Harry merely holds on and looks down, wide-eyed. The slab finally breaks off and this precipitates a sequence of obviously "tricked" shots taken at close range in which Harry is seen supposedly sliding down the cliff on the slab. The trick sequence conveys no sense whatever of any real danger as in the action and thrill sequences in some of Lloyd's and Keaton's films, or of any skill or ingenuity on Harry's part in surviving.

The antithrill sequence in *Three's a Crowd* is another sequence that involves intercutting but no suspense. In this sequence, Harry accidentally falls through the trapdoor in the floor of his shack. Harry's shack clings to the side of a building several stories above street level. As he falls through the hole in the floor, Harry grabs on to a corner of the carpet. There is a cut to an exterior shot of Harry dropping down and pulling the carpet down through the hole with him. Then there is a cut to the interior of Harry's shack. In this shot, the rug is seen being drawn into the hole and the trap door is seen flipping down just in time to close on the remaining piece of carpet. This is followed by a cut to an exterior shot in which Harry's downward plunge ends abruptly as the carpet is pulled taut by Harry's weight midway to the ground.

This is a cause/effect edit construction, but it is one in which the effect has not been motivated by any effort on Harry's part. The sequence continues in the form of intercutting from exterior, long, and medium shots of Harry climbing up the carpet to interior close-ups of less and less of the remaining carpet slipping bit by bit through the opening each time Harry pushes the trapdoor up to climb back inside. In terms of basic structure, this sequence resembles a simple suspense sequence. However, the effect of the intercutting from interior to exterior and of the causal connections thus established is neutralized by the pace of the cutting. All of the shots in the sequence are continued on screen longer than is necessary for the purposes of conveying information and adequately depicting the action, and last too long to create any suspense. The sequence does not culminate but ends when Harry finally comes to the end of his rope, or more precisely, carpet, and finally plunges into a snowdrift on the street below.

If one compares these two sequences with that exemplary thrill sequence in Harold Lloyd's *Safety Last,* it is obvious that in Langdon's film the length of shots, and thus the pace of editing, corresponds to the pace of Langdon's performance, and that the pace of Langdon's performance is much too slow to foster suspense. It is also obvious in this comparison that, rather than suspense, the real object of Langdon's antithrill sequences is to make the viewer aware of the long time it takes Harry to recognize the danger of the situations he is in and allow the viewer to appreciate the slowness of Harry's reflexes as well as the inadequacy and inefficiency of his attempts to escape.

The object in situations in which Harry is confronted by the hostile or amorous advances of some aggressive antagonist is to allow the viewer to appreciate the long time it takes Harry to discover that he is threatened—if he does at all—and the long time it takes Harry to respond inappropriately or not at all. Even in situations of comic interaction involving Harry and up to four other characters, as in the fistfight in *Saturday Afternoon,* the characters are arranged and move within the space of a single frame. One of the aesthetic implications of presenting such an incident in this way rather than in the form of the standard edit sequence of intercutting action and reaction, as comic aggression between characters is traditionally presented, is that the temporal continuity of Harry's slow response or failure to respond as the object of aggression is maintained as a function of spatial contiguity.

To imagine Harry Langdon's comic characterization and performance in terms of the synthetic time and space of montage as ventured here is to recognize and understand the degree to which a mode of presentation based on the formal principle of spatiotemporal continuity is integrally linked to Langdon's comic charcterization and performance.

7
Langdon as Metteur-en-Scène

Langdon's unique comic style prescribes not only a basic filmic format of spatiotemporal continuity but also determines formal specifications of individual shots. The mise-en-scène scheme of Langdon's films is simply this: the spatial and temporal specifications of individual shots are accommodated not to the comic or virtuosic content of Langdon's performance (there isn't any to speak of) but to the spatial and temporal coordinates of Langdon's performance. Camera setup accommodates the space of the frame to the spatial relation between Harry and a particular fact of life, antagonist, or one or more alternatives. The length of each take is accommodated to the duration of that confrontation and/or transition.

An example is the shot that follows the one in which Harry is given directions by the doorman to the place where he can find Mary Brown in *The Strong Man*. Harry is already standing several feet from the doorman in a leftward-leaning position with one leg extended in that direction when he extends his arms in the opposite direction toward the doorman to thank him. Since the doorman does not extend his hand and Harry does not move closer to the doorman, Harry's hand does not reach the doorman's and he is not able to shake hands. The places of Harry and the doorman (or to put it another way, the several feet of space between them) define the outermost bounds of the frame. Harry's figure marks the left frameline and the doorman's marks the right frameline. Their full figures also determine the vertical dimension of this full shot. The space in between the two, along with the amount of time Harry hesitates there between getting to Mary Brown as fast as he can and thanking the doorman for his assistance, conveys Harry's indecision, excitement at the prospect of meeting Mary

Camera setup and time of take conform to the spatial relationship between Harry and the character or thing he is confronting and to the duration of that confrontation. A scene from *Heart Trouble*.

Brown, and gratitude to the doorman for helping him find her. The duration of this shot conforms to that amount of time.

Langdon's filmic mise-en-scène provides the time and space for Harry's transitions from sleeping to waking, from a conscious to an unconscious condition, and vice versa, and for Harry's transitions to cognition. Langdon's mise-en-scène also provides the time and space for Harry's inappropriate physical responses to the various demands of waking life that confront him in his semiconscious condition.

One might say that the formal specifications of each shot in Langdon's films are precisely determined in terms of the following prerequisites. They must provide the space to include Harry and some fact of life, antagonist, or one or more alternatives within plain sight of Harry or at point-blank range as the only instigation to intellection or some other emotional or sexual awakening and as the only instigation of Harry to action. Those formal specifications must provide the space for Harry to respond in these situations in the form of a too great or too little expenditure of physical energy as the manifestaton of Harry's psychological under- and overreactions for as long as it takes Harry to comprehend—correctly, incorrectly, or not at all—and to act—inappropriately or not at all. That space may be the deep space of a long shot, the shallow space of a medium close-up, or something in between. The only cutting "scheme," per se, in Langdon's films is cutting from Harry to Harry as a means of reframing Harry and his surroundings to accommodate screen space to the spatial relation between Harry and a particular fact of life, antagonist, or alternative.

In Langdon's pantomimed transitions between waking and sleeping and consciousness and unconsciousness, the time of the take is normally equivalent to the time it takes for Harry to gain or lose consciousness. These shots represent one of only two types of situations in Langdon's films in which Harry appears alone in the frame. (The other type of situation is discussed in the pages that follow.) In *Feet of Mud*, the shot in which Harry inhales the opiate incense that is burning under his nose and the shot in which Harry is hit on the head with a brick last as long as it takes Harry to succumb to their effects.

The shot in *The Sea Squawk* in which Harry is revived from the effects of a blow with a swig of whiskey and the shot in *Saturday Afternoon* in which Harry is revived from the effects of a blow from a swig of gasoline each last as long as it takes Harry to gradually regain consciousness. In the lengthy opening sequence of *Three's a Crowd*, Harry makes the slow and difficult transition from sleeping to waking in several shots, each of which lasts as long as it takes Harry to rouse himself and fall back asleep, and vice versa. Later, Harry sits in the baby's cradle and rocks the child to sleep in two shots that last as long as it takes Harry to start to nod off himself.

His Marriage Wow contains a long take of Harry at his wedding dinner that is equal to the time it takes for Harry to succumb to the sedative influence of the wine. The time of another long take solo shot in *Tramp*,

Tramp, Tramp is the time it takes Harry to fall asleep after eating a handful of sleeping pills and washing them down with whiskey while, throughout the shot, his insistence that he cannot sleep gradually gives way to the more insistent urge to close his eyes. When Harry tries to cross the room to a chair in *His Marriage Wow* and to a pitcher of water in *Tramp, Tramp, Tramp*, the time of each take is the time it takes Harry to cross a certain space in his intoxicated condition before collapsing in the middle of the floor in both cases to sleep it off.

In Harry's slow and difficult transitions to cognition, the time of the long take is normally equivalent to Langdon's slow take 'em. The time of the long take is the long time it takes Harry to comprehend an intellectual, emotional, or sexual revelation and absorb the psychological impact of such a profound awakening and the shock of momentarily gaining presence of mind. As Harry never exhibits intellectual curiosity or a capacity for abstract thinking, he must confront the material manifestation of some highly provocative fact of life, such as the cow's udder in *Soldier Man* and the kissing and making of eyes between Vernon and his girl friend in *Saturday Afternoon*, which is in plain sight or at point-blank range, for a long time as the necessary precondition for making these transitions to cognition. Therefore, none of these long takes of slow take 'ems by Langdon are solo shots of Harry. In *Long Pants*, Harry and the woman's bare thigh are squeezed into the background and foreground, respectively, of a tight-fitting medium close-up so that Harry cannot miss noticing this normally private portion of the female anatomy. (Even so, Harry nearly does miss noticing it.) Then, after looking at it a while, he finally does perceive the erotic implication of the bare thigh in a single shot that lasts as long as it takes Harry to go through all of this.

Other profound awakenings precipitated by highly provocative facts of life revealed in plain sight of Harry are the static tableaux in *Three's a Crowd* and in *The Strong Man*. The duration of the two long takes in which Harry is temporarily paralyzed by the sight of Gladys and her newborn baby in *Three's a Crowd* and by the revelation in the garden in *The Strong Man* of the fact that Mary Brown is blind is equivalent to the length of time Harry remains physically incapacitated by the affective impact of these revelations. The duration is also equivalent in each case to the time it takes Harry standing absolutely still and beholding those sights to comprehend their significance.

The medium-long-shot camera setup in *The Strong Man* is determined by the space between Harry and Mary, which is determined by the fact that, having told him she is blind, Mary turns away from him and walks toward the camera, groping in foreground left for the bench to sit upon. The space between them is also determined by the fact that Harry cannot cross the garden to help her because he has succumbed to paralysis and remains standing in background right. The filmic dimensions of the static tableau in *Three's a Crowd* are determined by the space between Harry and Gladys and

Harry experiences a profound awakening when he discovers that Mary Brown is blind in *The Strong Man*.

the child, who are sleeping in the right foreground of this medium long shot. The space between Harry and the two is determined by the fact that, after entering the shack, Harry is stopped in his tracks in the middle of the room at the moment he first sets eyes on them and remains in this arrested pose throughout the duration of this very long take.

The time and space for action on Harry's part as an overt physical response to the instigation of some fact of life, antagonist, or choice between alternatives is the time and space Harry takes to run around frantically in circles or in a completely erratic trajectory and get nowhere, teeter and totter, and overshoot a logical objective. Harry's kinetic expressions of excitement at confronting the fact of his dream come true is thus accommodated in *Three's a Crowd* by a medium long shot of the interior of Harry's shack. Another example is seen in *The Strong Man* at Harry's first sight of Mary Brown through the backstage door. In this case, the camera is positioned at medium-long-shot distance from the door. The space in between the camera and the door is the space for Harry to run back and forth and around in circles backstage, stop and start, and bypass the door to the garden before he is able to compose himself and venture out to introduce himself to Mary.

Instances in which Harry is confronted by the advances of a hostile antagonist are often presented in the deep space of a street that recedes into the background of a long shot. This provides ample space for Harry to run or walk up and down for a long time without getting anywhere. A good example is the long shot in *Lucky Stars* in which Harry stages his inefficient escape from the angry mob on a San Tabasco street. Harry dawdles as he looks around for the doctor, then dawdles some more as the doctor runs past him until Harry finally decides to follow him out of the frame. Another example is a long shot in *Fiddlesticks* in which Harry is left behind and dawdles in a narrow alley as his fellow musicians escape the barrage from their unappreciative audience.

The filmic dimensions of shots in which Harry overshoots a logical objective are determined by the requirement to include Harry, his logical objective, and adequate space for Harry to approach and then bypass that objective. These shots conform to Harry's action in temporal as well as spatial terms by presenting Harry's action whole—from approaching to overshooting. In the fistfight in *Saturday Afternoon*, the mise-en-scène is arranged along a plane perpendicular to the surface of the screen in a long shot. This allows Harry to enter from background right, run past Vernon, who is at the mercy of the jealous boyfriends, and past their girl friends in center frame, and stop some distance beyond them in the foreground to practice his moves. The camera setup of an earlier shot, after he smashes the storefront window, provides the time and space for Harry to hesitate, fluctuate, stop, start, retrace, and re-retrace his steps; overshoot Vernon's car; and go back along a trajectory diagonal to the surface of the screen.

As Harry is incapable of abstract thinking, he must be able to stand and/or move between the options or alternatives that confront him for a long time as the necessary precondition for intellection. Harry's physical relation to those manifest and spatially differentiated alternatives, and the amount of time he must run back and forth between them before arriving at a decision are the factors that inform the formal specifications of shots in which Harry is confronted by a moral, logical, or intellectual decision. The spatial dimensions of the shot in *Saturday Afternoon* in which Harry must decide between being courteous to the man who asks him for a light or being home from work on time are defined by Harry's two alternatives. The duration of this shot is defined by the amount of time Harry shuttles indecisively along a diagonal trajectory between the man, who marks the far left corner of the frame, and the departing streetcar, which marks the near right corner of the frame of this medium long shot.

In a shot in *His Marriage Wow*, the space of the frame is defined along an axis perpendicular to the screen by the wrong minister with the offering box containing Harry's money at full-shot range at the head of the center aisle of the wrong church in the foreground, and by the front door of the church at the opposite end of the aisle at medium-long-shot range in the background. The duration of this shot is defined by the length of time Harry hovers indecisively in the aisle between his two alternatives of economy (retrieving his money from the offering box), and expediency (exiting through the door to get to the right church in time for his wedding).

A medium long, slight high angle shot in *Tramp, Tramp, Tramp* provides the space for Harry to sit, stand, look, and walk and run back and forth in between two possible Betty Burtons for a long time in order to discern which one of them is the real Betty Burton. Harry is situated between the real Betty Burton, who is standing absolutely still in foreground left, facing Harry and away from the camera, and Betty's mirror image on a billboard that faces Harry and the camera in the background on the right side of the frame.

The formal properties of shots in which Harry has no logical objective, concrete alternative, or clearly demarcated course of action in plain sight are accommodated to this situation, just as they are in those shots cited earlier in which camera setup and duration of take are accommodated to Harry's relation in space and time to a specific object or alternative. The lateral proportions of these medium long shots are defined as the few feet within which Harry teeter-totters or runs back and forth without getting anywhere along an axis that is parallel to the surface of the screen with no such objective, alternative, or course of action in sight. These shots usually last until he finally comes to a halt or walks out of the frame in one direction or the other. (This is the only type of situation, other than Harry's transitions between sleeping and waking and consciousness and unconsciousness, that may be considered a solo performance by Langdon.)

One of these is seen in *Tramp, Tramp, Tramp* when Harry emerges from the family shoe store having resolved to raise the money for the mortgage. Facing the camera on the sidewalk in front of the store, Harry bobs from side to side, first on one foot, then the other, from a point at center frame. Another is an almost identical shot in *Lucky Stars* in which Harry does the same thing when he is advised by the astrologer to follow his lucky star.

The incident in *The Strong Man* in which Harry keeps losing and regaining sight of his objective, Lily, when Harry lets go of her hand on the busy sidewalk is presented in a slight high angle, medium long shot. This is the only possible camera setup in which Harry's disposition, movement, and direction at any moment with respect to Lily and her disposition, movement, and direction as he loses and regains sight of her, and with respect to the movement of the crowd of people surrounding him on the sidewalk, can be presented for the duration of Harry's ordeal and reunion with Lily.

Plotting the vectors, or lines of trajectory of Harry's movement, is one way to describe the parameters of the shot in *His Marriage Wow* in which Harry, with nothing more than a traffic cop's verbal directions to go on, tries to get to the church where he is to be married. In this shot, it is plain to see the way in which formal specifications of individual shots in Langdon's films conform to Langdon's mime and movement. Harry is first seen talking with the traffic cop in the middle of an intersection at medium-long distance from the camera. After exiting with the usual difficulty at screen left, Harry eventually reappears deep in the background of this same shot at long-shot distance from the stationary camera, having gone around the block in a circle. He makes his way up the intersecting street toward the traffic cop from background to midground, runs on past him, and finally stops in full-shot range in the foreground of this shot. Here he runs from side to side and settles to a stop in the center of the street, sucks on his finger, and then turns and runs back to the cop for another reconfirmation of the directions.

In *The Strong Man,* Harry falls over the front pew in an auditorium at Ellis Island while trying to escape an irate baggageman and precipitates a domino effect. He stands and watches the first three pews fall before following the toppling benches with his arms helplessly outstretched. He undershoots a logical objective when he makes his way up the aisle just behind the toppling benches from background to foreground and from medium-long- to medium-shot range of the stationary camera. He stops, sways in place, and totters from side to side as he lets his hands drop, then raises them again futilely, stepping up his pace and then slowing down. The time of the shot is precisely measured as the time it takes for Harry, with a delayed start of three benches, to move up the aisle at the same slow rate that it takes each bench to knock over the next and for Harry to then make his way just as uncertainly back down the aisle after reaching the end of the row of benches, three benches too late.

The specifications of another shot in *The Strong Man,* a medium two-shot, are measured in terms of the length of time Harry sits in close proximity beside the man on the bus, scowling, glaring, and wielding his fist in retaliation without making contact. The proportions of this medium shot are precisely determined by the close proximity of the two characters to each other and the distance between Harry's fist and the man's nose. The specifications of two other medium two-shots, one in *The Strong Man* and one in *Tramp, Tramp, Tramp,* are measured in terms of the length of time Harry sits in close proximity beside the objects of his desire without making

The time of this shot in *The Strong Man* is the time it takes for all the benches to topple and for Harry to follow with a delayed start of three benches after the first bench to fall.

The specifications of this shot are based on the length of time Harry sits in close proximity to his antagonist and the distance between Harry's fist and the man's nose. *The Strong Man.*

physical contact. In these shots too, the space of the frame is based on the close proximity of Harry and Mary sitting together on a bench in the garden in *The Strong Man* and of Harry and Betty Burton sitting together on a park bench in *Tramp, Tramp, Tramp,* and the distance between Harry's fingertips and the two girls' faces.

The camera distance and duration of most shots in which Harry is seen with a woman are determined by the safe distance Harry maintains or tries to maintain between himself and the woman. For instance, the aftermath of Lily's "seduction" of Harry in the cab is presented in medium shot. This medium shot camera setup includes both Harry and Lily in close proximity in the back seat of the cab, and the space between them as the most space Harry can put between himself and Lily by cringing in his corner of the cab. The long duration of this shot is equivalent to the long time Harry remains in that protective position, keeping a watchful eye on Lily.

In one shot of Harry and Lily on the sidewalk in front of her apartment building, Lily's body in full shot in the right foreground marks the point nearest the camera. The street corner at the end of the block at medium-long distance in the left background is the point farthest from the camera. The safe distance that Harry maintains in this shot is the space between that far point at the left frameline and halfway between that point and Lily, who is lying inert on the sidewalk at the apartment building entrance at the opposite end of the block at the right frameline. The time of this take is the amount of time that Harry moves too much back and forth along a diagonal axis between these two points as evidence of his emotional overreaction to the situation.

Langdon as Metteur-en-Scène

Cinematic specifications of this shot in *The Strong Man* are based on Harry's physical relationship with Lily's inert body.

In the shot in which Harry is trying to escape from Lily's apartment, Harry is standing in the space between the locked door in right background and Lily with the key in the left foreground. In this shot, the camera setup is accommodated to Harry's situation between Lily and the door. The time of the take is accommodated to the unduly protracted time it takes Harry to cross that space to get the key.

In all of these examples, the formal filmic specifications of camera distance and duration of take of individual shots conform to Langdon's performance as it describes and is inspired by Langdon's comic characterization. In all of these examples the specifications of filmic space and time conform to the spatial and temporal coordinates of Langdon's performance, through which Harry's disoriented relation to the world is demonstrated. This conformity of film form to Langdon's performance is seen, perhaps most obviously in the tracking shot of the beginning of the cross-country walking race in *Tramp, Tramp, Tramp*.

The ever-widening divergence between Harry and the other racers as he runs past and veers away from the pack is directly related to the long time Harry remains unaware that the other racers are no longer behind him. A medium high angle, medium long tracking shot in depth of long duration that is frontally centered on Harry is the one and only cinematic treatment in which this interrrelationship and Harry's exact position in relation to the other racers at every moment can be made explicit. The formal specifications of this shot provide the space and time for Harry, in this situation, to demonstrate his impaired perception, lack of motivation, and consequent inability to direct his movement with respect to a specified objective. The formal specifications of this shot are, therefore, precisely determined by the spatial and temporal coordinates of Langdon's physical disposition with respect to the other racers—the increasing disparity in distance and direction between Harry and the others, and the long time Harry remains unaware that he has gone astray.

In all of Harry Langdon's silent comedy films (except perhaps those first two he made for Mack Sennett), the spatial and temporal specifications of individual shots—the filmic mise-en-scène—were Langdon's own domain. Whether as featured performer or as performer-director, Langdon himself is metteur-en-scène. In the opening sequence of Harry awakening in the morning in *Three's a Crowd*, for example, the action is not analyzed by editing. Rather, Langdon just goes about the action—of trying to wake and falling back to sleep—in his own time. The very slow overall edit rhythm of that sequence and the temporal boundaries of each shot that makes up the sequence correspond to Langdon's pantomimed impression of someone hovering between sleeping and waking.

This slow rhythm or pace is an essential feature of the comic character conceived by Langdon as one whose rational faculties and motor functions are impaired, sometimes to the point of incapacitating Harry, because of his perpetually semiconscious condition. That slow rhythm or pace is inscribed by Langdon's performance directly into the rhythm of the films in which he appears through the extensive use of long takes. Mack Sennett's comment, "We had to give him a hundred feet of film or so to play around in, do little bits of business, and introduce himself," should be recalled here. Sennett's comment and other information on the production of Langdon's films as provided by Sennett and Capra, plus the manner in which the rhythmic structure of Langdon's films conforms to the rhythm of Langdon's performance, indicate that it is Langdon, as performer, who provides the formative influence on the temporal structure of Harry Langdon's silent comedies.

Any of the examples described thus far illustrate how the rhythmic structure of Langdon's films conforms to the slow rhythm of Langdon's performance. These include the long takes that correspond to Langdon's slow take 'ems in Harry's confrontations with the woman's bare thigh in *Long Pants,* the prolonged kiss in *Saturday Afternoon,* the cow's udder in *Soldier Man,* the brawl between Bebe and Betty in *Long Pants,* and Gladys and her newborn child in *Three's a Crowd.*

Other examples are the long takes of Langdon's pantomimed transitions between waking and sleeping and consciousness and unconsciousness, as when Harry slowly succumbs to the effects of the opiate incense in *Feet of Mud,* and when he puts himself to sleep while rocking the baby to sleep in *Three's a Crowd.* In other long takes, Harry hovers about the picnic table without ever eating anything in *Remember When,* stands by the palm reader's window with a brick in his hand without ever throwing it in *Three's a Crowd,* and holds a chicken over a frying pan waiting for it to lay an omelette in *The Chaser.*

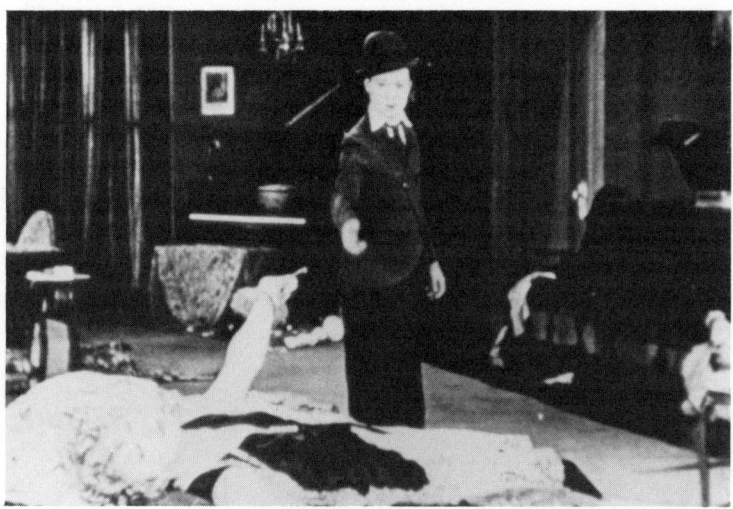

Here camera setup is accommodated to Harry's situation between Lily on the couch and the door of her apartment in *The Strong Man*.

In edited sequences such as the attempted murder of Priscilla in *Long Pants*, Harry's preparation of a pie from a frozen diaper in *Three's a Crowd*, and the antithrill sequences in which Harry hangs from a nail over the cliff in *Tramp, Tramp, Tramp* and hangs over the street from a carpet in *Three's a Crowd*, the action unfolds almost in slow motion and edit rhythm follows suit at a slow and constant pace.

On examination of Langdon's Sennett films, it also becomes apparent that Sennett's comment, "We had to give him a hundred feet of film or so to play around in," refers not only to filmic time but to filmic space as well. In films, Langdon generally worked in a space basically equivalent to full stage—the medium long shot. It was a space whose adoption he, as featured comedian, imposed not for its own sake or merely because this was the space he was accustomed to working in onstage. It was imposed by him because the comic conception he developed onstage—the comic persona and style of performance, the relation of character and performance, and the relation of both character and performance to mise-en-scène—required the conditions of spatiotemporal continuity.

The various confrontations between Harry and the minister in the wrong church in *His Marriage Wow*, Harry and the man in the street who wants a light in *Saturday Afternoon*, Harry and Lily on the sidewalk in front of her apartment building in *The Strong Man*, Harry and the vamp on her balcony in *Lucky Stars*, and Harry and the two Betty Burtons in *Long Pants* all take place in the space of a single medium long shot. Those static tableaux in which Harry beholds Gladys and the infant in *Three's a Crowd*, the brawl between Bebe and Betty in *Long Pants*, and Mary Brown groping

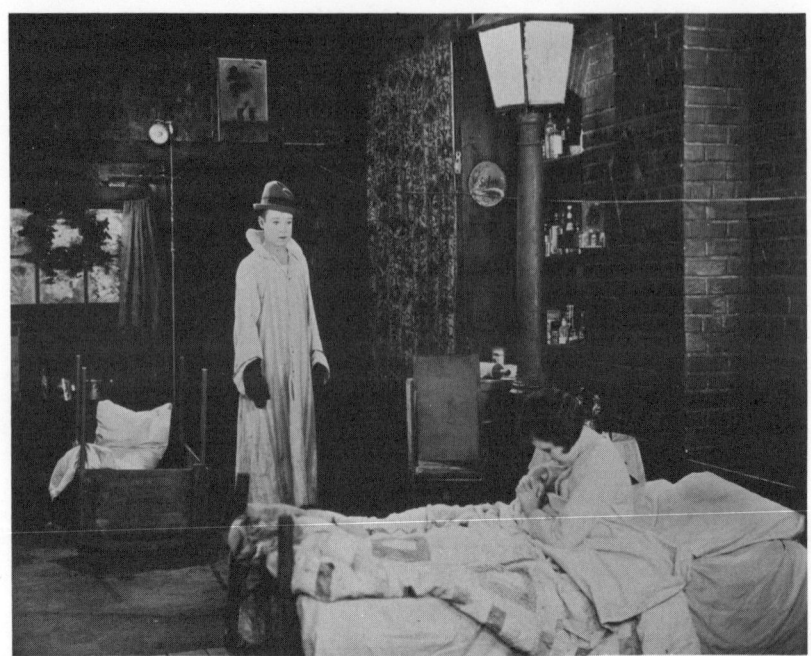

Two examples of a typical Langdon mise-en-scène—Harry and a point of reference in medium long shot. *Three's a Crowd* (above) and *The Chaser* (below). (Courtesy of Gladys McConnell)

her way to the bench in the garden in *The Strong Man* are all presented in medium long shot, with Harry seen in medium shot in the foreground in *Long Pants* and the objects of his gaze in the foreground in the other two shots.

In *Soldier Man*, the entire exposition of the dream sequence story is presented in a single shot in which the characters are all carefully arranged on four levels in depth in a medium long shot. The drunken king (whose resemblance to Harry, the soldier, is more than merely physical) is seen in the right foreground at medium close-up distance. A servant at medium-shot range to the king's left serves him a cocktail. The chief minister is seen in full shot in between the king and the servant, trying to coax the king to sign a peace treaty to end the war. The other ministers who are conspiring with the chief minister to coerce the king to sign the treaty are seen in the background at medium-long distance peeking from behind a palace archway. The king is completely oblivious to everything that is going on around him and lapses into unconsciousness during the course of the shot.

Harry's attempted escape from his bride and her family after having drunk too much wine at the wedding dinner (which he thinks is poison) is elaborately acted out in the "full stage" space of a medium long shot in *His Marriage Wow*. Harry drunkenly bobs and weaves around the room in foreground, midground, and background in a foggy response to the appearance or advance of various members of the wedding.

Another elaborate routine is performed in a single medium long shot in *Remember When*. Harry stands unnoticed beside the sheriff as the sheriff shoves the bunch of hoboes Harry has joined across the state line. At first, the sheriff and Harry are seen in midground at full-shot distance, both with their backs to the camera, watching the group of hoboes tramp off into the background. As they do, Harry turns and starts walking in the opposite direction, toward the camera into the foreground. As Harry does so, the sheriff turns and glares at him, at which point Harry turns around again and starts to follow the rest of the bums into the background of the shot. The sheriff now turns his back to Harry a moment to mount his horse and as he does, Harry reaches for a rock. The sheriff turns back around just in time to catch Harry in the act. Harry replaces the rock and continues on his way, finally disappearing over the horizon in medium long shot as the sheriff rides into the foreground past the camera and out of the frame.

Langdon, as comedian and metteur-en-scène, also transcended in film the more or less fixed spatial dimensions of the proscenium, which had placed a certain limitation on Langdon's theatrical mise-en-scène. He did not change his comic style, but he did discover, in the medium of film, ways to employ and even exploit the greater plasticity that is unique to film in order to implement his original comic conception in ways he could not have done on stage. Langdon employed and exploited the expanded spatial parameters of film in a natural, more or less intuitive manner through his performance. This is the same manner in which he imposed a filmic style

Langdon in *Heart Trouble* gives himself the time and space "to play around in."

that is now generically referred to as the "mise-en-scène" style upon all the films in which he appeared and this is the grounds on which Harry Langdon, the comedian, can be declared metteur-en-scène.

Langdon took advantage of the possibility that film offered to alter the mise-en-scène more easily and freely than he could do on stage. Now, working within the more flexible spatial dimensions of film, Langdon utilized the possibility of working in a space that was shallower than that of working "in one" and of working in a space deeper than "full stage."

It cannot be merely coincidental that in Langdon's films for Sennett, frequent and optimal use is made of a three-dimensional rendering of the illusionistic, deeply recessive two-dimensional space of the boulevard drop Langdon had designed for his vaudeville sketch, "A Night on the Boulevard." This space is reconstituted in the form of the deep streets of Sennett's Glendale Boulevard lot and actual Los Angeles locations. In his first encounter with film at Sennett's, Langdon took advantage almost immediately of the much greater depth available in film than the space of full stage in which to move or not move. Langdon could now work in the space of his old boulevard drop. A street set constructed in three dimensions or an actual location continued to serve Langdon as a scene for action or stasis in stationary long shots and in tracking shots.

Langdon also exploited a special kind of reciprocal relationship of spatial and temporal properties that pertains to film as it does not pertain to the stage. The commonly used camera setups in a deeper or shallower space than that available on stage and tracking shots through deep screen space are employed in Langdon's films as a means of providing Langdon more time as a function of more or less space than is available on stage. This more plastic filmic space offered Langdon the opportunity to enhance a primary feature of his performance and a significant element of characterization by allowing him to exaggerate the slowness of Harry's mental and physical functions beyond the limits of what he could effectively sustain on stage.

The more expansive space of film allowed Langdon in some cases to extenuate the duration of those simple situations of confrontation. This allowed him to further exaggerate his slow-witted and slow-moving under- and overreactions to the demands of waking life included in the shot and thus "milk" or get the most from single, simple bits of business. Those facts of life, antagonists, and alternatives are placed at a greater distance from Harry and from each other than on stage. In the long shots involving screen space deeper than that of full stage, Harry and up to four other characters are placed, and their movement with respect to one another is elaborately worked out, within the space of a single frame.

Perhaps the most elaborate of the routines in which Langdon uses the more expansive playing space of film to milk a situation and exaggerate the character's indecisiveness occurs in the two-reeler *Lucky Stars*. In this shot, Harry hovers between business and pleasure in the deep space of a street in

San Tabasco as he passes the entrance to a saloon on his way with the doctor to the town square to begin the medicine-show performance. The action takes place in three very long takes (two long shots and a medium long shot) as follows. In the first shot, a long shot, Harry and the doctor are seen at the end of the street, coming forward into the camera. As the two pass the saloon entrance on the left side of the frame at midground depth, Harry is distracted from his course by the light that shines from under the swinging doors. He stops in his tracks and kneels down under the doors to peer inside while the doctor proceeds on course into full-shot range in the foreground of the shot, unaware as yet that Harry is no longer at his side.

Harry now starts to follow the doctor, then goes back, kneels, and looks into the saloon again while the doctor continues to proceed forward. Harry calls him just as the doctor bypasses the camera and leaves the frame in the right foreground. Harry now stands alone beside the saloon door and points to it, facing the camera at medium-long distance and midground depth. He comes forward a bit, still pointing back toward the door, and then starts running back to the door while beckoning to the doctor, who is offscreen, to follow him. Harry kneels and looks inside again, comes forward those same few steps while pointing back toward the door, and then tips over backward to his former position at the saloon entrance and crawls inside. After a moment, Harry emerges from the saloon doors with a beer in his hand and stands there, facing the camera, holding it aloft and pointing at the saloon.

The next shot is also a long shot in which the camera is at a slightly greater distance from the action and takes in the doctor, who was just offscreen in the previous shot and is now at medium-long-shot range in the foreground. Harry is now seen at long-shot range in the midground, pointing at the glass of beer and coming forward a few steps, then stopping to take a sip while the doctor watches with his back to the camera and calls Harry impatiently. As the doctor continues to demand that Harry come, Harry hesitates and finally puts the glass of beer down on the ground. The doctor now turns toward the camera and starts off out of the frame again in the same direction as in the previous shot. Harry starts to follow him, but as soon as the doctor's back is turned, Harry runs back to get his beer.

Before Harry gets to the beer, the doctor, now at full shot in the right foreground, turns back in time to catch him and calls Harry once more. Harry turns to face the doctor, stops, stares, and hesitates, circling the glass of beer in the street. Harry then comes forward as the doctor again turns toward the camera and again starts off out of the frame. After taking those same few steps forward, Harry stops again, turns around, and creeps back toward the beer as the doctor, not quite out of the frame, notices and turns around to face Harry again. The doctor watches Harry creep the rest of the way to the beer, and then scolds and calls him back. Harry stands up, then kneels down again, but stands back up when the doctor yells at him once more from the foreground. At this last reprimand, Harry comes forward a step or two, scratches his head, extends his arms in a plaintive gesture, backs up again, comes forward a step, backs up, and continues to totter back and forth between the doctor and the beer until the doctor finally ventures into midground to get him.

The third shot is a medium long shot in which Harry is seen standing between the beer on the ground and the saloon entrance, looking at the doctor, who enters the shot and advances on Harry from the right foreground. Harry turns back to the door, backs up a few steps, and then runs into the saloon as the doctor follows him inside. After a moment, the two emerge wiping their lips and proceed slowly together toward the camera. Harry stops in his tracks once more when they are a few steps beyond the beer that is still sitting in the street. Harry looks back momentarily, takes a step forward, and then turns back to get the beer. The doctor pulls Harry away before he can retreat again and the two continue walking forward toward foreground left. When they reach full-shot range, Harry and the doctor stop and the doctor crosses to foreground right to get his bag. As soon as the doctor turns away, Harry looks and then scurries back into the background for his beer. By the time Harry kneels to pick it up, the doctor is there with his bag pulling Harry back. The two finally make their way forward, crossing the frame diagonally, and exit at medium-shot distance at screen right.

In Langdon's film comedies, the moving camera conforms closely to Langdon's performance by imitating Harry's movement. The camera generally moves along in front of or behind Harry at the same slow pace at which Harry is moving and hesitates and halts when Harry hesitates and halts. In *Fiddlesticks,* the moving camera follows Harry down the street at full-shot range after he leaves his bug-infested room. Harry begins walking at a relatively fast pace, for Harry, then abruptly breaks into a slightly faster-paced skip for several steps while scratching the seat of his pants as the camera also picks up a bit of speed. Harry and the camera now continue on at Harry's former, slower pace as Harry continues to scratch. The camera stops for a moment when Harry stops to devote his undivided attention to the still unsatisfied itch.

Harry then skips ahead another few steps as the camera follows for the same distance at the same rate while Harry starts to scratch again. Harry and the camera now continue on for a few more steps, gradually slowing together, until Harry comes to a stop again to direct his undivided attention to smacking at the bug in his pants. The camera pauses here for a time while Harry, still seen from the rear in full shot, tries to shake the pest out of his pants leg, jumps out of the way when it drops out, and then grinds it into the sidewalk. Harry kneels down to examine the bug, steps on it again, and finally continues on his way.

Following a sequence in which Harry is seen as a little boy in *Remember When,* he is introduced as an adult in a moving camera shot in which the camera follows and then precedes.him in a second shot at the same slow pace at which Harry ambles along a country road with a bundle on a stick over his shoulder. A moving camera dollies out in front of Harry in *Long Pants* in a series of shots, all at the same medium-shot distance and normal angle, in which Harry is seen returning home after his adventure with Bebe. He walks out of jail, through a wooded landscape, through the front gate of his parents' home, and through the front door and into the dining room where his family is saying grace at the table. In each of these shots, the moving camera moves at the measured, zombielike pace at which Harry is walking.

Like the static long shots, tracking shots also provided Langdon more space than that available on stage in which Harry could take a longer time to recognize and comprehend or fail to comprehend the nature and significance of his circumstances, and to respond or fail to respond. For instance in *Remember When*, Harry is walking along another country road, carrying a live beehive that he has inadvertently picked up on the end of his hobo stick. In this long take, the camera tracks out in front of Harry at full-shot range at Harry's slow pace. Throughout the duration of the shot, Harry is never more than slightly annoyed by the bees buzzing around the hive just over his shoulder. Once, he even turns around to look behind him, naturally sees nothing there, and continues on his way. Another such example is the moving camera shot that tracks out in front of Harry as he lags behind, catches up with, surpasses, and then veers off course away from the pack of racers in *Tramp, Tramp, Tramp*.

Like the stationary long takes in deeper and shallower space than available on stage, moving camera shots were another element of filmic mise-en-scène that afforded Langdon the opportunity to exaggerate the slow pace of his mime and movement beyond what he could do on stage as a way of more effectively impressing the viewer with the slowness of the character's physical and mental functions than he could on stage. The tracking shot in depth, like the other deep and shallow stationary shots in Langdon's films, is also a filmic form in which the proximity and simultaneity of Harry's response (which may include the absence of any overt physical response) and the instigation of that response, as well as the duration of that interaction or lack of interaction, are maintained.

The camera generally moves in depth in Langdon's films and is centered upon Langdon, as usual, as the focal point of the shot at full-shot or medium-long-shot range, from a frontal or following point of view. There is no orientation of Harry's movement with respect to a point of departure or destination. These tracking shots emphasize duration rather than distance. This is seen in the shot of the walking race in *Tramp, Tramp, Tramp* and the shot in *Remember When* in which Harry walks along with the live beehive over his shoulder. The time of the latter tracking shot is not the time it takes Harry to get from one place to another—Harry usually moves without getting anywhere—but is equivalent to the long time Harry can walk around carrying a live beehive and remain unaware of it.

The tracking shot through deep screen space, like the deep and shallow stationary camera setups commonly used in Langdon's films, is another example of a cinematic treatment that conforms to and derives from Langdon's own comic persona and performance. The lateral tracking shot in which the camera moves along an axis parallel to the surface of the screen is uncommon in Langdon's films because it does not conform to and derive from Langdon's persona and performance. The lateral tracking shot does, on the other hand, conform to a comic persona and performance such as Buster Keaton's, in whose films fast-moving lateral tracking or panning shots often follow Buster's fast movement. The lateral tracking or panning shot in Keaton's films also graphically features challenging topography and/or obstacles and emphasizes the long distance traversed by Buster with Buster seen against a panoramic background. The distance traversed is usually extended in Keaton's films by the editing together of a series of such shots.

Such a sequence is seen in *Seven Chances* in which Buster, trying to escape hundreds of eager brides-to-be, runs down a steep hill while he dodges huge boulders that are rolling down the hill in a torrent after him. Another such sequence occurs in a Keaton two-reeler entitled *The Paleface* in which Buster is chased by hostile Indians over steep and rugged Western terrain. Sequences such as these are a demonstration of the strength, speed, and endurance of a very different comic character and style of performance than Langdon's.

The limited depth of full stage had imposed a limitation on Langdon's vaudeville performance, although Langdon did, to a certain extent, successfully overcome that limitation by means of the cleverly contrived stage effects of his curtain call. The limited intimacy of performing "in one" as the shallowest space in which to work in vaudeville also seems to have imposed a certain limitation on Langdon's stage performances. Perhaps these are the considerations that initially encouraged his interest in working in films.

Langdon not only took advantage of a filmic space that was deeper than that of full stage, he also utilized a shallower, more intimate space than the space in which he had worked on the stage. Like the long takes in deep screen space, these long takes in shallow screen space also fulfill the prescription that is implicit in Langdon's conception of comic persona and performance to maintain the spatiotemporal unity of Harry's physical responses and the instigation of those responses. These medium shot and medium close-up camera setups allowed Langdon to further retard the slow pace of Harry's transitions between sleeping and waking and consciousness and unconsciousness, his transitions to cognition, and his more intimate under- and overreactions to encounters with the facts of life or antagonists which confront him at point-blank range. Langdon could retard those slow transitions and take 'ems for a longer time than he could effectively sustain such physically reductive pantomime from the greater fixed distance of the stage.

Langdon must have felt this limitation when he presented the final version of his long-running vaudeville act, called "After the Ball," in which he toured just prior to his entry into film. "After the Ball" was received by reviewers as an experiment that was not entirely successful. This amounted to a failure for Langdon, whose act did not often receive unfavorable comments. "After the Ball" consisted of three "scenes," or comic episodes: "In the Ruff," "Treated Ruff," and "Ruff Riding." The first, which lasted six minutes, was set "in one" on a golf course and featured Harry as a quiet caddy for two talkative lady golfers. In the second scene, the comic business was set "in full" in front of the clubhouse and lasted eight minutes. The third was a condensed version of Langdon's automobile routine featured in the two earlier versions of his act, and included the two women and a cop. It was set "in two" in front of a hospital drop, which Langdon later changed to a café drop, where Harry's trick auto becomes stalled. The third scene lasted nine minutes.

Prior to "After the Ball," Langdon had presented his act in full stage with only an opening and final curtain, which was followed by Langdon's special "curtain call" effect. The innovation on Langdon's part of dividing the act up into three scenes, each of which was presented in a different stage setting and in a different stage space, must have had something to do with another development in Langdon's performance in that final version of his long-running sketch. According to descriptions in reviews in the trade papers, Langdon's performance in "After the Ball" was, physically and in terms of comic content—gags, comedy talk, and business—his most highly refined. He presented this highly refined comic performance (in other words, he did less) at a slower pace than he had ever done before on stage. It was of "After the Ball" that a *Variety* reviewer quoted in chapter 2 said:

> Harry Langdon got a halting start with the golf prolog to his auto burlesque. In his new vehicle . . . he humors his slow personality a bit too much. It is a unique and laughable technique, but it does slow up business. He closed to very little, having tired the audience with repetition of gags and draggy delivery. The act, of course, is of high grade, as its nucleus is "Johnny's New Car," which had developed into one of the surest skits of years when Langdon decided to experiment.[1]

A *Billboard* writer noted, "his act drags and missed fire. It is about fifteen minutes and nothing much else."[2] Others simply preferred the old automobile routine of the three scenes.

In "After the Ball," distractions probably interfered with the audience's appreciation of Langdon's physically subtle performance and with its sense of the long time it took for Harry to respond or fail to respond as an element of his characterization. The possibility of adjusting the film frame by changing camera setup as though it were an infinitely adjustable proscenium has the effect in long-take medium shots and medium close-ups of reducing distractions. In these shots, Langdon is working in less space than had been available to him on stage to do less for a longer time than he could effectively sustain on stage.

The long takes in shallow screen space in Langdon's films include full shots, medium shots, and medium close-up two- and three-shots. The full shot is a screen space that can be compared to working "in one" on stage. This is the space before a drop in the first entrance behind the proscenium that is normally reserved for the solo specialty number. In Langdon's films, the full shot is normally a two-shot—of Harry and the indifferent doorman in *The Strong Man;* of Harry and the indifferent sergeant in *All Night Long;* of Harry and the inanimate and therefore indifferent and inert telephone pole in *His Marriage Wow;* of Harry and his angry and inert wife in *Saturday Afternoon;* of the persistent cabbie and Harry, who is indifferent in *Tramp, Tramp, Tramp;* and of Lily and Harry, who is unaware that she is circling around him on a busy street with her hand inside his jacket in *The Strong Man*.

The medium shot and medium close-up in Langdon's films are commonly two- or three-shots. These medium shots include long takes of those intimate scenes between Harry and Mary Brown on the bench in the garden in *The Strong Man*, between Harry and Betty Burton on the park bench in *Tramp, Tramp, Tramp*, between Harry and Lily in the back seat of the cab in *The Strong Man*, and between Harry and the man on the bus in that film. They also include the shot in which Harry cuddles up to the vamp in *Lucky Stars* and starts to doze while she raises a dagger over his head, and the shot in *Soldier Man* in which the queen pulls a dagger on Harry as she embraces him while Harry munches from the fruit bowl.

The medium shots of Harry's slow take 'ems or slow transitions to cogni-

In this full, two-shot in *The Strong Man*, the viewer sees that Harry is unaware that Lily has her hand in his jacket.

tion include the two-shot of Harry and the bearded lady in *Remember When* and the three-shot in *Saturday Afternoon* of the kiss between Vernon and his girl friend with Harry in the middle. Other slow take 'ems and slow transitions are seen in medium close-up two-shots of Harry and the woman's thigh in *Long Pants* and Harry and the cow's udder in *Soldier Man*.

Harry's solo transitions between sleeping and waking and between consciousness and unconsciousness include a medium close-up of Harry's protracted surrender to the effects of the opiate incense in *Feet of Mud*. Other examples are medium shots of Harry awakening in the morning, and falling asleep while trying to rock the baby to sleep in *Three's a Crowd;* a long-take medium shot of Harry surrendering to sleeping pills and whiskey in *Tramp, Tramp, Tramp;* and a long-take medium shot of Harry succumbing to the effects of too much wine at his wedding dinner in *His Marriage Wow*.

Though Langdon's performance is by definition not a solo performance and Langdon rarely appears alone in a shot, Langdon's position in the frame is the focal point of the majority of shots in a Langdon comedy. Thus, Langdon as performer is the formative influence on the spatial as well as the temporal structure of Langdon's films, regardless of who the producer, writer, or director was.

The fact that the spatial and temporal properties specific to film are exploited in Langdon's films for the purpose of further developing, refining, and enhancing the same comic conception to which Langdon had already devoted twenty years in vaudeville to developing, refining, and enhancing establishes a continuum between Langdon's work as a comic performer and metteur-en-scène on stage and in film. It is also evidence of a progressive development of a single-minded artistic preoccupation.

It does seem that Langdon tried to alter the less plastic properties of the stage to better accommodate that comic vision, as in the experimental "After the Ball." The way in which Langdon broke up his act into three scenes, each of which was presented in a different stage space, suggests an aspiration on Langdon's part to achieve the plasticity that is possible in film.

It would be presumptuous to claim that the failure of Langdon's experiment in "After the Ball" precipitated him into film as Eisenstein claimed concerning the failure of the latter's production of *Gas Masks*. However, in the way in which Langdon's performance utilizes filmic time and space to enhance his comic conception, it does seem that he recognized that film was ideally suited as the medium in which to continue to develop that conception as he could never have done on stage. In fact, Langdon was interested in "breaking into the movies" throughout his vaudeville career and indicated a desire to direct his own films from as early as the time that *The Strong Man* went into production. (There are also two articles on comic theory and the making of film comedy signed by Langdon and at least seven articles based on interviews with Langdon in which he discusses these topics. These articles are cited in the bibliography. In none of these, however, does Langdon suggest that the filmic mise-en-scène scheme described here was intellectually preconceived by him as such.)

Langdon's attempts in his vaudeville act to artificially expand the space of the stage to enhance the slow rhythm of his performance is additional evidence of a single, formative artistic intention in Langdon's work as metteur-en-scène on stage and as metteur-en-scène in film. To this end, Langdon employed elements of theatrical mise-en-scène: scenic design; lighting and mechanical effects; placement of props and actors on stage; and timing of action, of curtain, and of action and curtain together to enhance the slow rhythm of his performance. He subsequently utilized elements of filmic mise-en-scène to this same end.

For example, the "curtain call" with which Langdon concluded his vaudeville act can be considered protocinematic. It is protocinematic not only in terms of his creation of a highly realistic illusion of a recessive space that is much greater than the actual depth of full stage and his combination of lighting and scenic effects to simulate the slow movement of the automobile into that space, but also on the basis of the formal similarity of Langdon's theatrical effect to the filmic long take and fade-out. These two filmic devices act in Langdon's films to enhance the viewer's impression of the slow rhythm of his performance and to inscribe the rhythm of his mime and movement into the structure of the film—just as the "curtain call" effect did in his vaudeville act.

Only in film could Langdon fully realize his kind of comedy. Langdon's last two surviving silent features, *Three's a Crowd* and *The Chaser*, are the logical outcome of his continuing development of a comic conception that originated when Langdon decided to abandon the technical virtuosity which was featured in his blackface specialty act for a performance without virtuosic attractions and a style of mime distinguished by its lack of mimetic specificity. At the same time, Langdon also adopted the whiteface persona now well known from Langdon's films. This adoption of a new persona and style of performance was made in conjunction with the Langdon's decision to abandon the space of the specialty for full stage in which to present his new comic persona and performance.

In the evolution of Langdon's vaudeville act from "A Night on the Boulevard" to "Johnny's New Car" to "After the Ball," Langdon gradually reduced the comedy talk, jokes, and gags and introduced more and more pantomime. He also devoted more attention to developing scenic, lighting, and mechanical effects and increasingly relied upon these elements for comic effect. *Three's a Crowd* and *The Chaser* are more clearly than any of the other films the product of this evolution and of the kind of experimentation that Langdon undertook on stage in "After the Ball."

In the two very long static tableaux that are seen in each of these two films, Langdon's comic performance is ultimately reduced. And that ultimately reduced performance is extenuated in two longer single takes than any of the many other long takes in Langdon's films. Each is nearly a

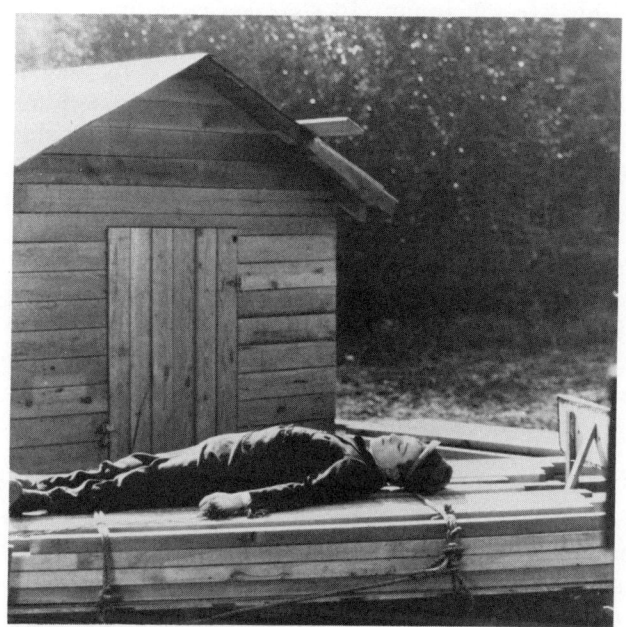

A scene in *Heart Trouble* similar to Harry's "suicide" in *The Chaser*. Langdon plays it in an immobile, prone position before an eventual awakening.

minute (or thirty feet in 16mm). In *Three's a Crowd* this is the shot in which Harry stands paralyzed and stares at Gladys and the newborn child that is finally concluded with a very gradual fade to black. In *The Chaser* it is the long take in which Harry lies inert on the kitchen floor, waiting to die after trying to poison himself with castor oil. This long take ends when Harry sits up suddenly when the effects of the castor oil impress upon him the fact that he is not dead. Throughout the duration of both of these tableaux, there is no movement whatever by Langdon—not of his body, or face, nor even a blink of the eyes. He is completely inert. In both shots, there is no other movement in the frame. Both are perfect instances of stasis.

In the shot from *Three's a Crowd,* the mise-en-scène—Harry's physical disposition with respect to the woman and child and the long time he stands there, paralyzed, and stares—completely assumes the burden of signification that is not borne by Langdon's mime. In the long take from *The Chaser,* Harry's inert body is seen in a medium long shot, stretched across the floor at the bottom of the frame in an otherwise deserted kitchen while Harry waits there to die. The gag is the viewer's own acute awareness of that extremely long take. The spatial and temporal specifications of Langdon's filmic mise-en-scène participate directly in the creation of pathos in the shot from *Three's a Crowd* and in the creation of comedy in the shot from *The Chaser.*

These two films survive of the three in which Langdon was director as well as producer and featured comedian. A renewed contract with First National Pictures to make these three films (including *Heart Trouble,* Langdon's third feature film under this contract and his last silent comedy, which has not been seen since its original release) for the first time granted Langdon complete financial and artistic autonomy in the control of every aspect of the production of those films. In *Three's a Crowd,* as in "After the Ball," Langdon ignores certain traditional notions of comedy and comic performance and ignores the conventions of film comedy construction that prevailed at the time it was produced even more blatantly than in any of his previous, normally unconventional comedies. This is seen in the pace of Langdon's performance, the pace of editing, narrative construction and continuity, and the film's virtual absence of gags.

Like Langdon's experimental "After the Ball," *Three's a Crowd* and *The Chaser* were not considered successful by the critics. *Heart Trouble* was largely ignored by them. Their objections are represented in the following selection of excerpts from reviews of those films. The *Variety* reviewer said of *Three's a Crowd:*

> Those who don't like Langdon aren't going to be won over by this release. It's too quiet and lacks the necessary explosive mirth to overcome that handicap. . . . There are spots in the picture where Langdon is brilliant, but on the other hand slow passages also creep in. It's not a high geared vehicle and Langdon has held down the hoke, which may explain.[3]

Harry, at home, in *Heart Trouble*.

Quinn Martin in *The New York World* wrote of *Three's a Crowd*:

> For some reason or other Mr. Langdon has gone intensely tragic; and in recurring scenes, showing the actor gazing forlornly down into the face of a sleeping girl whom he has come to love, he appears to have forgotten for the time all he has ever learned of the value of movement and life in the making of comic pictures.[4]

Another reviewer claimed:

> "Three's a Crowd" . . . is poor from start to finish. Its gags are old and badly developed, its continuity is choppy and, worst of all, the film drags on interminably. . . . Now that Mr. Langdon has had his fling at art, perhaps he will snap out of it and give us another "Strong Man."[5]

Yet another critic noted:

> Langdon directed this one himself. He devotes hundreds of feet to close-ups of himself, which mean absolutely nothing to the action, of which there is none. There are no outstanding gags—the life of a comedy—to build up to any climax.[6]

Rose Pelswick said of *The Chaser* (which was not widely reviewed) in *The New York Journal:*

> There is reel after reel of Harry facing the camera, batting his eyelashes, looking wistful and running about in circles. Each of these mannerisms is extremely funny—but, admitting that Langdon's appearance is in itself a comedy gag, there is, he should realize too much of a good thing.
>
> "The Chaser" is a succession of close-ups, long shots and medium-shots of the star. The plot would have made a good two-reeler, but stretched to its present length, it snapped.[7]

Chester Smith summarized his objection to *The Chaser* in *Motion Picture News* as follows:

> There is hardly the thread of a story in this picture; there is no continuity and the direction, by Langdon himself, is poor. The gags are only fair and what there are of them are poorly executed. They are allowed to drag out to such length that they lose what little humor there is to them.

One critic of *Three's a Crowd* singled out the "recurring scenes, showing the actor gazing forlornly down into the face of a sleeping girl whom he has come to love." Langdon with Gladys McConnell. (Courtesy of Gladys McConnell)

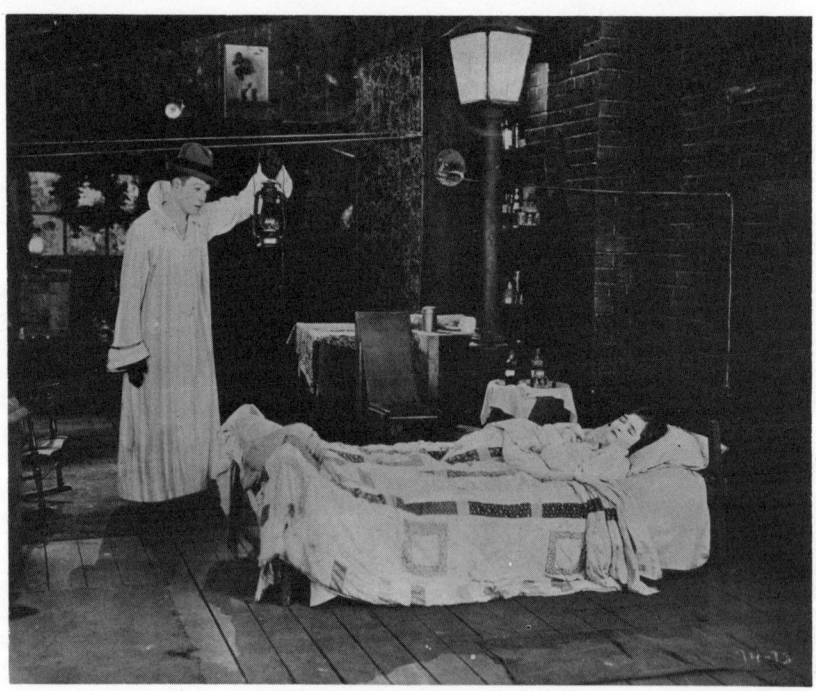

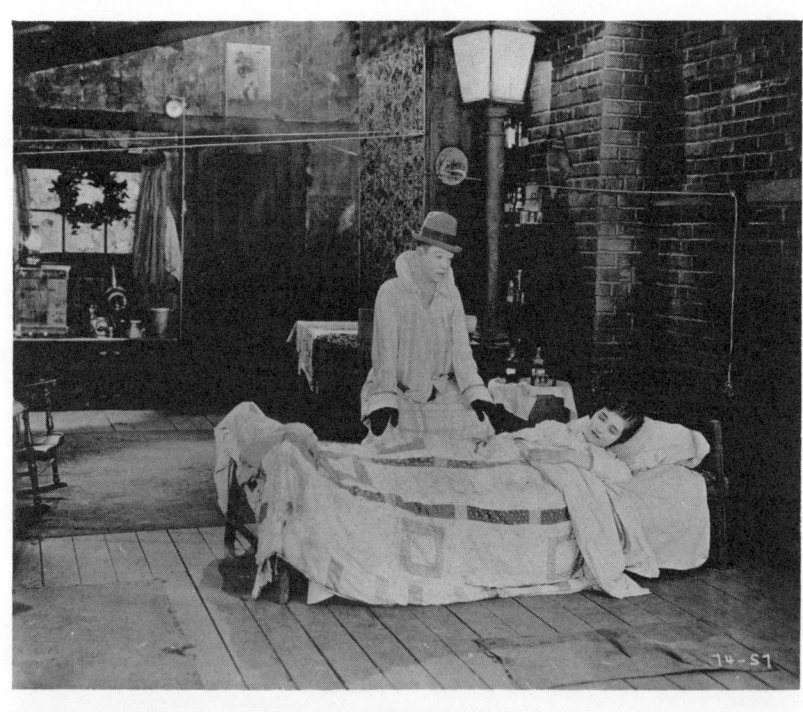
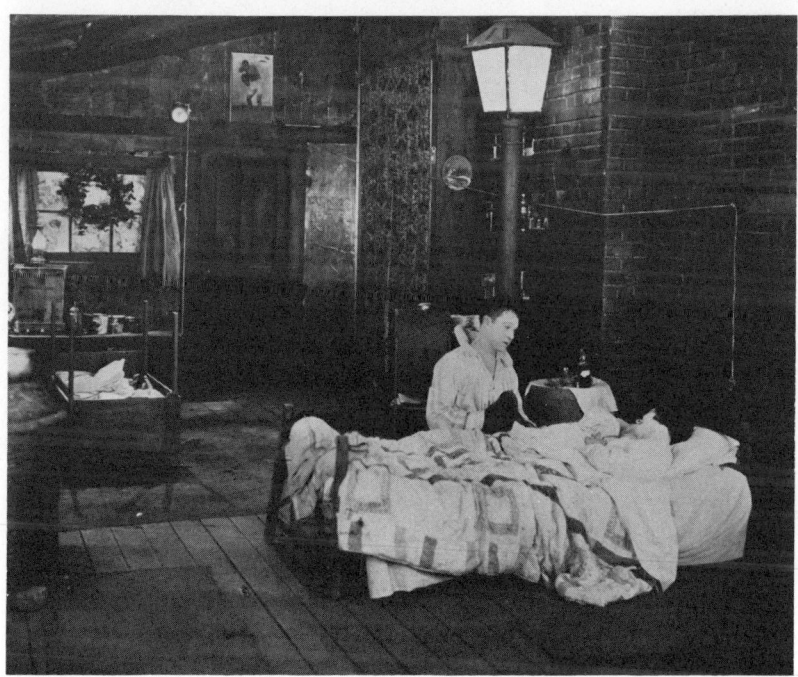

Langdon unfortunately is the whole works. There is not another role in the story that is worthy of mention, and aside from his usual comical make up, he falls absolutely flat. He slowed down what might have been a fair two-reeler to the lackadaisical and languid pace of the personal character he always assumes. There are not as many gags nor as much action in this full feature-length film as usually characterize the two-reeler, though the picture is styled after the two-reeler. Langdon needs better material than this and far better direction if he is again to assume the popularity he once enjoyed.[8]

Langdon now also had the opportunity to exert a direct influence on photography, lighting, and set design beyond the formidable influence on filmic mise-en-scène he invariably exerted as performer. Special attention is given in these two films to art direction, lighting, graphic composition, and special visual and cinematic effects such as fades and dissolves that is not apparent in previous films.

The set of the house interior in *The Chaser* is ingeniously designed with certain comic functions and even particular shots in mind. Nearly all of the

The interior of Harry's shack in *Three's a Crowd*, which, in exterior shots, clings to the side of an old warehouse three stories above the street with a long, narrow stairway leading to it. Langdon with Gladys McConnell. (Courtesy of Gladys McConnell)

Langdon as Metteur-en-Scène

The versatile house set in *The Chaser*. Langdon with Gladys McConnell. (Courtesy of Gladys McConnell)

action in the film takes place in three sets: the house, the backyard, and a park. Of these, the most action takes place in the house. The set is a living room with a stairway to the unseen upstairs rooms on the right side. With the camera in the living room, one can see through the doorway of the living room into the dining room and through a second doorway into the kitchen. By a slight change of camera position, a number of different comic incidents involving Harry and a number of characters, or Harry alone, are staged on this single set.

For instance, one camera setup in which the camera is placed in the living room includes the stairway. One such shot follows Harry's attempted suicide when nature's urgent call alerts Harry to the fact that he is not dead. This shot also includes the kitchen, seen through the living room and dining room doorway in the background. In this shot, Harry hurries into the living room and up the stairs. The camera holds on the empty rooms and stairway for some time after Harry is gone in a long take and then fades out. In other shots, Harry goes upstairs and comes down after a while with some kind of prop, such as a baby carriage to return to the salesman who treats Harry as the lady of the house. (Harry has been ordered by a judge to exchange roles with his wife.)

At other times, the living room is seen from a slightly different angle that includes the front door on the left and excludes the stairway. In this setup too, the kitchen is seen through the dining room in the background. This is

The house set in *The Chaser* from a slightly different angle following Harry's suicide attempt. (Courtesy of Gladys McConnell)

Harry brings the baby carriage downstairs to return it to the salesman in *The Chaser*. (Courtesy of Gladys McConnell)

the space in which the final comic situation in the film is set. Harry's wife has discovered a suicide note from Harry and, in this shot, Harry's wife and mother-in-law return home in despair after searching vainly for him. As they enter the front door at screen left, Harry is seen sweeping the kitchen floor in the background at screen right. Both Harry and the floor are covered with the flour he has spilled. As the shot continues, Harry's wife is being comforted by her mother in the living room while Harry now makes

The house set in *The Chaser*, including the front door and excluding the stairway, just before Harry appears to his grieving wife. (Courtesy of Gladys McConnell)

his way from the kitchen into the living room, looking like a ghost, as the audience awaits the wife's reaction.

The set was also designed to be, in a sense, turned with its side to the camera (although it is actually the camera that is moved around to the side of the set) so that the camera can track along with the characters as they move through the three rooms in certain shots. Lateral tracking shots are not commonly used in Langdon's films, but there are several lateral tracking shots in *The Chaser* that are used specifically in conjunction with this special set. In one of these, Harry walks from the living room through the dining room, into and through the kitchen all the way to the back door, pursued by his mother-in-law, who is followed by his wife. The culmination of the shot and of the comic action presented in the shot occurs when Harry reaches the back door and opens it for his mother-in-law, who is several paces behind Harry. She walks out and Harry closes the door behind her. In another lateral tracking shot, the camera follows Harry from the front door, where he has just indignantly expelled the baby carriage salesman for making a pass at him, through the dining room and kitchen to the back door, where he answers the bell. This time, in a rare instance of forethought, Harry prepares to defend his virtue with a weapon in hand before he opens the door to admit the milkman.

This kind of set reduces the necessity for cutting, and even simple cuts to change camera distance and angle on a single subject or action are very sparse. The set therefore contributes significantly to the viewer's impression of the film's slow pace. *The Chaser* displays the same attention to creating a space in which to perform and the same ingenuity and expertise in stagecraft that was displayed in Langdon's vaudeville act and that was noted so often in the reviews.

Special attention to lighting and composition is apparent in *Three's a Crowd*. *Above:* **Gladys secretly leaves home to elope with her lover, of whom her parents disapprove, in a sequence cut from the final version of the film.** *Below:* **Gladys struggles through a snowstorm after deserting her dissolute husband. (Courtesy of Gladys McConnell)**

The influence of Langdon's background in stagecraft upon *Three's a Crowd* is indisputable. This influence is most obvious in the opening and closing sequences of the film. A conscious effort is apparent in these two sequences to create an impressive moment by means that bear a blatant similarity to the combination of elements of theatrical mise-en-scène which

Langdon employed to create the effective opening and closing curtains of his vaudeville act.

The boulevard drop originally used by Langdon in "A Night on the Boulevard" as depicted in theatrical photographs and described in contemporary reviews is replicated complete with "lighting effects" in the three-dimensional set that is featured in both the opening and closing sequences of *Three's a Crowd*. As it was finally released, *Three's a Crowd* opens with the title, "Lest we should forget—," followed by a close-up of an alarm clock that establishes the early hour. The third shot, a long shot, is composed by the receding perspectival lines of a street which dominates the frame. The set is actually a working model of the painted boulevard drop. This shot is dimly lit as in predawn and highlighted by the soft gauze-diffused glow of a row of street lamps which line the street. A horse-drawn milk wagon moves through the street at a leisurely pace. Its path and slow progress from background to foreground is traced through the frame by the highlight of a lantern that hangs at the front of the wagon and grows more prominent as the wagon approaches the camera. The effect is that of Langdon's curtain call in reverse. In that case, the progression of Johnny's new car along the winding road into the distance was traced by its diminishing taillights.

A gradual overlap-dissolve transition is then made in the film to a shot of the same set from the same camera setup with the shot now lit in medium key and the street full of people. The slow pace of the action, the long duration of the shots and dissolve transition, and the soft visual tone of this opening sequence prepares the viewer for Harry's introduction, which follows in a long and slow-paced pantomime routine of Harry waking from a night's sleep. The dissolve serves as a means of executing a lighting effect and of effecting a scenic transformation rather than as a montage transition and was surely inspired by the lighting and electrical effects that Langdon developed and featured in his vaudeville act.

In the final sequence of the film, after his "family" is taken away by the husband and father, Harry makes his way from his shack down to the street. He enters into the background of the same long shot of the same "boulevard" set that is seen in the opening sequence of the film. As before, the street is dimly lit and the shot is highlighted by the soft illumination of the row of street lamps, though it is now night and the street is covered with snow. Standing at the far end of the street, Harry raises the lantern he is carrying to blow out the light. He does so in the next three-quarter shot. As he finishes, again in long shot, all of the street lamps go out in unison as an expression of Harry's melancholy mood, which his facial expression or posture does not convey.

This comparison of aspects of *Three's a Crowd* and *The Chaser* with Langdon's work in vaudeville reveals the use of some common techniques, but, more significantly, again reveals a single artistic intention. That intention is to integrate with persona and performance, the elements of mise-en-scène that are specific to each of the mediums in which he worked as constituents of his comedy and pathos.

There is documentary and other extrafilmic evidence to corroborate that Langdon did have a comic vision and an ambition to implement and develop this notion in his films, as analysis of his work on stage and in film suggests. This evidence includes reports of Langdon's early interest in appearing in films and, later, in directing his own films, and the comments of Hal Roach concerning Langdon's stubborness about working in his own way before the camera. Langdon worked in two-reel sound comedies for Roach soon after producing, directing, and starring in his last silent comedy feature, *Heart Trouble,* in 1928. Roach recalls further from his experience with Langdon during 1929 and 1930 that Langdon had an "insane idea that he wanted to stay longer on the scene than any comedian ever stayed on the same scene." Langdon's idea of "holding a scene long in time," in Roach's words, "got to be an obsession with him," and Roach says that Langdon "got to the point where he thought that was his achievement, that that was his basic bid to fame as a comedian."[9]

This was the only difficulty that Roach and his staff had with Langdon in those films and, according to Roach:

> it was constantly.... As soon as the camera started he went down to this—it was like slow motion—and the scene didn't justify the length of time it took. It didn't make any difference what scene it was. If it was just an insignificant scene, he was just as slow in that as he was in the more important scenes.

As far as Roach was concerned, this "difficulty" with Langdon made it impossible for anyone at his studio, including himself in one exasperated attempt to try to direct Langdon, to work with him (although Roach and Langdon remained personal friends).

The Dreiser interview with Mack Sennett indicates that, when working at the Sennett studio, Langdon did have, as Sennett puts it, "'his own ideas, exactly, of how everything should be done.'" In this 1928 interview, Sennett offers quite a different view of Langdon's personality and attitude toward his work than that offered twenty-six years later in Sennett's autobiography. Far from being the "obedient puppy," as Sennett characterizes Langdon in his autobiography, Langdon, in Sennett's 1928 account, "'wants to do a monologue all the time; he wants to be the leading lady, cameraman, heavy and director all in one.'" Sennett goes on to compare Langdon with Chaplin, who had also worked for Sennett, in terms of temperament:

> "And in Langdon the same restless energy and criticism of everything. Why, nothing was ever right, because, like Chaplin, he had his own ideas, exactly, of how everything should be done. And he didn't want to be

interfered with, although, of course, he was there under contract and had to take direction from others."[10]

This earlier account precedes the full impact of Langdon's popular and financial decline and Frank Capra's subsequent career as one of Hollywood's most successful and highly regarded directors.

There is a popular contention that the decline of Langdon's career as a popular and critically respected film comedian was directly related to Langdon's assumption of responsibility for the production of his films. (Langdon was assisted by Arthur Ripley, who remained with Langdon as the writer of his last three features.) A superficial summary of Langdon's career in film (which is the most that is offered in any of the published commentaries on Langdon and his films) bears some resemblance to one of the familiar archetypes of Hollywood mythology—the "shooting star" whose sudden ascendance is astonishing and whose fall from the heights of fame and fortune is tragic and just as abrupt. Langdon's popular success in Mack Sennett two-reelers was great enough that only a little over a year after his first Sennett comedy in 1924, Langdon was making a feature-length comedy for Sennett, *His First Flame*. Sennett held back *His First Flame*, along with *Fiddlesticks* and *Soldier Man*, also produced in 1926, until Langdon's popularity reached a peak in feature comedies for First National. These three films were not released until 1927. In 1925, Langdon was offered a million-dollar contract by Pathé, the releasing company for Langdon's Sennett comedies, to produce his own feature comedies—six of them in two years. According to the publicity on the deal, Langdon was to replace Harold Lloyd, who had gone to Paramount the previous year.

Langdon accepted a better offer from First National Pictures. Within the next two years, 1926 and 1927, Langdon's own production company, The Harry Langdon Corporation, produced and First National released four more feature comedies starring Langdon to ever-mounting popularity and critical enthusiasm. *Variety* included Langdon after Harold Lloyd and Charles Chaplin under "Comedy Stars" in its list of "Leading Film Stars of 1927," an annual ranking of stars according to their box-office drawing power. Langdon was constantly being compared with Chaplin in the reviews of his films. In a September 1926 review of *The Strong Man*, Richard Watts, Jr., warned that Chaplin might soon be surpassed by Langdon as the world's foremost clown.[11]

However, by 1928, Langdon was "washed up" in films. The option in Langdon's contract with First National to make more films was dropped soon after the release of *The Chaser*, his fifth feature for First National, in February 1928. At this point Langdon, along with the last film provided for in that contract, *Heart Trouble*, were literally abandoned by that studio. By 1929, Langdon was back in vaudeville and two-reelers. In 1931, he declared bankruptcy and was mired in numerous civil lawsuits.

The convenience of this coincidence of the summary facts of Langdon's film career with popular mythology may be one reason that there has been heretofore no examination of Langdon's life and work in a broader scope and greater detail. Though a more detailed examination perhaps lacks the melodramatic appeal of the summary approach, such an investigation is ultimately more useful in coming to terms with Langdon as an artist and in correctly interpreting his role in the creation of his films. Material on Langdon's long and successful prefilm career has shown that his rise to fame and fortune as a comedy star in motion pictures was not actually so sudden. Likewise, the documentary material that is available on this later period of decline in Langdon's career indicates that Langdon's fall was also not so abrupt. Nor can the decline in Langdon's popularity and financial failure be simply explained by ascribing it to sheer incompetence on Langdon's part in discharging the added responsibilities he took on in his last three films. This is the reason for Langdon's failure that has traditionally been offered by Mack Sennett, Frank Capra, and by others who have taken their word for it. Langdon's decline was more likely the result of a more complicated combination of factors and circumstances.

One possible contributing factor to Langdon's problems was the certain respect in which Langdon can be said to resemble the comic character he impersonated. Langdon seems to have been in some ways out of touch with his circumstances. He apparently had difficulty communicating with people other than a small group of family members and longtime friends. Yet, according to several articles based on interviews with Langdon, he was highly susceptible to personal criticism or criticism of his work by anyone.[12] Langdon is described by those who knew him well and by those who hardly knew him at all as quiet, introverted, and even antisocial. Among those who hardly knew Langdon at all were most of those who worked with him every day during the production of his films, both silent and sound. Langdon did not socialize with them off the set, and during the making of his features, he was completely preoccupied with the films' production.

Langdon's offscreen behavior might easily have led some people to identify him with the childlike character he impersonated on the screen. He is often described by columnists in newspaper stories and fan magazines of the period as "not a fluent talker" and "a tough bird to interview."

Another circumstance that may possibly be relevant to the decline of Langdon's career is the fact that, even though Langdon's contract with First National, as renewed following the release of *Long Pants,* specified that he would have exclusive personal supervision over every aspect of the production of his films, it was renewed with the reservation that the option to make further films depended on the box-office showing of the films that were provided for under the present contract. *Three's a Crowd* did not bring in enough money according to the discretion of First National. Attempting to apply some pressure on Langdon to deliver "comedy features that meet market requirements and which would obtain wide distribution and grosses,"[13] First National publicly reminded Langdon in the trade publications of the terms of his contract and his probationary status. At one point, First National announced that they were grooming Douglas McLean as Langdon's replacement, and publicly presented Langdon with an ultimatum that unless the box-office receipts of his next film were better than those of *Three's a Crowd,* he would be dropped.[14]

According to the contract terms, First National could not directly inter-

Heart Trouble. Langdon, as a small-town boy, and Doris Dawson as his sweetheart, a farmer's daughter, decide to elope.

Heart Trouble. **Harry gets caught up in The Big Parade and decides to join the army.**

vene in the production of those films and this was the only way the studio could attempt to influence Langdon. The only apparent evidence of the influence that this sort of pressure might have had on Langdon is the extensive cutting of all three films, to which Langdon acceded, based on the reception of preview audiences.

The receipts of *The Chaser,* a fifty-eight-minute silent film released in February 1928 in competition with the first talkies and part-talkies, predictably were not much better than those from *Three's a Crowd,* and Langdon was immediately dropped by First National. Following the cancellation of his option, Langdon was completely abandoned to go through the motions of carrying out the provision of his contract for a third film on what remained of his budget. That film was *Heart Trouble.* First National gave more publicity to the cancellation of Langdon's contract during the production of *Heart Trouble* than they gave the film on its release. *Heart Trouble* was released with a running time of fifty-eight minutes. It opened in one theater in New York City as half of a double bill and played there for only one day.

First National, like the other studios in the years 1927 to 1929, was involved in effecting the major industrial transformation to sound. This situation was complicated by the fact that First National had been having its own share of financial difficulties for some time. The studio executives,

Heart Trouble. **In a tearful meeting, Harry tells Doris that, instead of eloping with her, he is off to join the army.**

busy arranging to merge with Warner Brothers (which occurred in 1929), probably had little patience with Langdon's diffidence or "artistic" experiments. Langdon, on the other hand, was temperamentally ill equipped to ingratiate himself with those who might help him secure his position amidst the pressures and turmoil of studio politics, particularly at a time when First National was experiencing a financial crisis and at the same time the imminent reality of a changeover to sound.

After a second marriage in 1929 and a second divorce in 1933, Langdon married for a third time in February 1934. By his third wife, Langdon became the father of his first and only child, a son, born in December of that year. Langdon receded from celebrity status to the isolation of a very private and modest life with his wife and child, working whenever he could, doing whatever he could in order to live comfortably and quietly with them until his death late in 1944.

Notes

1. *Variety,* 5 May 1922, p. 17.
2. *Billboard,* 27 May 1922, p. 14.
3. Sid., review of *Three's a Crowd, Variety,* 5 October 1927.
4. Quinn Martin, review of *Three's a Crowd* in unidentified newspaper, in "Weinberg Scrapbooks of Film Reviews," 3 vols., ed. Herman G. Weinberg, vol. 2: "1927," in the Library of the Museum of Modern Art, New York, New York.
5. "Harry Langdon in 'Three's a Crowd' at the Strand," review of *Three's a Crowd* in an unidentified newspaper, in "Weinberg Scrapbooks of FIlm Reviews," vol. 2: "1927."
6. "Langdon's Latest," review of *Three's a Crowd* in unidentified newspaper, in "Weinberg Scrapbooks of Film Reviews," vol. 2: "1927."
7. Rose Pelswick, review of *The Chaser, New York Journal,* in "Weinberg Scrapbooks of Film Reviews," vol. 3: "1928."
8. Chester J. Smith, review of *The Chaser, Motion Picture News,* 21 April 1928, p. 1272, in "Harry Langdon" clipping file in the Film Study Center of the Museum of Modern Art, New York, New York.
9. Hal Roach to author, Bel Air, California, 17 June 1974.
10. Theodore Drieser, "The Best Motion Picture Interview Ever Written," *Photoplay* 34 (August 1928): 126–27.
11. Richard Watts, Jr., "An Attempt to Philosophize about the Comic Mr. Langdon," in unidentified newspaper, 12 September 1926, in "Weinberg Scrapbooks of Film Reviews," vol. 1: "1925–1927."
12. Dorothy Herzog, "The Wistful Mr. Langdon," *Motion Picture Magazine* 34 (October 1927): 18–19; J. R. Milne, "Whoopee Isn't Fun," *Omaha* (Neb.) *World-Herald,* 26 April 1931, Sunday magazine section, p. 1; Katherine Albert, "What Happend to Harry Langdon," *Photoplay* 4 (February 1932): 40, 106; Sonia Lee, "Good Luck or Bad Luck—Bebe and Harry Can Take It!" *Motion Picture* 44 (January 1933): 56–57.
13. "First National Holds McLean for Langdon's Place," *Variety,* 23 November 1927, p. 9.
14. Ibid.

8
Langdon, Lloyd, Keaton, and Chaplin

A common critical attitude toward Langdon has been to consider him an inferior imitation of Chaplin. In this chapter, Langdon's work is compared to that of his most important rivals in terms of popular and critical recognition: Harold Lloyd, Buster Keaton, and Charles Chaplin. This comparison suggests that Langdon is the author of a highly original comic conception which, within the richest period in the history of American film comedy, distinguishes his work in every respect from that of his contemporaries.

This comparison is not based merely on narrative values, as is much traditional writing on film comedy. It is rather concerned with the relation of characterization to performance and the relation of characterization and performance to cinematic form. Applying this analytic approach to Lloyd, Keaton, and Chaplin as it has been applied to Langdon shows how the films of each comedian display a distinctive filmic style. This approach also reveals, as in Langdon's work, the unique relationship in each case of that distinctive film style with a distinctive comic persona and performance style.

Lloyd and Keaton have in common the fact that they are, as film comedians, fundamentally unlike Harry Langdon at every level. As comic characters, both Lloyd and Keaton are highly motivated. The action and attractions that constitute their performances are specifically oriented with respect to an explicitly defined goal or end, in pursuit of which both characters exhibit the traits of initiative and fierce determination. These attributes are wholly antithetical to the nearly incoherent character conceived by Langdon, described by Langdon's performance, and defined by Langdon's mise-en-scène. The performances of both Lloyd and Keaton are distinguished by indefatigable energy. Their films include virtuosic displays of physical strength, endurance, and acrobatic skill as compared to the display in Langdon's films of Harry's complete physical ineptitude. Montage is a significant element of the cinematic style of the films of both Lloyd and Keaton, whose films are, to a large degree, conceived and constructed in terms of edit analysis of action and intershot associations.

The comic characters of Lloyd and Keaton offer a sharp contrast to Langdon's, in which qualities such as motivation, initiative, ambition, insight, foresight, and the capacity for premeditation are absent. The only action initiated by Harry is a spontaneous, instinctual, or reflex response to the provocation of some urgent biological need or somatic stimulus, or some highly affective or aggressive instigation that is physically manifest in close proximity to Harry. Even at that, Harry's reflexes and instinctual responses of self-preservation and self-defense are retarded, impaired, or inoperative. Harry cannot act on the most elemental impulses. He does not fall when he is hit, he cannot feed himself when he is hungry, he cannot quench his thirst, and he cannot run away when pursued. He is unable to concentrate his attention and therefore he cannot direct and structure his movement either away from or toward a specified point or objective.

The vertical ascent is an attraction that symbolizes the relation of characterization and other narrative values to performance in the films of Harold Lloyd. Within the narrative context of a Harold Lloyd film, the vertical ascent represents the character's perseverance as a social climber up the ladder of success toward a pinnacle that is defined in materialistic terms. In fact, this metaphoric scheme is the design of a number of Harold Lloyd's "building-climbing" comedies, all of which feature a "human fly" stunt. These are: *Look Out Below,* an early one-reeler; *High and Dizzy,* a two-reeler made in 1920; *Never Weaken,* a three-reeler made the following year; the feature, *Safety Last,* of 1923; and *Feet First,* a feature comedy with sound made in 1930.

Lloyd's highly goal-oriented ambition in these sequences may be contrasted to the situation in Langdon's *Lucky Stars* in which the astrologer advises Harry to "follow that star and you'll win fame and fortune!" Harry begins his forecast career as a doctor on the wrong foot when he merely totters within the space of a few short steps, first in one direction, then the other, and then gets on the wrong train. When the conductor informs Harry of this, Harry sticks his finger into his mouth and runs frantically up and down the aisle. Harry is thus diverted from the pursuit of his lucky star. His pursuit of the medical career it forecasts takes a purely arbitrary turn when he is recruited by a medicine-show charlatan beside whom Harry happens to be seated on the train.

In Lloyd's comedies, the character's execution of some feat of physical strength and athletic skill in overcoming innumerable obstacles and in the face of overwhelming odds is absolutely integral to the melodramatic formula that serves as the basis for the scenarios of Lloyd's films. Harold's obstacle course is plotted vertically in the building-climbing comedies and horizontally in the films in which an elaborate race or chase sequence is the lateral alternative of the vertical ascent. The spectacular race to the church in *Girl Shy* in which Harold runs, jumps, and dives from vehicle to vehicle in order to reach the girl before she is married to the villain is notable among these lateral pursuits. Another is Harold's hair-raising ride through the busy streets of Los Angeles on a runaway bus in *For Heaven's Sake*. During the ride, Harold tries to keep from being pitched off and to pilot the speeding bus safely through oncoming and intersecting traffic while fending off a busload of rowdy drunks.

One might compare the sequence in Lloyd's *Girl Shy* to Langdon's *His Marriage Wow*. In the latter film, Harry goes to the wrong church for his wedding; runs up and down the aisle when he discovers this; walks around in a circle after he has been given directions to the right church; and, after the ceremony, gets into a cab and rides away without his bride, and then gets into the wrong cab and rides off with the wrong bride.

Usually, the stunts in Lloyd's films are genuinely difficult and dangerous, and Lloyd went to great lengths, or more properly—in the case of the building-climbing comedies—heights, to make the viewer aware of this. Such a difficult and dangerous feat generally serves as the dramatic climax of Lloyd's feature-length comedies. It represents the moment of self-recognition when the character, heretofore a hopeless boob, discovers previously unknown inner resources through an extraordinary display of energy that is directed with relentless determination toward the accomplishment of the desired end.

A situation in Langdon's *Tramp, Tramp, Tramp* offers a convenient basis for comparison with Lloyd at the level of characterization. This is the situation in which Harry's white-haired father explains to Harry in desperation that the mortgage on the family shoe store is about to be foreclosed and that they are going to be put out in the street. To this dire news Harry replies, "Does this mean I don't get my new bicycle?" As his father tries to impress Harry with the seriousness of the situation, Harry gazes distractedly out the door of the shop at Betty Burton's picture on a billboard. His father finally charges him, "The money must be raised in three months—*it's up to you*."

This is just the sort of challenge that sets the plots of Harold Lloyd comedies into motion and the character Harold into action at a breathtaking pace. Harry, on the other hand, resolves to "get the money in three months if it takes a year," charges out the door of the shop, and is stopped in his tracks when different parts of his body go off in different directions. He then paces from side to side within the space of a single medium long shot and gets nowhere until he finally comes to a standstill in the middle of the sidewalk, where he stands and scratches his head. This bewildered standstill symbolizes the relation of Langdon's character to his performance. Harry's course of action is arbitrarily determined again here when the landlord comes around on his way to a cross-country walking race and Harry decides to accompany him as his assistant by spitting into the wind.

In the Lloyd comedies, characterization and motivation are articulated and developed through the narrative values of the basic melodramatic formula described previously, which was used over and over in Lloyd's films. The editing of Lloyd's films conforms to narrative development and to the characterization of Harold as a social climber. The ladder to material success is, in terms of narrative construction, a structure on which to build a melodramatic climax. It is, in terms of cinematic construction, a structure on which to build a montage climax to a suspense sequence of a sort peculiar to Lloyd's own comic specialty—the elaborate "thrill comedy" climb and race/chase sequences. And it is, at the same time, a structure on which to build the culmination of a kind of comic momentum that is created by a method known as "gag construction" and which is designed to elicit an ascending order of responses from the spectator (described by James Agee in the jargon of screen comics and gagmen as the "titter," the "yowl," the "belly laugh," and the "boffo").

The building-climbing sequence in Lloyd's *Safety Last* consumes well over half the running time of this feature comedy. In this sequence, Harold's pal, a human fly by trade, is supposed to climb a department-store building in a publicity stunt that Harold has devised. Harold wants to marry the girl, Mildred, but cannot because he is only a department-store clerk. When he overhears the store manager offer a hundred dollars for a new idea to bring in more business, Harold thinks of the stunt as a way to "make good" so he can marry Mildred. On the day of the stunt, Harold's pal is being pursued by a cop and Harold must start the climb himself. As his pal is chased into the building, he assures Harold that he will shake the cop and take over the climb on the next floor.

There is intercutting at regular intervals throughout the sequence to Harold's pal calling to him from the windows of successive floors to "keep on going . . . just one more floor." This montage device extends the sequence to a point at which Harold finally reaches the top of the building. It also serves a narrative function as the means by which Harold is made to test and prove his own ability to himself.

The basic editing structure of this sequence creates a rhythm of tension and relief. This is brought about in large part by the cutting away, as in a classic suspense sequence, from Harold on the outside of the building to shots that inform the viewer of various dangers and obstacles that lie along Harold's upward course just before he encounters them. For instance, at one point Harold is seen clinging to a window ledge. This shot is followed by a cut to an interior shot of some painters positioning a long scaffold in an office, unaware that Harold is hanging from the ledge outside the window. In the next exterior shot, the scaffold shoots out the office window at Harold, who grabs onto the end in the nick of time and rides it out over the street below, dangling by his fingertips.

At another point during the climb, Harold's pal throws him a rope from an office window that is just above Harold. Just as Harold's pal is about to tie the end of the rope around a desk leg, the cop enters the office and chases him out. This is followed by an exterior shot of Harold reaching for the other end of the rope, which is dangling from the window. Now there is a cut to a close-up of the desk leg and the unattached rope; then another shot of Harold reaching for the rope again, grabbing it, and falling out of the frame. In the next shot, Harold's pal reenters the office just in time to grab the loose end.

In another sequence of shots, Harold climbs up to the relative safety of a ledge as in the next shot, a close-up, a mouse scurries out onto the ledge. Harold stands up on the ledge in the following shot, which is followed by a cut to a close-up of the mouse disappearing up his pant leg. In the next shot, Harold dances around on the narrow ledge trying to shake the mouse out of his trousers. The relief is effected in each of these situations as the cutting also details Harold's escape from these and a succession of various other precarious situations.

This rhythm of tension and relief is also conveyed to the viewer by the cutting away from Harold on the side of the building to people in the crowd on the street below, who react either with gasps of apprehension or applause, depending on the shot of Harold that precedes or follows. These sequences, and cuts away from Harold to onlookers who are watching, commenting, or yelling suggestions from the windows also create a certain anxiety in the viewer, whose attention is also riveted on Harold, because his or her glance is constantly being pulled away from him.

Harold's climb, as a whole, is composed of many different camera distances, angles, details of, and viewpoints on the action. Among these are the subjective point-of-view shots from Harold's viewpoint of the crowd of onlookers on the street far below him, and shots of Harold clinging to or dangling from the side of the building seen from the point of view of the crowd and of individual members of the crowd. This kind of intercutting precisely fixes Harold's position in relation to the ground at various points throughout the sequence as Harold climbs higher and higher. The shocked expressions of Harold and the crowd in subsequent reaction shots tend to reinforce the viewer's own sense of danger. The shots that are photographed from a camera position on the building face that represent Harold's point of view also contribute to the suspense by serving to identify the viewer with the character by placing him or her into Harold's extremely precarious situation. In many other shots of Harold, he is seen alongside the building in the foreground at one side of the frame and the urban landscape of Los Angeles is seen stretching out beneath him in the background of the same shot as a means of cinematically certifying the authenticity of the height and danger involved.

At the top of the building, the sequence is "topped." The comic momentum is culminated with a spectacular upside-down aerial swing by Harold (this stunt was actually performed by a circus acrobat standing in for Lloyd) suspended from a flagpole at the end of a rope. Harold falls off the roof after being dazed by the arm of a wind gauge but, luckily, he has tangled a foot in the rope. The "topper" is then "topped" when Harold lands on his feet on the roof and into the waiting arms of his girl friend.

The architecture of gag construction as demonstrated in the building-climbing thrill comedy sequence in *Safety Last* is described by Lloyd as follows:

> "We built as we went along, like building a house. Building was of great importance.
> We'd have a certain number of pieces of business, gags, that we knew we were going to do. They were called 'islands.' We knew we had to go there. But whatever we did between those was up to us."[1]

In another interview, Lloyd describes how, in the "building" of a gag sequence, a whole sequence could be developed from a single idea: "It led from one thing to another, and inside of that one idea were more little complex ideas." He describes how "one gag led into the other." He also describes the "building of a gag" as "pyramiding . . . where if it wasn't for the original piece of business you couldn't possibly do the second, and naturally not the fifth."[2]

Thus the interrelation of comic persona, performance, and cinematic form in Lloyd's comedies is quite unlike that which characterizes the films of Harry Langdon. The attraction, or feat, of overcoming a vertically or horizontally plotted obstacle course is central to the narrative structure of a Harold Lloyd film as a climax and as a moment of recognition. It also provides the basic architectural structure of the thrill comedy sequence in terms of both montage construction and comedy or gag construction. In comparison, the cinematic treatment of the "antithrill sequences" seen in some of Langdon's films conforms to Langdon's comic persona and performance.

The comedies of Buster Keaton also offer a distinct contrast to those of Harry Langdon. Keaton's performance demonstrates his comic character's ingenuity, perceptual acuity, superior intellect, and Keaton's own physical agility and acrobatic expertise. These qualities are displayed in comic situations in which Buster solves the problems that confront him and adjusts to the abrupt changes of fortune and circumstance that constantly beset him.

For instance, while Keaton as Johnnie Gray is pursuing the enemy locomotive in *The General*, one of the unforeseen problems that arises is that the enemy has jettisoned some of the wooden beams carried as fuel along the track to derail, or at least stop, him. Johnnie spots the first beam; slows his train; climbs out of the cab, over the engine, and slides down onto the cowcatcher; and runs on ahead in time to pick the beam up off the track so that his train can proceed without stopping. The cowcatcher scoops Johnnie up off the track before he can dispose of the beam. While he is pinned to the cowcatcher by the heavy beam in his arms, he spots a second beam on the track just ahead.

The camera now tracks out in front of Johnnie and the beam appears in the foreground of this shot as Johnnie's train comes nearer and nearer the obstacle. Unless it is removed, the beam will derail the train, since Johnnie is unable to get to the controls to stop the locomotive before it reaches the obstacle. As the cowcatcher approaches the second beam, Johnnie raises the first beam over his head and drops it on one end of the second beam, bouncing it off the track and, along with the first one, out of the path of his train. Thus Johnnie continues his pursuit without having to stop the train to dispose of the first obstacle in his path, solves the problem of freeing himself from the burden of the heavy beam that is pinning him to the cowcatcher without having to replace it on the track, and meets the emergency of an imminent derailment owing to the fact that there is no engineer in the cab to stop the train as it approaches the second obstacle.

Harry not only lacks the mental and physical facility to bring about a change in his circumstances in order to improve his situation, but, in the case of a fortuitous turn of events, he remains unaware of it and is therefore not able to take advantage of it. For instance, while Harry is pounding rocks with his tiny hammer on the chain gang in *Tramp, Tramp, Tramp,* the other prisoners are making an escape. One of them runs by and hands Harry a pistol, which Harry merely substitutes for his hammer and keeps on pounding. Later, when a railroad car runs over the chain and cuts the iron ball loose from Harry's leg, Harry does not notice and continues to carry the heavy ball around with him.

As the vertical ascent is for Lloyd, Buster Keaton's long-distance dash is an attraction that symbolizes the relation of characterization and other narrative values to performance in Keaton's films. It is an exhibition of strength, speed, and endurance. Buster runs at top speed either toward or away from something, or toward and away at the same time, according to an explicitly defined trajectory that is always as near as possible to the shortest distance between two points.

For example in the feature *Seven Chances,* the start and finish lines and the time in which to complete the course are clearly defined for Buster by his desire to escape the hundreds of brides who are gathered at the church to marry him, and to get to the girl he loves by a certain, precise time—7:00 P.M. on his twenty-seventh birthday—and not a second later. If he gets to the ceremony on time, he can marry the girl, claim his inheritance of seven million dollars, and live happily ever after. There are even cuts from Buster to a clock at various points during the race that indicate exactly how much time remains for Buster to reach his goal. There is also editing to increase the distance covered by Buster in a long-distance dash in a single shot, by combining a number of shots of Buster running into one very long-distance dash in the artificial time and space of montage. This enhances the viewer's impression of Buster's strength and endurance.

The walking race in Langdon's *Tramp, Tramp, Tramp* offers a convenient comparison with Keaton. The start and finish as well as Harry's entry into the race are arbitrarily determined as far as Harry is concerned. Harry is merely tagging along as the champion's assistant and has no intention of entering the race to win the twenty-five-thousand-dollar prize to pay off the mortgage on the family shoe store (as Harold Lloyd would certainly have thought of doing). Harry enters the race because Betty Burton, the girl on the billboard, spots him in the crowd, feels sorry for him, and brings him a form to sign to register as a contestant. Even as she holds the form for him to sign, Harry is so distracted by her that he stabs himself in the tonsils with the pencil.

As the race begins, Harry dawdles around the starting point, already far behind the pack, and is finally chased on his way by the photographers who rush in behind him to cover the start of the race. Harry sees Betty in the crowd of onlookers and after only a few steps, he stops to give her a silly love note. As a consequence of his problems with cognition, perception, and simple locomotion, Harry veers off course and away from the pack before he is even out of sight of the starting line. His trajectory is erratic to say the least, including sojourns into a farmer's berry patch, doing time on a chain gang, becoming involved in a jailbreak, and encountering a twister in a small prairie town. Harry wins the race in his own slow time and only in spite of himself. He wins the girl, who happens to be the big shoe manufacturer's daughter, and the prize money and saves the family shoe business, but not as the result of any design or effort on his part.

A long-distance dash is actually included in the story of *Tramp, Tramp, Tramp* and is simply deleted in Langdon's performance. After the jailbreak, Harry is supposedly pulled along forty miles of countryside after he hoists the heavy ball onto a train and is not able to climb on by the time it starts to pull away. Rather than a series of lateral tracking or panning shots, as a long-distance dash such as this would be presented in a Keaton film, Harry is seen skipping alongside the train as it slowly pulls away in one shot. This is followed by the title, "Forty miles later," which is followed by another shot of Harry, hobbling along, tired out, as the train slows to a halt.

In *Safety Last,* Lloyd employed the analytic and synthetic properties of montage to create suspense, to create comic momentum, and also to create an impression of the greatest possible height of the building climbed by Harold to enhance the viewer's impression of the danger of Harold's situation. Lloyd actually climbed several different buildings. Shots taken on the several different buildings were combined to create a single, artificial building that was taller than any one of them, but which Lloyd could climb and be photographed upon properly and in relative safety.

The use of montage in Keaton's films also involves edit analysis of action by alternation of camera distance and angle and the creation of a thoroughly synthetic space through intershot associations. Keaton invokes the Kuleshov effect in full force in sequences in which the character's mental as well as physical agility is demonstrated. The cutting in these sequences explicitly specifies the details of the problem with which Buster is confronted or of the adverse circumstances in which he finds himself. It also carefully elaborates the ingenious plans of action that Buster conceives as solutions, clearly establishing goals or objectives.

In *The General,* once Johnnie Gray overhears the details of the Union plan of a surprise attack, he resolves, "We've got to get back to our lines somehow and warn them of this coming attack." From this moment until the end of the film, the editing lays out a tightly interwoven chain of events instigated by Johnnie to accomplish this end. These events are elaborated in a rather complex montage structure of causal interaction that presumably is determined according to a complex process of logical thinking on the part of the character.

One of this series of interconnected incidents occurs shortly after Johnnie has accomplished his initial objective of recovering "The General" from enemy hands. To effect his escape and speed his progress back to Confederate lines to warn of the attack in time, Johnnie stops "The General" at a safe distance from the enemy camp. A series of shots detail Johnnie's actions as he lassoes a telegraph pole and ties the other end of the rope to the last car of the train. Johnnie climbs over the cars to the cab, starts the train moving forward at a slow speed, and starts back across the top of the cars. In the next shot, the noose tightens around the telegraph pole and pulls it over onto the track as seen from a camera mounted on top of the last car of the moving train.

This shot is followed by a parallel cut to the effect of Johnnie's action. A Union telegraph operator and officer are seen making the discovery that they are not able to continue wiring ahead word of the capture of "The General" nor can they send orders to stop Johnnie. In the next shot, Johnnie cuts the telegraph pole loose from the car and "The General" pulls away, leaving the pole lying across the track. Several shots later, in another cutaway from Johnnie aboard "The General," now at some distance down the line, the result of this particular detail in Johnnie's plan is seen when the enemy train that is pursuing Johnnie, followed by a supply train, comes upon the downed telegraph pole and has to stop while the soldiers get off to clear the track. A subsequent sequence includes shots of Johnnie inside the baggage car of "The General," chopping away at the rear wall and finally dumping it and the car's contents onto the track. These shots are intercut with shots of the enemy locomotive stopping as it approaches each of these obstacles as the men get off to clear the track.

In another sequence of shots, Johnnie puts another plan into effect to waylay the pursuing locomotive. Johnnie stops "The General" again just beyond a point where the tracks intersect and gets out to hook a chain to the track. He then turns the track switch and signals to the girl to start "The General" moving. This is followed by a close shot of the chain pulling taut, bending the rail, and snapping. Buster then enters the frame to inspect his work. A later sequence of shots presents the effects that Johnnie had in mind in the previous sequence: the two enemy trains are diverted onto an elevated side track and are not able to proceed on the main track because Johnnie has successfully jammed the switching mechanism. Throughout the remainder of the film, there are parallel cuts from shots of Johnnie making his way to Confederate lines carrying the news of the surprise attack and shots of Confederate troops mobilizing after Johnnie conveys the news, to shots of the Union soldiers and officers foiled in their attempts to repair the track or standing around it in helpless consternation.

Now that he has successfully waylaid his pursuers, Johnnie can put his next plan into action. There is a shot of the Union soldiers discovering that the track switch is jammed after they maneuver the two trains back onto the main track to recommence their pursuit. This is followed by a cut to a sequence of shots which range from extreme long shots to medium shots. This sequence includes a moving camera shot and a wide variety of angles and viewpoints on the action that detail Johnnie's activities as he piles up some firewood in the middle of a wooden bridge that spans a deep chasm and douses it with kerosene from "The General"'s headlight.

Thus the overall design of Johnnie's scheme is revealed. Parallel cuts during this sequence away from Johnnie serve to interconnect the various events of: (1) Johnnie setting the bridge on fire behind him; (2) the Union officers and men standing around the broken rail in a quandary, their pursuit of Johnnie foiled and their mission to deliver supplies to the Northern division of Union troops at the bridge delayed; and (3) the troops of the Northern division nearing the bridge to meet the supply train.

Shortly afterward, Johnnie reaches Confederate headquarters and alerts the commanding general of the attack. The immediate result of this is seen in cutaways from Johnnie explaining to the general the details of the Union plan, to shots of Confederate infantry and cavalry mobilizing to meet the attack. Meanwhile, back at the bridge, the effects of Johnnie's earlier firing of the bridge are seen in the next sequence of shots. A Union general orders the first train (which, in the meantime, has finally been switched onto the right track) to cross the smoldering bridge, and the bridge collapses under its weight. The end result of Johnnie's efforts is that the Union army has been held up on the opposite side of the chasm long enough for the Confederate forces to take their positions and eventually turn back the Union advance. Johnnie adds the finishing touch to the Confederate victory when he fires a big artillery gun in one shot (a film "shot") that, in the next shot, strikes the supply train and derails it, cutting off the Union retreat.

It is discovered later that Johnnie has also captured a Union general. This prize is a result of an incident presented at the beginning of this lengthy and elaborate chain of events. When Johnnie first finds himself in the Union camp, he poses as a Union soldier and, to remain inconspicuous, joins in with the other soldiers who are loading the captured "General" with firewood and supplies. Johnnie picks up a stick of firewood and follows the others to the fuel car. When Johnnie chooses to carry a stick of firewood, it serves both to disguise him and as a weapon. With it, Johnnie knocks out the Union general in the cab of "The General" in order to recover the train and use it as a vehicle with which to reach Confederate lines and warn of the Union attack. Neither the capture of the Union general nor, for that matter, the Confederate victory are accidentally or arbitrarily brought about. Both events were engineered by Johnnie Gray. The montage structure of the sequence as a whole and its various incidents presents those events as conceived and carried out by him.

The cinematic style of Harry Langdon's films is also distinct from that of Charles Chaplin's, even though generally in the films of both Langdon and Chaplin, comedy is not created from the relationships between shots. Both Langdon and Chaplin reject montage in favor of the primacy of a pantomime performance, which is presented within a basic filmic context of spatiotemporal continuity. Thus, the film style of Chaplin's comedies may also be termed "mise-en-scène." However, the filmic mise-en-scène scheme employed in Chaplin's comedies is different from Langdon's because it is linked to a comic persona and style of performance that are, like Lloyd's and Keaton's, very different from Langdon's persona and performance.

Chaplin's performance is like that of Lloyd and Keaton and unlike that of Langdon in that it significantly features the virtuosic display. Chaplin's performance is one of extraordinary balletic grace, agility, skill and timing, and pantomimic acting of virtuosic eloquence. The relation of this kind of performance to characterization and narrative structure defines the distinctive nature of the comedy of Charles Chaplin to a great extent. Whereas Langdon's performance describes a comic character that is barely conscious, and is in fact is often unconscious, Chaplin's performance describes a character that is extremely self-conscious—an exhibitionist. As such, it is a comic character that can be closely identified with the egocentric artist himself.

Chaplin's gestures, movement, and mime, like Langdon's and unlike Lloyd's and Keaton's, characteristically are not motivated by some utilitarian purpose or structured with regard to a particular predetermined objective. The motivation for Charlie's virtuosic exhibitions—of dancing, of dancing on roller skates, of tightrope walking, of juggling, or of balancing—is often merely the egotistical urge to show off. In *Modern Times*, Charlie skillfully and gracefully skates around on the department store mezzanine, boasting to the girl, "Look, I can do it blindfolded!"

These exhibitions of technical virtuosity usually occur as solo set pieces that are basically independent of narrative continuity, and have little or no direct bearing on the development of plot. The function of the virtuosic display as a set piece within the narrative context of Chaplin's films is even further emphasized by the continual references by the character to the presence of an actual or imaginary proscenium and his frequent acknowledgment of the audience by opening with a nod or flourish and concluding with a bow to the camera.

In *The Rink,* Charlie makes his entrance and takes his bows between the portals of the doorway to the skating rink floor and then proceeds literally to skate rings around the heavy, Eric Campbell, and, figuratively, around everyone else on the floor. The skating routines in Chaplin's films probably derived from "Skating," a sketch that he performed in music hall and vaudeville as a member of the Fred Karno Company. Charlie emerges in the same way in *The Cure* from a curtained bath house dressing booth as if it were a theatrical proscenium, performs a little ballet, and takes his bows to the camera.

Tidying the back room in *The Pawnshop* with a broom, Charlie sweeps a piece of string across the floor. When Charlie spots it, he starts walking it as if it were a tightrope, using the broom as a balance beam, and then bows into the camera. In *The Circus,* Chaplin presents an impressive exhibition of equilibrium as Charlie, the circus clown, practices to become a tightrope walker. He also practices his flourishes to the crowd, finishing with bows into the camera. In his dream in *The Gold Rush,* Charlie presents the famous set piece of the "Oceana Roll" to the girls at his party and to the audience of the film in the miniproscenium of a medium close-up in very low-key lighting with highlighting on his face and hands that gives the effect of footlighting.

As in *The Rink* and *The Cure,* Charlie formally and ceremoniously introduces another virtuoso performance in *Pay Day.* Following the title, "Preparing for what is to come," Charlie, as a bricklayer, takes his place on a scaffold above Syd, as his fellow worker, on the ground below, whose job is to throw bricks up to Charlie. Charlie prepares by throwing a handkerchief back and forth between himself and Syd in the same way acrobats begin their act at the circus. Charlie then catches a series of bricks behind his back and puts each one in place in rapid succession as seen in reverse motion photography. Chaplin's skill is exhibited in his movement, gesture, and timing in actually picking off and dropping the bricks with the reversal of motion in mind. In *The Circus,* Charlie is tossing some food up to the girl who is on a trapeze above him. When her cruel stepfather who has forbidden her to eat comes along, Charlie starts to juggle the food and instinctively takes a bow.

In *The Pawnshop,* Charlie foils a robbery and wins the girl. In the end, he shows off with a bow to the camera and gets a kiss from the girl. Charlie is a waiter in *Modern Times* about to make his debut as a cabaret singer. While he waits in the kitchen before going on, Charlie rehearses his song into the camera with a normal angle, full shot camera setup forming the proscenium. Charlie then goes on and presents his song and dance on the nightclub floor, facing away from the majority of the nightclub audience seen behind him in the background of the shot, and into the camera toward the larger film audience. Other evidence of Charlie's self-consciousness, as seen in Chaplin's conscious acknowledgments of camera and audience, is found in Chaplin's Mutual two-reeler, *Behind the Screen*. The film ends with Charlie kissing the girl and winking into the camera. Charlie also kisses the girl in the final shot of the feature, *The Gold Rush*, and in this case, waves the camera away.

Some other set pieces in Chaplin's films are the acrobatic and balletic boxing routines in *The Champion* and *City Lights*, the latter a masterpiece of comic timing and choreography. In *The Circus*, Charlie flies up a flagpole when he is frightened by a lion. He tries to compensate for exhibiting his fear before the girl with another exhibition atop the flagpole in the form of a balletic interpretation of flying as the girl looks on. Chaplin's set pieces also include balletic expressions of exuberance as in *The Great Dictator* when Hynkel dances with the globe while he contemplates world domination.

These can be compared to Harry's dances of delight at his first sight of Mary Brown in *The Strong Man* and in *Long Pants* after Harry intercepts a love note from Bebe, believing that it is intended for him. Langdon's dances do not display physical grace or require technical virtuosity. They are merely displays of Harry's lack of coordination. In other situations in which Harry expresses his exuberance, as at the evidence of a dream come true, he runs around frantically in a completely erratic trajectory. This occurs in *Tramp, Tramp, Tramp* when Harry first sees the girl from the billboard in the flesh.

The basic cinematic structure of Chaplin's films, like that of Langdon's, is based on spatiotemporal unity. The informal mise-en-scène scheme exhibited in Chaplin's films is uniquely suited to present Chaplin's own comic persona and style of performance, just as Langdon's is to his own persona and performance. However, Chaplin's persona and performance are different from Langdon's and the filmic mise-en-scène scheme exhibited in the films of each is therefore also different. Langdon's filmic mise-en-scène conforms to a comic performance that is nonvirtuosic and a style of mime that is basically nonreferential. Chaplin's filmic mise-en-scène conforms to a comic performance characterized by solo set pieces of technical expertise and by a pantomime style that is highly articulate and rich in allusion.

Space in Chaplin's films may be considered a cinematic modification of traditional theatrical space. Spatial specifications, or camera setup, of individual shots in Chaplin's films represent the optimum vantage point on Chaplin's performance at any moment. For example, Chaplin's virtuoso solo set pieces like those mentioned are most often presented in long takes in a fixed normal angle, full shot or medium long shot. These are, by far, the two most commonly used camera setups in Chaplin's films. The fixed spectator viewpoint on Chaplin's performance in these shots approximates that of one seated in front or fifth row center in a theater. As did Langdon,

Chaplin also took advantage of the possibility of cutting in film to freely and easily adjust the film frame to accommodate screen space to his performance. In Chaplin's films, this potential of film was utilized to provide an idealized proscenium for the solo specialty.

Sometimes, rather than full shot or medium long shot, medium shot is the camera setup that provides the viewer with the optimum vantage point on Chaplin's performance. A normal angle, medium shot is the optimum vantage point in the case of Chaplin's adept handling of a customer's alarm clock in *The Pawnshop*. Chaplin's performance is presented in two long-take medium shots with a single reaction shot of the customer in between. Sometimes a medium close-up camera setup provides the optimum vantage point on Chaplin's pantomime performance. This applies to the famous dinner scene in *The Gold Rush* in which Charlies dines on the sole of his shoe as if he were enjoying a turkey dinner. Charlie twirls the shoelaces around his fork and sucks them into his mouth as if they were spaghetti, and sucks on and savors the nails from the sole as if they were the bones in several medium close-ups of rather long duration. These shots are intercut occasionally with shots of his companion, Big Jim, who is not enjoying the shoe's uppers.

Sometimes a medium shot or a medium close-up or close-up camera setup captures the eloquence and subtle psychological nuances of a Chaplin posture, gesture, or facial expression better than a full shot or medium long shot. In *The Tramp,* after leaving Edna a farewell note and just before departing, the tramp turns his back to the camera in a medium shot to fondle her hat in a moment of pathos in which his posture conveys his feelings of sorrow and disappointment. In *City Lights,* a close-up is the optimum vantage point from which to see Charlie's provocatively ambiguous facial expression in the long-held final shot of the film after he reveals himself to the beautiful flower girl as her benefactor.

As in the films of Harry Langdon, the time of the long take in Chaplin's films corresponds to the time of the performance. However, unlike that of Langdon's, the duration of Chaplin's performance is based on the dramatic or technically virtuosic content of that performance. Both spatial and temporal specifications of individual shots in Chaplin's films are based on the dramatic or technically virtuosic content of Chaplin's performance.

There is no such content in Langdon's performance. Therefore, even though Langdon is the focal point of the majority of shots in his films, Langdon rarely appears alone in a shot. Langdon's is not a solo performance; it must be referred by the viewer to some point of reference in order to derive significance from Langdon's essentially inarticulate pantomime and to appreciate his highly reductive comic performance. (Another event coincidental with Langdon's abandonment of his solo specialty act around 1905, along with his adoption of a new comic persona and a different space in which to work on stage, was his first marriage. Langdon's marriage began a vaudeville partnership that lasted throughout the duration of

Langdon's vaudeville career.) In contrast to Langdon's comedies, Chaplin's two-reel Mutual comedy, *One A.M.*, is a strictly solo performance of a drunk routine probably taken from Chaplin's Karno sketch, "The Mumming Birds" (known as "A Night in an English Music Hall" in the United States).

The significant difference in the work of Langdon and Chaplin as metteurs-en-scène is the fact that, in Langdon's films, the spatial and temporal elements of Langdon's mise-en-scène take on a signifying capacity with respect to characterization and become, themselves, constituents of comedy and pathos. In Langdon's comic conception, the quantitative coordinates of Langdon's performance—Harry's spatial relation, in time, to a particular point of reference as one of a system of emblems that represent objective reality in Langdon's films—bear a qualitative significance. In Langdon's films, these quantitative coordinates *are* the content of Langdon's performance. This is shown in the confrontation between Harry and Lily on the sidewalk in front of her apartment building in *The Strong Man*, the confrontation between Harry and the dummy cop in *Long Pants*, the start of the cross-country walking race in *Tramp, Tramp, Tramp*, and many other examples.

This point can also be demonstrated through a comparison of tableau shots in the films of Chaplin and Langdon. The long shot is the least common camera setup in Chaplin's films. In fact, long shots are rarely used in Chaplin's films except for metaphoric tableaux such as the final shot of *The Tramp* in which the tramp is seen as a lone figure plodding dejectedly away from the camera along a country road after being rejected by the girl. He stops midway, kicks up his heels, and continues on down the road at a quickened pace as the shot irises out. In a cursory reading of the simple humanistic statement represented in this image, the country thoroughfare may be interpreted as the road of life, the figure of the tramp as a universal symbol of all humanity, and the tramp's gesture of kicking up his heels and continuing on with renewed optimism may be interpreted as symoblic of the resiliency and indomitable optimism of the human spirit.

In *The Circus*, too, the girl whom Charlie loves, loves another. In one of the final shots of this film, the circus wagons that carry the girl away with her new husband roll out of the frame. Charlie remains standing alone in the center of a circle that has been left on the ground by the circus ring. This is followed by closer shots of Charlie and an insert close-up of a leftover paper star. Charlie is seen in the final shot, a long shot, kicking the crumpled paper star away behind him and walking slowly and dejectedly away from the camera toward the horizon. As in the final shot of *The Tramp*, Charlie recovers, jauntily swings his cane, and continues on in this long take, which also concludes with an iris-out.

Chaplin's posture, movement, or gesture is always the most important feature in the symbolic tableaux in his films. As such, the tramp is seen as the central figure in the symbolic images described earlier. In *The Tramp*,

Charlie is seen at center frame in the middle of the road, which reaches across the frame into the background of the shot at a slightly oblique angle to the surface of the screen. In *The Circus,* he is seen in the center of the circus ring in the center of the two long shots.

There is no such priority in the composition of the tableau shots in Langdon's films. In the shot in *Three's a Crowd* in which Harry stands as if paralyzed and stares at Gladys and the child, he is seen across the room in background left with Gladys and the baby in foreground right. In the shot in which Harry stands in an arrested pose and looks on as Mary Brown blindly gropes for the bench in the garden in *The Strong Man,* Harry is seen in the background as Mary moves into the foreground. In the shot in which Harry watches the brawl between Bebe and Betty in the nightclub dressing room in *Long Pants,* Harry sits in foreground center with his back to the camera and remains absolutely motionless throughout the duration of the shot while the two women are seen fighting it out before him.

These symbolic images in Langdon's films cannot be read and are not intended to be read as universalized philosophical metaphors, as Chaplin's symbolic tableaux often are and are usually meant to be. Langdon's symbolic tableaux have a much more specialized significance. The time that Harry stands expressionless and motionless in plain sight of such highly provocative facts of life as those mentioned is actually an indexical indication of the extent of Harry's innocence, inexperience, and naiveté; the difficulty with which he comprehends such facts and makes the transition to cognition or emotional maturity; and the profound psychological impact of such a discovery upon him. This significance is conveyed to the viewer through all of the elements in the mise-en-scène of each of these shots as a whole—through their spatial relation to one another and their coexistence in time.

To imagine Harry Langdon's comic persona and performance in terms of the synthetic time and space of montage that Lloyd and Keaton employed, or in terms of the cinematically idealized proscenium for a solo specialty which Chaplin employed, or in any cinematic form other than that which Langdon's comedies actually take, is to recognize the originality of Langdon's comic and cinematic style. By comparing the work of these three comedians on the basis of the relation of persona to performance, and of the relation of persona and performance to cinematic style, one recognizes the significance of formal factors in the comedy, not only of Harry Langdon but of these other comedians as well.

Notes

1. Kevin Brownlow, *The Parade's Gone By . . .* (New York: Alfred A. Knopf, 1968), p. 534.
2. Hubert I. Cohen, "The Serious Business of Being Funny," *Film Comment* 5 (Fall 1969): 54.

9
Footnote: Arthur Ripley and the Dark Side of Langdon's Comedies

It has been maintained in this study that Langdon's silent comedies are dominated stylistically by Langdon's performance and that their narrative elements were always subordinate to that performance. The view has also been expressed that, as Mack Sennett and Frank Capra have claimed, such things as story, plot development, and integrity of characterization were relatively unimportant to Langdon. It is suggested in chapter 1 that whatever sophistication at the narrative level is to be found in Langdon's films can probably be traced to Langdon's gag and story writers, Frank Capra and Arthur Ripley.

There is a clearly conscious use of certain narrative techniques and development of certain themes in Langdon's silent films, although none of these is ever fully developed into a coherent, unified narrative structure in those films. The significant narrative unit is the individual episode, with little integration or development from one episode to the next. Most of the themes and devices outlined in this chapter are more coherent when seen on paper in the written scenarios for the films and when they are discussed out of context than when they are seen in the context of Langdon's translation of them in the films. The written scenarios suggest interesting potential narratives that remained to be developed by Capra and Ripley in their own later films.

Some of these narrative elements are discussed in chapters 1 and 2 as evidence of Capra's contribution to the stories of Langdon's films. Capra's contributions might be classified as the brighter side of the Langdon comedies. These include the theme of good triumphing over evil, the clear-cut assignment of character types into these two camps, and the characterization of the struggle in the films as a moral one.

Much has been written on Frank Capra, his early career as a Sennett gag writer, his relationship with Langdon, and his role in the production of Langdon's films. In addition to his own account in *The Name above the Title* and Sennett's complimentary comments about Capra in *King of Comedy*, several books, monographs, and numerous articles have been published on the films of Frank Capra. Capra has made himself available in his retirement for talks, interviews, and seminars, out of which several lengthy interviews have become available in print. By comparison, there is very little available on Arthur Ripley, and almost nothing, except in Capra's autobiography, is available in print on Ripley's contribution to the Langdon screen stories.

The present study presents a view of Langdon and his work that is, in a number of ways, an alternative to the prevailing, traditional view of Langdon's comedy. It is perhaps appropriate then to include as an expanded footnote to this work, a brief chapter on narrative values that emphasizes Arthur Ripley rather than Frank Capra, and the dark side rather than the bright side of Langdon's comedies. The narrative elements that constitute this darker side of Langdon's films are traced here to Ripley.

Ripley collaborated with Capra on the stories of the Sennett two- and three-reelers and the Sennett feature *His First Flame*. Ripley wrote and Capra directed *The Strong Man* and *Long Pants* for the Harry Langdon Corporation. Capra left the Langdon company during the production of *Long Pants* when it became clear that it was Capra, on one side, versus Langdon and Ripley on the other. Ripley remained with Langdon and wrote the stories of Langdon's next, and last three silent features: *Three's a Crowd, The Chaser,* and *Heart Trouble.* Ripley had high hopes of success for his association with Langdon. However, these hopes faded as Langdon's success faded at the end of the silent film era. Thereafter, Ripley inhabited the Hollywood demimonde of the "B" film and comedy shorts as a writer and director. He ended his career as director of the Motion Picture Division of the Theatre Arts Department at the University of California at Los Angeles. Ripley died in 1961.

In assessing Ripley's contribution to Langdon's films, it is interesting to consider Capra's description of himself and Ripley as "opposites." The seemingly Manichaean division of their respective contributions to Langdon's films proposed here is based on Capra's observation and on a comparison of Langdon's films in terms of narrative values with the later films of Capra and Ripley. A comparison of character types, plot devices, and thematic motifs of some Langdon films with those of later Capra-directed

Harry's wife and mother-in-law lay in wait for him when Harry stays out late one night. Helen Hayward and Gladys McConnell in *The Chaser*. (Courtesy of Gladys McConnell)

films is included in chapter 2. Capra's own view of the Langdon character was a version of the "Christian innocent," a prototype of the heroes who appear in Capra's subsequent films. Capra's contribution to Langdon's films is optimistic and overt.

Ripley's contribution, in contrast to Capra's, can be sensed as a perverse undertone. Ripley seems to have seen something quite different than Capra in a comic character that is on the surface at once both man and child. Ripley exploited the bizarre eroticism that was latent in the character's amorphous sexual identity. In gags, comic situations, and stories, the Langdon films are full of thinly disguised references to homosexuality and transvestism and obvious metaphors for sexual impotence, virginity, and rape.

None of these censored subjects was uncommon in silent comedy. However, Langdon's physical appearance offered a ripe source for these kinds of allusions. Thematic motifs in his films include incest and the linking of sex and violence. The use of dream, sexual fantasy, and nightmare are also common in Langdon's films as seen in chapter 3, inspired surely by the somnambulistic characteristics of the comic character that Langdon had earlier created in vaudeville.

These elements do not conform to Capra's view of the character as an elf whose only ally was God, and Capra would certainly disavow those darker elements that appear in the Langdon films on which he collaborated. These covert elements surface in later Ripley-directed "films noir." Ripley's later

Harry evades a murder attempt by his mother-in-law when he comes home late in *The Chaser*. Langdon with Helen Hayward and Gladys McConnell. (Courtesy of Gladys McConnell)

When Harry's wife returns home from a night out with the girls, she discovers a farewell note and evidence of Harry's suicide attempts. Gladys McConnell in *The Chaser*. (Courtesy of Gladys McConnell)

films and screenplays are laden with Freudian implications. His characters inhabit nightmarish milieus. The stories are either tragedies, or near-tragedies like *Waterfront* (1939). In this film, a young waterfront tough seeks the killer of his brother and mistakenly almost murders his own bride. In the Ripley-scripted and -directed *Prisoner of Japan* (1942), a drunken, pacifist American astronomer finds love, death, and spiritual redemption on a remote Pacific island as the two lovers sacrifice themselves for the American cause in World War II.

Violence is also significant in Ripley's post-Langdon dramatic films. It is usually subtle, though it is sometimes expressed in a spectacular outburst, as in *Thunder Road* (1958). Ripley's outlaw hero runs moonshine by night and eludes Treasury men on dark mountain highways in his high-powered car. The grand finale of *Thunder Road* is the hero's immolation in a fiery explosion when his car careers into a high-voltage power station.

Voice in the Wind (1944), written, directed, and independently produced by Ripley, is the hopeless story of two lovers, victims of Nazi tyranny, who are separated as the film begins and are reunited at the end in their deaths. The heroine lies in a coma, dying, from the beginning of the film and the hero suffers from brain damage caused by his former captors. Their tragedy is set against the misery of other refugees trapped on the fog-bound island of Guadeloupe. The hero sometimes works for a trio of gruesome brothers (two of whom eventually kill each other off) who operate a "murder ship." They promise groups of the stranded refugees pas-

Harry's wife fondles the pants he was ordered to trade for her skirts as she mourns his seeming demise. Gladys McConnell and Helen Hayward in *The Chaser*. (Courtesy of Gladys McConnell)

Harry submits to a peck on the cheek from the milkman in *The Chaser*. (Courtesy of Gladys McConnell)

sage to America and then rob them of their valuables and drown them once they are out at sea.

The prevalence of dream and fantasy in the Langdon stories can be traced to Ripley through evidence of this same preoccupation in Ripley's later work. Of the five features directed by him, three—*Voice in the Wind; The Chase* (1946), about a shell-shocked ex-G.I. who becomes involved in a woman's murder, then wakes to find it was only a bad dream; and *Thunder Road*—feature dreams as a significant thematic element or structural device. The nightmare worlds of each of these films are enhanced visually by heavy shadows and murky, low-key lighting. A Ripley-focused reading of the Langdon stories shows Langdon's offbeat character plunged into a psychological limbo of utter confusion whenever his dreams and fantasies do or do not come true.

In a certain respect—specifically, with respect to this Ripley-focused reading of Langdon's film stories—Langdon's comedies can be considered "black comedies" in the same way, in terms of narrative, that Ripley's later dramatic films are considered "films noir." *The Chaser* is a comedy in which Harry escapes his mother-in-law's attempt to murder him only to attempt suicide, once by hanging, then by stabbing, shooting, and finally by poisoning. Harry has been ordered by a judge to exchange roles and clothes with his wife in a court action she has brought against him for philandering. Harry tries to kill himself to put himself out of the misery of having to endure humiliation by a salesman, the iceman, and the milkman who make passes at him.

Two shots that suggest the bizarre touch of Arthur Ripley. Gladys's mascara runs as she cries over Harry's apparent suicide. (Courtesy of Gladys McConnell)

Harry's physical relationship with women—keeping a safe distance—is a demonstration of his psychological relationship with women. It lets the viewer know of his naiveté, virginity, and fear of women. Judging from the gags and comic situations in which Harry is placed, Harry has every reason to be afraid of women. His experiences with sex are almost always associated with violence. In a Ripley-focused reading of the dark side of Langdon's screen stories, Harry's fear of women is a fear of castration.

It is often unclear whether the advances of the aggressive women who constantly confront him are amorous or hostile. In *Soldier Man* and *Lucky Stars,* the queen and the sultry Latin vamp kiss and caress Hary while each holds a dagger over his head about to plunge it into his back. When Harry is up in Lily's room in *The Strong Man,* she chases him around the room at knife-point. Under the threat of death, Harry finally yields and kisses her. As he does, Lily breaks a bottle over his head, where upon Harry climbs into bed and curls up in the fetal position to sleep it off. Harry and Lily are seen together in a series of ambiguous postures while she wrestles with him on the bed, trying to get at the stolen bankroll hidden in his clothes. Then she kisses him while she tears open his back pocket with the knife and reaches in to get the money. In *His Marriage Wow,* Harry is convinced that his new bride has poisoned him at their wedding dinner to get his life insurance.

The gags and situations in Langdon's films often present Harry's intimate encounters with these worldly, violent women as seductions, even rape. In *His First Flame,* Harry is seduced and abandoned by a female thief who is being chased by the police. She hits Harry on the head as he happens by, knocks him out, and drags him offscreen into a doorway. After a while, she comes out of the doorway in Harry's clothes. Harry emerges shortly afterward, dazed and dressed in her clothes. When Lily circles Harry from behind with her hand inside his jacket on the street corner in *The Strong Man,* it is a symbolic seduction. The incident in which she pulls him into the back seat of the cab with her and digs into Harry's clothes for the bankroll, along with the scene inside her room are symbolic of rape and the loss of Harry's virginity. The moment Lily touches him, Harry shrinks into a corner of the cab and cringes in a terrified defense of his virtue.

In *Long Pants,* Harry's harrowing, belated initiation into manhood by Bebe Blair is traumatic. She takes Harry, fresh out of short pants, on a crime spree and plunges him into a violent and sensuous milieu. In a nightclub back room, Harry watches her beat up another woman and then murder her lover in a shoot-out in which the lover also shoots her. The psychological impact of all this is conveyed in the mise-en-scène of this static tableau and in Harry's frozen stare as he heads for home. This impact is symbolized by Harry's gunshot wound in the arm. Harry retreats into the protective, repressive custody of his domineering mother and her chosen successor, Priscilla, Harry's fiancée.

Harry gets burned again in *Saturday Afternoon* when his latent manly

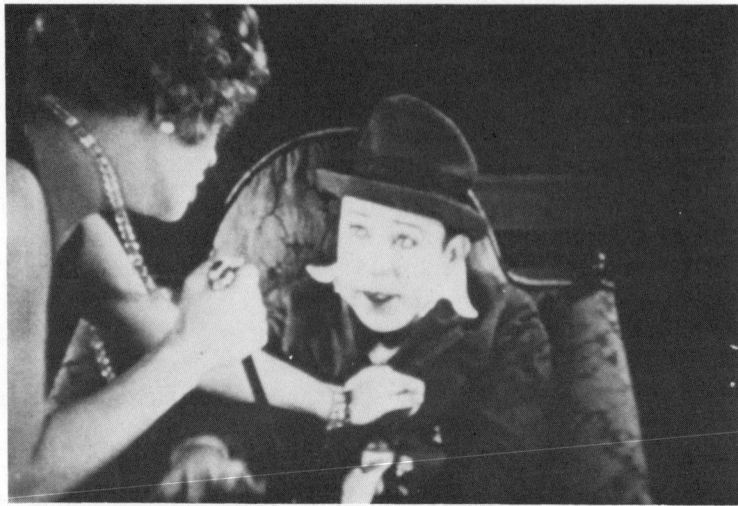

Harry's experiences with sex are almost always associated with violence. Here Lily threatens Harry with a knife in *The Strong Man*.

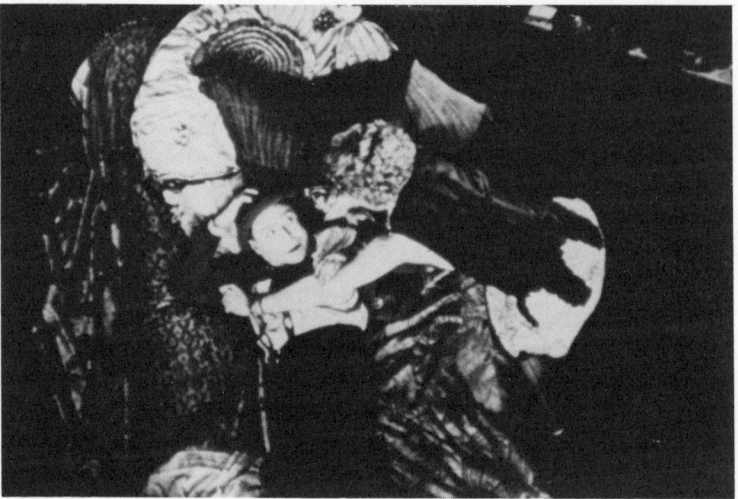

Harry and Lily are seen in a series of ambiguous postures on her bed in *The Strong Man*.

desires are aroused by an invitation from his pal to evade the surveillance of his wife and mother-in-law and join him for a fling with some girls. Harry ends up wrapped around a telephone pole after his encounter with the girls' surly boyfriends. Harry's wife comes by in the family car to collect him as two passersby unwrap him and put him in the seat next to her. Harry snuggles up to her bosom to sleep, retiring to the more secure and perverse role of his wife's child.

Harry is also "raped" by men. After Harry is undressed by the lady thief in *His First Flame* and dressed in her clothes, Harry tries to hitch a ride. One car finally stops, a man's hand beckons him into the back seat, and the car takes off. Before going very far, the car stops and Harry, flustered, climbs out.

Another gag situation in *The Sea Squawk* is laden with innuendo about transvestism, homosexuality, rape, and loss of virginity (and is very similar to one in a 1927 Laurel and Hardy two-reeler called *Putting Pants on Philip*). Harry, as a Scotsman, is searched by a detective who tosses Harry's tie around and ruffles his hair looking for a stolen jewel. When the detective reaches for the hem of Harry's kilts, Harry grabs his kilts and holds them down. The detective finally tackles him and wrestles him to the floor and out of the frame with only Harry's feet sticking up in the air. Then the detective gets up, brushes off one hand with the other, and walks offscreen left as Harry reemerges into the frame. Harry stares passively off left and blinks while he pulls his suspender straps back up. Later he goes to the ship's masquerade ball in drag where he charms the captain, his dance partner, and flirts with the crook, who is his cabin-mate. There is also the seduction in *The Chaser* when a big, burly iceman plants a big kiss on Harry's mouth on his way out of the kitchen after a delivery.

The potential theme of incest can be found in many comic situations in Langdon's films. As in *Saturday Afternoon*, Harry's wives are mothers. The way women are always dressing and undressing him, dusting him off, and tidying his clothes suggests a connection between Harry's mothers and Harry's lovers. All the women involved with Harry in *Long Pants* do this at one time or another—his mother, his fiancée, and Bebe, the vamp. Another hint of Harry's perverse relationship with women is the way he nestles up to sleep with his head on their bosoms. In *Lucky Stars*, Harry curls up in the vamp's lap and cuddles up to her to sleep while she kisses and caresses him and raises a stiletto to kill him.

His New Mama is a two-reel comedy version of O'Neill's *Desire under the Elms*, complete with all its Oedipal implications, in which Harry, a virginal farmer boy, gets a sexual initiation from his future stepmother. She is a "typical vamp," according to the synopsis, who has charmed Harry's widowed father in a plot to get his money. When Harry is introduced to his new mother, the scenario says she "gives Harry a kiss. It is not the kiss of a mother and both Harry and the old man notice this" and "the old man shows a little bit of jealousy." In the synopsis, Harry goes outside and "sits on the cold steps, removes his hat and gloves, then rubs handfuls of snow on his head to cool off."

Again according to the scenario, when Harry's father gives a party to introduce his future bride to the neighbors, "some kissing games are played and Madeline contrives to kiss Harry a number of times, much to the annoyance of the old man." Later that night, Madeline asks Harry to get her some more bedclothes and "Harry takes them off the old man and

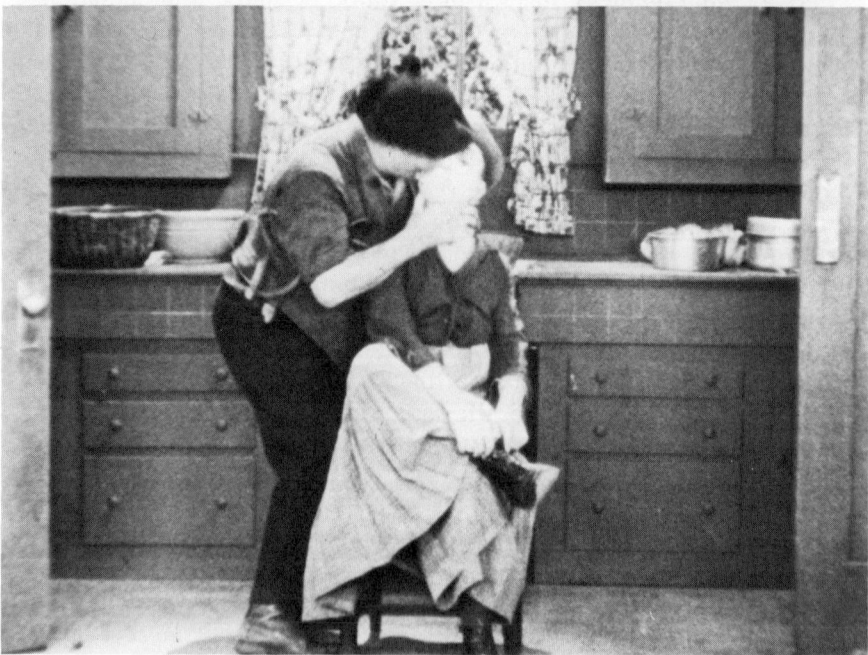

The Chaser includes references to transvestism and homosexuality. (Courtesy of Gladys McConnell)

goes to Madeline's room with them. She stays in bed and calls to him to come in and put them on the bed. Harry does so a bit hesitatingly." Harry's father wakes up and Harry hides in her closet. His father discovers him and chases him with Madeline's bed poster out into the snow and tells Harry never to darken his door again. The eroticism and Oedipus theme are more overstated in the written scenarios and synopses of this and other films than they are in the actual films, where much of the narrative unity is lost in the translation by Langdon.

One also finds many comic references to sexual potency and impotence in Langdon's films. Harry's physical inadequacy and ineptitude is often equated with sexual inadequacy, as in Harry's pitiful attempt to murder Priscilla in *Long Pants*. At first, Harry cannot get the pistol out of his pants. When he does get it out, he cannot fire it. He is pulled off his feet by a horse, rolls around in some barbed wire, puts his foot in a bear trap, and pulls a tree down on himself that knocks his top hat down over his head. Harry flails about trying to get the hat off, but cannot do it, and finally he sits down on a log in resignation. Priscilla comes over, removes the topper with ease, brushes Harry off, and tucks his shirttail neatly back into his pants. Then adding insult to injury, she does what he cannot do when she fires the gun for fun at a photo of Bebe and hits it between the eyes.

The exploitation of Harry's diminutive stature is another indirect reference to his lack of sexual prowess. *Boobs in the Wood* is the two-reeler in which the girl shows Harry what he is supposed to do as she tries to get him to kiss her when they are in the woods. Harry is introduced in this film in a long shot, dwarfed by the tall tree trunks that tower above him. Langdon is usually teamed up with a big sidekick, Vernon Dent. In *Boobs in the Wood*, Dent plays a bully lumberjack who is Harry's rival. While Vernon chops down a big tree, Harry knocks down a tiny twig.

Occasionally the tables are comically reversed when a gag calls for a display of sexual prowess on Harry's part, but even here, sex is expressed in violent terms. In *Boobs in the Wood*, Harry the milquetoast becomes sheriff when the last volunteer for the job is killed off. Harry enters the saloon in a too-large gunbelt with his gun hanging down in front and, surprisingly, subdues a crowd of roughnecks and wins the girl.

Presumably in expectation of sexual conquests, Harry dons his lodge uniform and ceremonial sword for an excursion into the park with his pal in *The Chaser*. After Harry is accosted by a female masher, he tries the same thing on another girl who faints dead away at Harry's embrace and kiss. The girl's companions and their large, matronly chaperone discover the girl sprawled out unconscious at Harry's feet. The girls' shocked expressions and the matron's threat, "Somebody will pay for this—with his life!" suggest rape, even murder, rendering Harry a real lady-killer.

Not all of Harry's encounters with women are violent; some are merely humiliating. When a girl who Harry thinks is Mary Brown yells at him for following her in *The Strong Man*, she warns, "If you don't stop following

Langdon with Babe London, according to First National publicity, one of his "five romantic conquests" in *Long Pants*. This episode, which involves a comically reversed reference to stature as an indication of sexual prowess, was deleted from the final version of the film along with two other "romances."

me, I'll turn you over to a truant officer!" while a crowd of women stand around and laugh. When Harry whistles and waves out of his attic window to a couple of neighborhood girls in *Long Pants,* one tells him, "Little boys should be seen and not heard," and the two girls giggle at him as they walk on by.

But Harry is not a little boy in *Long Pants*. According to the plot, which

Harry as a lady-killer in *The Chaser*. (Courtesy of Gladys McConnell)

describes a comic *American Tragedy,* Harry is a sexually repressed adult who lives with his parents and hides in the attic indulging in clandestine erotic fantasies. In fact, Harry's dreams, fantasies, and nightmares are all about

Frankie Darro plays Harry as an overprotected child in another early sequence trimmed from *Long Pants* after its initial release. Gladys Brockwell and Alan Roscoe play Harry's parents. (Courtesy of New York Public Library)

his sexual ability. His dreams and fantasies are wish fulfillments in which Harry displays incredible sexual potency. The nightmares are dreams of anxiety about impotence and emasculation.

In Harry's first fantasy in *Long Pants*, he pictures himself as the hero of a Ruritanian romance. He outduels the villain (in a segment trimmed from this sequence in the final version of the film), scales a wall to the beautiful heroine's balcony, sweeps her into his arms, and kisses her passionately. Later, when he gets his first pair of long pants, and as soon as his parents leave the room, he pretends to caress his dream girl. Harry's other fantasy in *Long Pants* is a wish fulfillment in which he smoothly and coolly murders his fiancée in order to be free to marry Bebe, a dope smuggler on the lam, whom Harry sees as the incarnation of his dream girl. When Harry tries to carry out the murder, it becomes a nightmare of frustration and humiliation.

When Harry kisses the queen in his dream in *Soldier Man*, she swoons and falls at his feet in another reference to Harry as lady-killer. When Harry wakes up, he tests his virility on his wife. Harry's kiss fails to faze her and he patiently submits as she finishes dressing him.

The excised dream sequence from the beginning of *Three's a Crowd* was a fulfillment of Harry's desire for Gladys. In existing stills from the missing sequence, she can be seen beckoning him to her through the long, dark cylindrical passage of Harry's telescope and coming to him in his room as he sleeps. Harry's second dream begins as a nightmare about his fear of inadequacy compared to Gladys's husband. In this heavily stylized se-

Harry subdues villain Pierre de Ramey *(above)* **and wins Alma Bennett** *(below)* **in the Technicolor fantasy sequence in the original release version of** *Long Pants*.

quence, some of the sets and props are distorted and misshapen. The acting and costumes are exaggerated and grotesque and the sequence is lit in low-key and sharp contrasts between highlight and darkness. The husband shows up in Harry's dream in a violent thunderstorm to take his wife and child from Harry. Harry fights for them in a boxing match that takes place in a dark void, except for one harsh overhead lamp. Gladys is the only spectator. Even though Harry is knocked out with the first punch, she still prefers him to her husband.

At least on the basis of narrative elements, a fear of castration on Harry's part would seem to be justified, as in the ending of *Saturday Afternoon*. At the end of *His Marriage Wow*, Harry's bride comes by to collect her new husband from the wreckage of an automobile after he gets into an accident trying to escape from her. In *All Night Long*, after some violent adventures, Harry's wife pushes her heavily bandaged and splinted husband and his rival home from the hospital in a big baby carriage. In *The Chaser*, Harry's sentence for stepping out on his wife is that he is to be "deprived of all the privileges of manhood." Harry later returns a baby carriage that has never been used to the salesman. Speaking of impotence, sex, and violence, Harry cannot even kill himself in this film as his only means of asserting his independence from the women he lives with and of freeing himself from their domination and tyranny.

Harry is sentenced in *The Chaser* to be "deprived of all the privileges of manhood." Langdon with Gladys McConnell. (Courtesy of Gladys McConnell)

In fact, many of Langdon's film stories have unhappy endings in which Harry resigns himself to the continued dominance of the mothers, wives as mothers, and mothers-in-law in his life after failing to establish his own sexual identity. These films include: *Saturday Afternoon, All Night Long, His Marriage Wow, Soldier Man,* and *The Chaser*. At the conclusion of *The Strong Man*, Harry is patrolling a quiet street in his oversized constable's uniform. After Mary brings him his lunch, he tells her, "Run along home, honey. I don't need any help." Mary pouts and Harry takes her hand and condescends to let her tag along as he walks his beat. As the two walk away from the camera, Harry trips and falls, and little, blind Mary picks him up, dusts

The last shot in *The Chaser*. Many of Langdon's comedies end as Harry resigns himself to the continued dominance of the mothers, wives, and mothers-in-law in his life. (Courtesy of Gladys McConnell)

Harry in a world of domineering women. Langdon with Gladys McConnell in a production still from *The Chaser*. (Courtesy of Gladys McConnell)

him off, and fixes his clothes. Priscilla does the same in *Long Pants* after the display of impotence and ineptitude he puts on in his frustrated attempt to murder her.

In the conclusion of *Long Pants,* Harry returns home from his harrowing

Scenes from Gladys's story, a kind of "film noir-within-a-film," which was cut from *Three's a Crowd* after previews. Gladys comes from a well-to-do home. Against the wishes of her father, she sneaks out at night for clandestine meetings with her lover and finally elopes with him. (Courtesy of Gladys McConnell)

adventure with Bebe and takes his place at the dinner table with his parents and Priscilla. He has been frightened into a passive acceptance of his former role as the child who now is passed on by a mother who kept him in short pants until it was time for him to marry, to another mother, Priscilla, who has already begun dressing him.

The two-reelers, *All Night Long* and *Lucky Stars,* are not only black comedies but, in the way visual style reinforces "dark" themes, they could also be called "films noir." "Film noir," a class of post–World War II American narrative films (including *Voice in the Wind, The Chase,* and *Thunder Road*), is a form of expressionism. These films project the paranoia, guilt, and anxiety of their time. In terms of both content (plots, themes, characterization) and cinematic form (low-key and high-contrast lighting, claustrophobic compositions, vertiginous angles), these films are dark. They reflect a mood of pessimism, perversity, and psychological disorientation. The incidents in these two Langdon films have a similar flavor and look.

All Night Long begins as Harry wakes up alone in a huge, dark, and empty movie theater. Harry scares himself with his own reflection in a mirror as he gropes his way through the theater corridors trying to find his way out. Most of the film is a flashback to Harry's war experiences, which includes night-for-night shots of Harry crawling around on a dark, barren battlefield that is occasionally lit up by flashes of enemy fire.

In one incident while Harry is on a "suicide mission," an explosion buries him upside down with only his legs sticking out of a mound of dirt. Another time, Harry's pants get caught while he is crawling under some barbed wire. He tries to free himself by pounding on the barbed wire with a live grenade. The flashback fades out on a classic Freudian anxiety-dream image of Harry clinging to the top of a tall telegraph pole, seen against the black void of a night-for-night sky while shells whizz by, gradually shooting the pole out from under him.

Lucky Stars is a reversal in negative of Harold Lloyd's American success story. Harry starts off pursuing his lucky star, which predicts romance, fame, and fortune for him as a doctor, by getting onto the wrong train. Before he even gets on the train, Harry loses all his worldly belongings when a baggage handler drops a crate on his trunk and flattens it. When he finds out that he is on the wrong train, Harry jumps off while the train is moving. The train stops, however, to pick up Harry's bruised and tattered remains. Harry is then seated next to a con man who promptly relieves him of his life savings. Harry has nothing left to do but tag along with the phony medicine-show doctor.

During his adventures as the doctor's assistant, the woman whom Harry decides is the beautiful, dark woman in his horoscope tries to stab him in the back. The film ends with the disconcerting image of Harry chased by an angry mob, dropping bottles of the nitroglycerine-spiked patent medicine along his way. The bottles explode and eerily illuminate Harry's flight against the night-for-night darkness of the San Tabasco street as he runs toward the camera and out of the frame.

Interestingly, the only Langdon feature that can be said to have a happy, "healthy" ending is *Tramp, Tramp, Tramp*—the only Langdon feature in which Arthur Ripley apparently did not take part in the production. The final sequence is a flash-forward from the end of the cross-country walking race, which Harry wins, along with the girl, through no effort on his part. In this ending, Harry and Betty, the proud parents, watch their baby son, played by Langdon, play in his carriage.

This look at the unexplored dark side of Langdon's film comedies and the role of Arthur Ripley will, it is hoped, shed some light on the work of Ripley, an intriguing though little-known figure in American film.

It is also hoped that the critical analysis of the comedies of Harry Langdon undertaken in this study has presented these films in a new and different light, and that it will prove to be a sample of a continuing examination of the American silent-comedy tradition in terms of form as well as content.

Harry Langdon Filmography

(Dates cited are release dates.)

Films in which Harry Langdon appears

(This list does not include appearances by Langdon in "soundies" [three-minute films made for jukeboxes] and guest appearances in two-reel sound films such as *Hollywood on Parade* and *The Voice of Hollywood*.)

Short films: silent

1. *Picking Peaches,* 2-3-24. Mack Sennett–Pathé. Director Erle Kenton; supervising director F. Richard Jones; photography George Spear; special photography Ernie Crockett; titles J. A. Waldron; with Irene Lentz, Alberta Vaughn, Ethel Teare, Dot Farley, Kewpie Morgan, Vernon Dent. 2 reels.
2. *Smile Please,* 3-2-24. Mack Sennett–Pathé. Director Roy del Ruth; supervising director F. Richard Jones; photography George Spear; special photography Ernie Crockett; titles J. A. Waldron; with Alberta Vaughn, Jack Cooper, Madeline Hurlock, Tiny Ward, Jackie Lucas, Andy Clyde, Louise Carver. 2 reels. [*Smile Please* was produced prior to *Picking Peaches* but its release was delayed pending clearance of title. *Smile Please,* therefore, is actually Langdon's first Sennett production.]
3. *Shanghaied Lovers,* 3-20-24. Mack Sennett–Pathé. Director Roy del Ruth; supervising director F. Richard Jones; photography George Spear; special photography Ernie Crockett; titles J. A. Waldron; with Alice Day, Kalla Pasha, Tiny Ward, Andy Clyde. 2 reels.
4. *Flickering Youth,* 4-27-24. Mack Sennett–Pathé. Director Erle Kenton; supervising director F. Richard Jones; photography George Spear, Bob Ladd; special photography Ernie Crockett; with Alice Day, Ray Grey, Charlotte Mineau, Louise Carver, Charlie Murray, Andy Clyde. 2 reels.

5. *The Cat's Meow,* 5-25-24. Mack Sennett–Pathé. Director Roy del Ruth; supervising director F. Richard Jones; photography William Williams, Lee Davis; special photography Ernie Crockett; titles J. A. Waldron; film editor William Hornbeck; with Alice Day, Kalla Pasha, Lucile Thorndike, Tiny Ward, Madeline Hurlock, Louise Carver. 2 reels.
6. *His New Mama,* 6-22-24. Mack Sennett–Pathé. Director Roy del Ruth; supervising director F. Richard Jones; photography William Williams; titles J. A. Waldron; film editor William Hornbeck; with Madeline Hurlock, Alice Day, Andy Clyde, Tiny Ward, Jack Cooper. 2 reels.
7. *The First Hundred Years,* 8-17-24. Mack Sennett–Pathé. Director Harry Sweet; supervising director F. Richard Jones; photography George Crocker, William Williams; titles J. A. Waldron; with Alice Day, Frank Coleman, Louise Carver, Madeline Hurlock. 2 reels.
8. *The Luck o' the Foolish,* 9-14-24. Mack Sennett–Pathé. Director Harry Edwards; with Madeline Hurlock, Marceline Day, Frank Coleman. 2 reels.
9. *The Hansom Cabman,* 10-12-24. Mack Sennett–Pathé. Director Harry Edwards; supervising director F. Richard Jones; photography Vernon Walker, Lee Davis; special photography Ernie Crockett; titles J. A. Waldron; film editor William Hornbeck; with Marceline Day, Charlotte Mineau, Andy Clyde, Madeline Hurlock, Leo Sulky. 2 reels.
10. *All Night Long,* 11-9-24. Mack Sennett–Pathé. Director Harry Edwards; story Vernon Smith, Hal Conklin; supervising director F. Richard Jones; photography William Williams, Lee Davis; special photography Ernie Crockett; titles J. A. Waldron; film editor William Hornbeck; with Natalie Kingston, Fanny Kelly, Vernon Dent. 2 reels.
11. *Feet of Mud,* 12-7-24. Mack Sennett–Pathé. Director Harry Edwards; supervising director F. Richard Jones; photography William Williams, Lee Davis; special photography Ernie Crockett; titles J. A. Waldron; film editor William Hornbeck; with Florence D. Lee, Natalie Kingston, Yorke Sherwood, Vernon Dent, Malcolm Waite. 2 reels.
12. *The Sea Squawk,* 1-4-25. Mack Sennett–Pathé. Director Harry Edwards; with Eugenia Gilbert, Christian Frank, Charlotte Mineau, Bud Rose, Leo Sulky. 2 reels. [*The Sea Squawk* was produced after *The Hansom Cabman* and prior to *All Night Long* but its release was delayed pending clearance of title.]
13. *Boobs in the Wood,* 2-1-25. Mack Sennett–Pathé. Director Harry Edwards; story Arthur Ripley; photography William Williams, Lee Davis; special photography Ernie Crockett; titles J. A. Waldron; film editor William Hornbeck; with Marie Astaire, Vernon Dent, Leo Willis. 2 reels.
14. *His Marriage Wow,* 3-1-25. Mack Sennett–Pathé. Director Harry Edwards; story Arthur Ripley; photography William Williams, Lee Davis; special photography Ernie Crockett; titles Felix Adler, A. H. Giebler; film editor William Hornbeck; with Natalie Kingston, William McCall, Vernon Dent. 2 reels.
15. *Plain Clothes,* 3-29-25. Mack Sennett–Pathé. Director Harry Edwards; story Arthur Ripley, Frank Capra; photography William Williams, Earl Stafford; special photography Ernie Crockett; titles Felix Adler, A. H. Giebler; film editor William Hornbeck; supervision J. A. Waldron; with Claire Cushman, Vernon Dent, Jean Hathaway, William McCall. 2 reels.

16. *Remember When?*, 4-26-25. Mack Sennett–Pathé. Director Harry Edwards; story Arthur Ripley, Clyde Bruckman; photography William Williams, Lee Davis; special photography Ernie Crockett; titles Felix Adler, A. H. Giebler; film editor William Hornbeck; supervision J. A. Waldron; with Natalie Kingston, Vernon Dent. 2 reels.
17. *Horace Greeley, Jr.*, 6-9-25. Principal Pictures–Pathé. Director Alf Goulding; story John Grey. 2 reels. [*Horace Greeley, Jr.* and *The White Wing's Bride* were produced by Principal Pictures Corporation prior to Langdon's association with the Sennett studio at some time from May to September, 1923. They were purchased along with Langdon's contract and subsequently released for the first time by Mack Sennett through Pathé.]
18. *The White Wing's Bride*, 7-12-25. Principal Pictures–Pathé. Director Alf Goulding; story John Grey. 2 reels.
19. *Lucky Stars*, 8-16-25. Mack Sennett–Pathé. Director Harry Edwards; story Arthur Ripley, Frank Capra; photography George Crocker; special photography Ernie Crockett; titles A. H. Giebler; film editor William Hornbeck; supervision J. A. Waldron; with Natalie Kingston, Vernon Dent, Andy Clyde. 2 reels.
20. *There He Goes*, 11-29-25. Mack Sennett–Pathé. Director Harry Edwards; story Arthur Ripley, Frank Capra; with Peggy Montgomery, Frank Whitson, Vernon Dent. 3 reels.
21. *Saturday Afternoon*, 1-31-26. Mack Sennett–Pathé. Director Harry Edwards; story Arthur Ripley, Frank Capra; photography William Williams; special photography Ernie Crockett; titles A. H. Giebler; film editor William Hornbeck; supervision J. A. Waldron; with Vernon Dent, Ruth Hiatt, Peggy Montgomery. 3 reels.
22. *Fiddlesticks*, 11-27-27. Mack Sennett–Pathé. Director Harry Edwards; story Arthur Ripley, Frank Capra; photography William Williams; special photography Ernie Crockett; titles Tay Garnett; film editor William Hornbeck; supervision J. A. Waldron; with Vernon Dent. 2 reels.
23. *Soldier Man*, 11-27-27. Mack Sennett–Pathé. Director Harry Edwards; story Arthur Ripley, Frank Capra; photography William Williams; special photography Ernie Crockett; titles A. H. Giebler; film editor William Hornbeck; supervision J. A. Waldron; with Natalie Kingston, Frank Whitson, Vernon Dent. 3 reels. [*Soldier Man* was actually produced after *There He Goes* and prior to *Saturday Afternoon*. *Fiddlesticks* and *Soldier Man* were released together after *His First Flame*.]

Short films: sound

24. *Hotter Than Hot*, 8-17-29. Hal Roach–MGM. Director Lewis R. Foster; story H. M. Walker; film editor Richard Currier; with Thelma Todd, Edgar Kennedy, Frank Austin, Edith Cramer. 2 reels.
25. *Sky Boy*, 10-5-29. Hal Roach–MGM. Director Charles Rogers; story Leo McCarey; story editor H. M. Walker; film editor Richard Currier; with Thelma Todd, Eddie Dunn. 2 reels.
26. *Skirt Shy*, 11-30-29. Hal Roach–MGM. Director Charles Rogers; story H. M. Walker; film editor Richard Currier; with May Wallace, Tom Ricketts, Nancy Dover, Charles Hall. 2 reels.

27. *The Head Guy*, 1-11-30. Hal Roach–MGM. Director Fred Guiol; story H. M. Walker; film editor Richard Currier; with Thelma Todd, Nancy Dover, Eddie Dunn, Edgar Kennedy. 2 reels.
28. *The Fighting Parson*, 2-22-30. Hal Roach–MGM. Directors Charles Rogers, Fred Guiol; story editor H. M. Walker; film editor Richard Currier; with Nancy Dover, Thelma Todd, Eddie Dunn, Leo Willis, Charles Hall. 2 reels.
29. *The Big Kick*, 3-29-30. Hal Roach–MGM. Director Warren Doane; story H. M. Walker; film editor Richard Currier; with Nancy Dover, Edgar Kennedy, Bob Kortman, Sam Lufkin, Baldwin Cooke, Charles McAvoy, Eddie Baker. 2 reels.
30. *The Shrimp*, 5-3-30. Hal Roach–MGM. Director Charles Rogers; story H. M. Walker; film editor Richard Currier; with Thelma Todd, Nancy Drexel, James Mason, Max Davidson. 2 reels.
31. *The King*, 6-14-30. Hal Roach–MGM. Directors James W. Horne, Charles Rogers; story H. M. Walker; dialogue H. M. Walker; film editor Richard Currier; with Thelma Todd, Dorothy Granger. 2 reels.
32. *The Big Flash*, 11-6-32. Educational-Fox. Director and producer Arvid E. Gillstrom; story Robert Vernon, Frank Griffin; with Vernon Dent, Lita Chevret, Ruth Hiatt, Matthew Betz, King Baggot, Jack Grey, Bobby Dunn. 2 reels.
33. *Tired Feet*, 1-1-33. Educational-Fox. Director and producer Arvid E. Gillstrom; story Robert Vernon, Frank Griffin; with Vernon Dent, Shirley Blake, Maidena Armstrong, Eddie Baker, William Irving, Les Goodwin. 2 reels.
34. *The Hitchhiker*, 2-12-33. Educational-Fox. Director and producer Arvid E. Gillstrom; story Robert Vernon, Dean Ward; with Vernon Dent, Ruth Clifford, William Irving, Chris Marie Meeker. 2 reels.
35. *Knight Duty*, 5-7-33. Educational-Fox. Director Arvid E. Gillstrom; story Dean Ward, William Watson; with Vernon Dent, Matthew Betz, Lita Chevret, Nell O'Day, Eddie Baker, Billy Engle. 2 reels.
36. *Tied for Life*, 7-2-33. Educational-Fox. Director and producer Arvid E. Gillstrom; story Dean Ward, Vernon Dent; with Vernon Dent, Nell O'Day, Mabel Forrest, Elaine Whipple, Eddie Baker. 2 reels.
37. *Marriage Humor*, 8-18-33. Paramount. Director Harry Edwards; producer Arvid E. Gillstrom; story Dean Ward, Vernon Dent; film editor Jack English; background music Lee Zahler; with Vernon Dent, Nancy Dover, Ethel Sykes, Eddie Schubert. 2 reels.
38. *Hooks and Jabs*, 8-25-33. Educational-Fox. Director Arvid E. Gillstrom; story Dean Ward, Vernon Dent; with Vernon Dent, Nell O'Day, William Irving, Frank Moran. 2 reels.
39. *The Stage Hand*, 9-8-33. Educational-Fox. Director Harry Edwards; story Harry Langdon, Edward Davis; with Marel Foster, Ira Hayward, Eddie Schubert. 2 reels.
40. *On Ice*, 10-6-33. Paramount. Director and producer Arvid E. Gillstrom; story Dean Ward, Vernon Dent; film editor Jack English; with Vernon Dent, Eleanor Hunt, Ethel Sykes, Kewpie Morgan, Ruth Clifford, Diana Seaby, William Irving. 2 reels.
41. *A Roaming Romeo*, 12-29-33. Paramount. Director and producer Arvid E. Gillstrom; story Dean Ward, Vernon Dent; film editor Jack English; with Vernon Dent, Nell O'Day, Jack Henderson, Les Goodwin. 2 reels.

42. *Circus Hoodoo,* 2-16-34. Paramount. Director Arvid E. Gillstrom; story Dean Ward, Vernon Dent; film editor Jack English; with Vernon Dent, Eleanor Hunt, Matthew Betz, Diana Seaby, James Morton, Tom Kennedy. 2 reels.

43. *Petting Preferred,* 4-27-34. Paramount. Director Arvid E. Gillstrom; story Jack Townley; adaptation Dean Ward, Vernon Dent; film editor Jack English; with Vernon Dent, Dorothy Granger, Eddie Baker, Alice Ardell. 2 reels.

44. *Counsel on de Fence,* 10-25-34. Columbia. Director Arthur Ripley; story and screenplay Harry McCoy; with Renée Whitney, Earle Foxe, Robert Frazer, Jack Norton, Babe Kane. 2 reels.

45. *Shivers,* 12-24-34. Columbia. Director Arthur Ripley; story Arthur Ripley; screenplay John Grey; film editor William Alyon; with Florence Lake, Dick Elliott. 2 reels.

46. *His Bridal Sweet,* 3-15-35. Columbia. Director Alf Goulding; story and screenplay John Grey; with Billy Gilbert, Geneva Mitchell. 2 reels.

47. *The Leather Necker,* 5-9-35. Columbia. Director Arthur Ripley; story Arthur Ripley; screenplay John Grey; with Wade Boteler. 2 reels.

48. *His Marriage Mixup,* 10-31-35. Columbia. Director Preston Black (pseudonym of Jack White); story and screenplay Vernon Dent; with Dorothy Granger. 2 reels.

49. *I Don't Remember,* 12-26-35. Columbia. Director Preston Black; story and screenplay Preston Black; with Geneva Mitchell, Mary Carr, Vernon Dent, Robert Burns. 2 reels.

50. *A Doggone Mixup,* 2-4-38. Columbia. Director Charles Lamont; story and screenplay Elwood Ullman, Al Giebler, Charles Melson; with Ann Doran, Vernon Dent, Bud Jamison, Eddie Fetherstone, Bess Flowers, Sarah Edwards, James C. Morton. 2 reels.

51. *Sue My Lawyer,* 9-16-38. Columbia. Director Jules White; story Harry Langdon; screenplay Ewart Adamson; with Ann Doran, Monty Collins, Bud Jamison, Vernon Dent, Cy Schindell, Don Brodie, Jack Long, Charley Dorety, Jack Lipson, Robert Burns. 2 reels.

52. *Goodness! A Ghost,* 3-8-40. RKO. Director Harry D'Arcy; producer Lou Brock; story George Jeske, Arthur F. Jones; screenplay Harry Langdon; film editor John Lockert. 2 reels.

53. *Cold Turkey,* 10-18-40. Columbia. Director Del Lord; story and screenplay Harry Edwards, Elwood Ullman; with Ann Doran, Monty Collins, Vernon Dent, Bud Jamison, Eddie Laughton. 2 reels.

54. *What Makes Lizzy Dizzy?,* 3-26-42. Columbia. Director Jules White; story Philip L. Leslie; screenplay Ewart Adamson; with Elsie Ames, Monty Collins, Lorin Raker, Dorothy Appleby, Kathryn Sabichi, Kay Vallon. 2 reels.

55. *Tireman, Spare My Tires,* 6-4-42. Columbia. Director Jules White; story Felix Adler; screenplay Clyde Bruckman; with Louise Currie, Emmett Lynn, Vernon Dent, Bud Jamison. 2 reels.

56. *Carry Harry,* 9-3-42. Columbia. Director Harry Edwards; story and screenplay Harry Edwards; with Elsie Ames, Barbara Pepper, Marjorie Deanne, Dave O'Brien, Stanley Blystone, Chester Conklin. 2 reels.

57. *Piano Mooner,* 12-11-42. Columbia. Director Harry Edwards; producer Hugh McCollum; story and screenplay Harry Langdon; film editor

Paul Borotsky; with Fifi D'Orsay, Gwen Kenyon, Betty Blythe, Stanley Blystone, Chester Conklin. 2 reels.

58. *A Blitz on the Fritz,* 1-22-43. Columbia. Director Jules White; story and screenplay Clyde Bruckman; film editor Edwin Bryant; with Douglas Leavitt, Bud Jamison, Vernon Dent, Louise Currie, Beatrice Blinn, Jack Lipson, Charles Berry, Al Hill, Kit Guard, Bud Fine. 2 reels.

59. *Blonde and Groom,* 4-16-43. Columbia. Director Harry Edwards; story and screenplay Harry Langdon. 2 reels.

60. *Here Comes Mr. Zerk,* 7-23-43. Columbia. Director Jules White; story and screenplay Jack White. 2 reels.

61. *To Heir Is Human,* 1-14-44. Columbia. Director Harold Goodsoe; story and screenplay Elwood Ullman, Monty Collins; with Una Merkel, Christine McIntyre, Eddie Gribbon, Lew Kelly, Vernon Dent, John Tyrrell. 2 reels.

62. *Defective Detectives,* 4-3-44. Columbia. Director Harry Edwards; story Harry Edwards; with El Brendel, Christine McIntyre, Vernon Dent, Eddie Laughton, John Tyrrell, Snub Pollard, Dick Botiller. 2 reels.

63. *Mopey Dope,* 6-16-44. Columbia. Director Del Lord; story and screenplay Del Lord, Elwood Ullman; with El Brendel, Christine McIntyre, Arthur Q. Bryan. 2 reels.

64. *Snooper Service,* 2-2-45. Columbia. Director Harry Edwards; story Harry Edwards; with El Brendel, Vernon Dent, Rebel Randall, Dick Curtis, Fred Kelsey, Buddy Yarns. 2 reels.

65. *Pistol Packin' Nitwits,* 4-4-45. Columbia. Director Harry Edwards; story Edward Bernds, Harry Langdon; screenplay Harry Edwards; with El Brendel, John Tyrrell, Brad King, Dick Curtis, Christine McIntyre, Tex Cooper, Victor Cox, Heinie Conklin, Vernon Dent. 2 reels.

Feature films: silent

1. *Tramp, Tramp, Tramp,* 3-21-26. Harry Langdon Corporation–First National. Director Harry Edwards; story Frank Capra, Tim Whelan, Hal Conklin, J. Frank Holliday, Gerald Duffy, Murray Roth; photography Elgin Lessley; titles George Marion, Jr.; with Joan Crawford, Edward Davis, Carlton Griffin, Alec B. Francis, Brooks Benedict, Tom Murray. 62 min.

2. *Ella Cinders,* 6-6-26 (guest appearance). First National. Director and producer Alfred E. Green; scenario Frank Griffin, Mervyn LeRoy; adapted from the comedy strip by William Counselman and Charles Plumb; photography Arthur Martinelli; art director E. J. Schulter; titles George Marion, Jr.; film editor Robert J. Kern; with Colleen Moore, Lloyd Hughes, Vera Lewis, Doris Baker, Emily Gerdes, Mike Donlin, Jed Prouty. 72 min.

3. *The Strong Man,* 9-19-26. Harry Langdon Corporation–First National. Director Frank Capra; story Arthur Ripley; adaptation Hal Conklin, Robert Eddy; production manager William H. Jenner; assistant director J. Frank Holliday; technical director Lloyd Brierly; lighting Denver Harmon; photography Elgin Lessley, Glenn Kershner; titles Reed Heustis; film editor Harold Young; comedy construction Clarence Hennecke; with Priscilla Bonner, Gertrude Astor, William V. Mong, Robert McKim, Arthur Thalasso. 60 min.

4. *Long Pants*, 4-10-27. Harry Langdon Corporation–First National. Director Frank Capra; story Arthur Ripley; adaptation Robert Eddy; photography Elgin Lessley, Glenn Kershner; comedy construction Clarence Hennecke; with Priscilla Bonner, Gladys Brockwell, Alan Roscoe, Alma Bennett, Betty Francisco. 61 min. [The seventy-minute version of *Long Pants* originally released included one reel in Technicolor.]
5. *His First Flame*, 5-8-27. Mack Sennett–Pathé. Director Harry Edwards; story Arthur Ripley, Frank Capra; photography William Williams; special photography Ernie Crockett; titles A. H. Giebler; film editor William Hornbeck; supervision J. A. Waldron; with Natalie Kingston, Ruth Hiatt, Vernon Dent, Bud Jamison, Dot Farley. 52 min. [*His First Flame* was produced after *Remember When?* and prior to *Lucky Stars* but its release was delayed by Sennett pending Langdon's appearance in features for First National.]
6. *Three's a Crowd*, 8-28-27. Harry Langdon Corporation–First National. Director Harry Langdon; story Arthur Ripley; adaptation James Langdon, Robert Eddy; photography Elgin Lessley, Frank Evans; with Gladys McConnell, Cornelius Keefe, Henry Barrows, Frances Raymond, Agnes Steele, Brooks Benedict, Bobby Young, Julia Brown, Joe Butterworth, Fred Warren, John Kolb, Arthur Thalasso. 56 min.
7. *The Chaser*, 2-12-28. Harry Langdon Corporation–First National. Director Harry Langdon; story Arthur Ripley; scenario Clarence Hennecke, Robert Eddy, Harry McCoy; photography Elgin Lessley, Frank Evans; titles A. H. Giebler; film editor Alfred de Gaetano; comedy construction Clarence Hennecke; with Gladys McConnell, Helen Hayward, William (Bud) Jamison, Charles Thurston. 63 min.
8. *Heart Trouble*, 8-12-28. Harry Langdon Corporation–First National. Director Harry Langdon; story Arthur Ripley; scenario Earle Rodney, Clarence Hennecke; photography Frank Evans, Dev Jennings; titles Gardner Bradford; film editor Alfred de Gaetano; with Doris Dawson, Lionel Belmore, Madge Hunt, Bud Jamison, Mark Hamilton, Nelson McDowell, Joseph Gerard, Jack Pratt, Kid Wagner, Pat Harmon, Bob Reeves, Clark Comstock, Thelma Salter, Edythe Chapman. 58 min. ["Comedy of a country boy, rejected in time of war as unfit. He unwittingly comes across information about a spies' base for sending supplies to enemy submarines. He saves an American officer, is captured by the spies, and captures the latter. He is then proclaimed a hero by all." *Motion Picture News Booking Guide, Volume 13*.]

Feature films: sound

9. *A Soldier's Plaything*, 11-1-30. Warner Brothers. Director Michael Curtiz; original screen story Vina Delmar; screen adaptation Perry Velcroff; dialogue Arthur Caesar; with Lotti Loder, Ben Lyon, Jean Hersholt, Noah Beery, Fred Kohler. 66 min.
10. *See America Thirst*, 11-24-30. Universal. Director William James Craft; story and dialogue Edward I. Luddy, Vin Moore; adaptation C. Jerome Harwin; with Slim Summerville, Bessie Love, Matthew Betz, Mitchell Lewis, Stanley Fields, Tom Kennedy. 89 min.

Filmography

11. *Hallelujah, I'm a Bum,* 1-27-33. United Artists. Director Lewis Milestone; producer Joseph M. Schenk; original story Ben Hecht; screenplay S. N. Behrman; music and lyrics Richard Rogers, Lorenz Hart; with Al Jolson, Madge Evans, Frank Morgan, Chester Conklin, Tyler Booke, Bert Roach. 100 min.

12. *My Weakness,* 9-22-33. Fox. Director and continuity David Butler; story and dialogue B. G. De Sylva; film editor Irene Morra; with Lillian Harvey, Lew Ayres, Charles Butterworth, Sid Silvers, Irene Bentley, Henry Travers. 75 min.

13. *Atlantic Adventure,* 9-10-35. Columbia. Director Albert S. Rogell; story Diana Bourbon; screenplay John J. Neville, Nat N. Dorfman; film editor Ted Kent; with Nancy Carroll, Lloyd Nolan, Arthur Hohl, Robert Middlemass, John Wray, E. E. Clive. 77 min.

14. *He Loved an Actress,* 4-11-38. Grand National. Director Melville Brown; producer William Rowland; screenplay John Meehan, Jr.; with Lupe Velez, Wallace Ford, Ben Lyon, Jean Collin, Cyril Raymond, Mary Cole. 77 min. [Musical made in England in color. Released in England in 1939 as *Mad about Money.*]

15. *There Goes My Heart,* 9-27-38. Hal Roach–United Artists. Director Norman Z. McLeod; producer Milton H. Bren; original story Ed Sullivan; screenplay Eddie Moran, Jack Jevne; film editor William Terhune; musical director Marvin Hatley; with Frederic March, Virginia Bruce, Patsy Kelly, Alan Mowbray, Eugene Pallette, Arthur Lake, Claude Gillingwater, Etienne Girardot, Nancy Carroll, Marjorie Main. 100 min.

16. *Zenobia,* 3-14-39. Hal Roach–United Artists. Director Gordon Douglas; producer A. Edward Sutherland; original story Walter De Leon, Arnold Belgard; screenplay Corey Ford; film editor Bert Jordan; musical score Marvin Hatley; with Oliver Hardy, Billie Burke, Alice Brady, James Ellison, Jean Parker, June Lang, Olin Howland, J. Farrell McDonald, Stepin Fetchit, Hattie McDaniel. 89 min.

17. *Misbehaving Husbands,* 12-12-40. Producers Releasing Corporation. Director William Beaudine; producer Jed Buell; original screenplay Vernon Smith, Claire Parrish, Charles A. Rogers; film editor Robert Crandall; with Betty Blythe, Ralph Byrd, Esther Muir, Gayne Whitman, Florence Wright, Luana Walters, Vernon Dent. 77 min.

18. *All-American Coed,* 10-13-41. Hal Roach–United Artists. Director LeRoy Prinz; original story LeRoy Prinz, Hal Roach, Jr.; screenplay Cortland Fitzsimmons; adaptation Kenneth Higgins; film editor Bert Jordan; musical score Edward Ward; with Frances Langford, Johnny Downs, Marjorie Woodworth, Noah Beery, Jr., Esther Dale, Alan Hale, Jr. 55 min.

19. *Double Trouble,* 11-17-41. Monogram Pictures Corporation. Director William West; producer Dixon R. Harwin; original story Harry Langdon; screenplay Jack Natteford; photography A. Martinelli; film editor Carl Pierson; with Charles Rogers, Catherine Lewis, Dave O'Brien, Frank Jaquet, Louise Curry, Benny Rubin. 77 min.

20. *House of Errors,* 3-26-42. Producers Releasing Corporation. Director Bernard B. Ray; original story Harry Langdon; screenplay Ewart Adamson, Eddie M. Davis; film editor Dan Milner; music director Lee Zahler; with Charles Rogers, Marian Marsh, Ray Walker, John Holland, Betty Blythe, Vernon Dent. 77 min.

21. *Spotlight Scandals,* 7-26-43. Monogram Pictures Corporation. Director William Beaudine; producers Sam Katzman, Jack Dietz; screenplay William X. Crowley, Beryl Sachs; photography Mack Stengler; film editor Carl Pierson; music director Edward Kay; with Billy Gilbert, Frank Fay, Bonny Baker, Butch and Buddy, Iris Adrian, The Radio Rogues. 89 min.
22. *Hot Rhythm,* 3-14-44. Monogram Pictures Corporation. Director William Beaudine; producer Lindsley Parsons; original story and screenplay Tim Ryan, Charles Marion; photography Ira Morgan; film editor Richard Currier; music director Edward Kay; with Robert Lowery, Dona Drake, Tim Ryan, Irene Ryan, Sidney Miller, Robert Kent. 89 min.
23. *Block Busters,* 8-15-44. Monogram Pictures Corporation. Director Wallace Fox; producers Sam Katzman, Jack Dietz; original story and screenplay Houston Branch; photography Marcel Le Picard; film editor Carl Pierson; with Leo Gorcey, Huntz Hall, Gabriel Dell, Billy Benedict, Jimmy Strand, Bill Chaney, Minerva Urecal, Roberta Smith, Noah Beery, Sr. 77 min.
24. *Swingin' on a Rainbow,* 8-27-45. Republic Pictures. Director William Beaudine; associate producer Eddy White; original story Olive Cooper; screenplay Olive Cooper, John Grey; photography Marcel Le Picard; film editor Fred Allen; music director Morton Scott; with Jane Frazee, Brad Taylor, Minna Gombell, Amelita Ward, Tim Ryan, Paul Harvey. 89 min.

Films in which Harry Langdon receives screenwriting credit

Short films

1. *The Stage Hand.*
2. *Sue My Lawyer.*
3. *Goodness! A Ghost.*
4. *Piano Mooner.*
5. *Blonde and Groom.*
6. *Pistol Packin' Nitwits.*

Feature films

1. *Blockheads,* 8-19-38. Hal Roach–MGM. Director John G. Blystone; associate producer Hal Roach; original story and screenplay Charles Rogers, Felix Adler, James Parrott, Harry Langdon, Arnold Belgard; photography Art Lloyd; film editor Bert Jordan; musical director Marvin Hatley; with Stan Laurel, Oliver Hardy, Billy Gilbert, Patricia Ellis, James Finlayson, Minna Gombell, Harley Woods, Harry Stubbs, William Royle. 55 min.
2. *The Flying Deuces,* 10-10-39. RKO. Director A. Edward Sutherland; producer Boris Morros; original story and screenplay Ralph Spence, Charles Rogers, Alfred Schiller, Harry Langdon; photography Art Lloyd; aerial photography Elmer Dyer; film editor Jack Denniss; musical director Edward Paul; music John Leipold, Leo Shuken; with Stan

Laurel, Oliver Hardy, Jean Parker, Reginald Gardiner, Charles Middleton, James Finlayson, Jean Del Val, Clem Wilenchick. 69 min.
3. *A Chump at Oxford,* 2-20-40. Hal Roach–United Artists. Director Alf Goulding; associate producer Hal Roach, Jr.; original story and screenplay Charles Rogers, Felix Adler, Harry Langdon; photography Art Lloyd; film editor Bert Jordan; musical score Marvin Hatley; with Stan Laurel, Oliver Hardy, Forrester Harvey, James Finlayson, Wilfred Lucas, Forbes Murray, Frank Baker, Eddie Borden, Gerald Rogers, Peter Cushing, Victor Kendall, Gerald Fielding, Charles Hall. 66 min.
4. *Saps at Sea,* 5-3-40. Hal Roach–United Artists. Director Gordon Douglas; original story and screenplay Charles Rogers, Felix Adler, Gil Pratt, Harry Langdon; photography Art Lloyd; film editor William Ziegler; musical score Marvin Hatley; with Stan Laurel, Oliver Hardy, James Finlayson, Dick Cramer, Ben Turpin, Harry Bernard, Eddie Conrad. 55 min.
5. *Road Show,* 2-20-41. Hal Roach–United Artists. Director Hal Roach; screenplay Arnold Belgard, Harry Langdon, Mickell Novak; based on the novel by Eric Hatch; film editor Bert Jordan; musical score Georgie Stoll; music and lyrics Hoagy Carmichael, Harris Robinson, Stanley Adams; with Adolphe Menjou, Carole Landis, John Hubbard, Charles Butterworth, Patsy Kelly, George E. Stone, Margaret Roach, Polly Ann Young, Edward Norris, Marjorie Woodworth, Willie Best, The Charioteers, Paul Stanton, Jack Norton. 100 min.
6. *Double Trouble.*
7. *House of Errors.*

Films directed by Harry Langdon

1. *Three's a Crowd.*
2. *The Chaser.*
3. *Heart Trouble.*
4. *Wise Guys,* 8-37. Fox-British. Director Harry Langdon; producer Ivor McLaren; story Alison Booth; screenplay David Evans; with Charlie Naughton, Jimmy Gold, Andrene Brier, Robert Mainby, Walter Roy, Sydney Keith, David Kier. 67 min. [Comedy Langdon directed while in England from December 1936 to April 1937.]

Bibliography

Books

Agee, James. "Comedy's Greatest Era." In *Agee on Film: Volume One*, pp. 2–19. New York: Grosset & Dunlap, 1969.

Brownlow, Kevin. *The Parade's Gone By. . . .* New York: Alfred A. Knopf, 1968.

Capra, Frank. *The Name above the Title*. New York: Macmillan Co., 1971.

Castelle, Giulio Cesare. *Il Divisimo, Mitologia del Cinema*. Torino: Edizione Radio Italiene, 1957.

Coursodon, Jean-Pierre. *Keaton et Cie, les burlesques américains du "muet."* Paris: Editions Seghers, 1964.

Durgnat, Raymond. *The Crazy Mirror: Hollywood and the American Image*. New York: Horizon Press, 1969.

Everson, William K. "Harold Lloyd: The Climb to Success." In *Harold Lloyd. The King of Daredevil Comedy,* pp. 168–75. Edited by Adam Reilly. New York: Macmillan Co., 1977.

Freud, Sigmund. *Jokes and Their Relation to the Unconscious*. Translated and edited by James Strachey. New York: W. W. Norton, 1960.

Gilbert, Douglas. *American Vaudeville: Its Life and Times*. New York: Dover, 1968.

Gómes Mesa, Luis. *Variedad de la Pantalla Cómica*. Madrid: Biblioteca Atlantico, 1932.

Kerr, Walter. *The Silent Clowns*. New York: Alfred A. Knopf, 1975.

Kyrou, Ado. *Le Surréalisme au Cinéma*. Paris: Le Terrain Vague, 1963.

Lahue, Kalton C. *World of Laughter: The Motion Picture Comedy Short, 1910–1930*. Norman: University of Oklahoma Press, 1966.

———, and Gill, Sam. *Clown Princes and Court Jesters: Some Great Comics of the Silent Screen*. Cranbury, N.J.: A. S. Barnes, 1970.

Langdon, Harry. "The Comedian." In *Breaking into the Movies*, pp. 90–94. Edited by Charles Reed Jones. New York: Unicorn Press, 1927.

Laurie, Joe, Jr. *Vaudeville: From the Honky-Tonks to the Palace*. New York: Henry Holt, 1953.

Levy, William, and Scherle, Victor. *The Films of Frank Capra*. Secaucus, N.J.: Citadel Press, 1977.

McCaffrey, Donald W. *Four Great Comedians: Chaplin, Lloyd, Keaton, Langdon*. New York: A. S. Barnes, 1968.

Maltin, Leonard. *The Great Movie Shorts*. New York: Bonanza Books, 1972.

Mast, Gerald. *The Comic Mind: Comedy and the Movies*. New York: Bobbs-Merrill, 1973.

Montgomery, John. *Comedy Films*. London: George Allen & Unwin, 1954.

Poague, Leland A. *The Cinema of Frank Capra: An Approach to Film Comedy*. New York: A. S. Barnes, 1975.

Robinson, David. *The Great Funnies: A History of Film Comedy*. New York: E. P. Dutton, 1960.

Sennett, Mack, and Shipp, Cameron. *King of Comedy*. Garden City, N.Y.: Doubleday, 1954.

Taibo, Francisco Ignacio. *Harry Langdon: El Mejor de Todos*. Mexico: Universidad Nacional Autónoma de Mexico, 1966.

Tichy, Wolfram, ed. and trans. *Lotte Reiniger—D. W. Griffith—Harry Langdon*. Frankfurt: Verlag Karl Maria Laufen, 1972.

Treadwell, Bill. *Fifty Years of American Comedy*. New York: Exposition Press, 1951.

Weinberg, Herman G., ed. "Weinberg Scrapbooks of Film Reviews." 3 vols., unpublished, in the Library of the Museum of Modern Art, New York, N.Y.

Periodicals

Albert, Katherine. "What Happened to Harry Langdon." *Photoplay* 4 (February 1932): 40, 106.

Allombert, Guy. "V.I.P. B.I.S." *Image et Son* (Paris) no. 269 (Summer 1973): 163–67.

Auriol, Jean George. "Harry Langdon." *La Revue du Cinéma* (Paris) no. 9 (April 1930): 3–15.

Billboard (Cincinnati), 15 September 1906–28 April 1923.

Brunelin, Andre G. "Harry Langdon." *Cinéma 60* (Paris) no. 49 (August–September 1960): 72–83.

Campassi, Osvaldo. "Comici Americani: Harry Langdon." *La Critica Cinematografica* (Parma) no. 8 (1948): 8.

Chevallier, Jacques. "Tramp, Tramp, Tramp." *Image et Son* (Paris) no. 247 (February 1971): 120–23.

Cohen, Hubert I. "The Serious Business of Being Funny." *Film Comment* 5 (Fall 1969): 46–57.

Columbat, Jacques. "Harry Langdon." *Image et Son* (Paris) no. 228 (May 1969): 30–37.

Curran, Doris. "The Sad-Faced Mr. Langdon." *Motion Picture Classic* 21 (July 1925): 62, 87.

Dreiser, Theodore. "The Best Motion Picture Interview Ever Written." *Photoplay* 34 (August 1928): 32–35, 124–29.

Dupuich, Jean-Jacques. "Harry Langdon." *Image et Son* (Paris) no. 274 (Summer 1973): 51–56.

Elkhart (Ind.) *Truth,* 7 September 1907.

Everson, William K. Letter. *Films in Review* 18 (November 1967): 582–83.

Fox, Fred W. "Out of the Past. Harry Langdon: Clown and Man." *Los Angeles Mirror News,* 1 April 1959, part II, p. 6.

Gilliatt, Penelope. "The Current Cinema. Langdon." *The New Yorker* 47 (24 April 1971): 130–34.

Gilson, Paul. "Harry Langdon ou la Maladie du Sommeil." *La Revue du Cinéma* (Paris) no. 3 (May 1929): no page numbers.

Goldfayn, Georges. "L'art de Harry Langdon." *L'Age du Cinéma* (Paris) no. 2 (May 1951): 20–22.

———. "Le Cinéma. Comme entreprise de transmutation de la vie." *L'Age du Cinéma* (Paris) nos. 4–5 (August–November 1951): 21–24.

Hall, Leonard. "Hey! Hey! Harry's Coming Back." *Photoplay* 36 (June 1929): 59, 102.

Herzog, Dorothy. "The Wistful Mr. Langdon." *Motion Picture Magazine* 34 (October 1927): 18–19, 84–85.

Kansas City Times, 15 April 1918.

Keene, J. H. "Harry Langdon." *Philadelphia Daily News,* 15 September 1930, pp. 22, 24.

Langdon, Harry. "The Serious Side of Comedy Making." *Theatre* 46 (December 1927): 22, 78.

Leary, Richard. "Capra and Langdon." *Film Comment* 8 (November–December 1972): 15–17.

Lee, Sonia. "Good Luck or Bad Luck—Bebe and Harry Can Take It." *Motion Picture* 44 (January 1933): 56–57.

McNamara, Brooks. "Medicine Shows: American Vaudeville in the Marketplace." *Theatre Quarterly* 4 (May–July 1974): 19–24.

Matzen, Madeleine. "That Funny Little Man." *Motion Picture Magazine* 32 (December 1926): 36–37, 96.

Milne, J. R. "Whoopee Isn't Fun." *Omaha* (Neb.) *World-Herald,* 26 April 1931, Sunday magazine section, p. 1.

Monks, Margaret G. "Harry, Harry, Quite Contrary." *Cinema Art* 5 (October 1926): 18–19.

New York American, 7 October 1920.

New York Dramatic Mirror, 7 April 1906–20 July 1907; 14 February 1920; 26 November 1921.

New York Evening World, 9 October 1920.

New York Star, 14 February 1914.

New York Telegraph, 11 November 1911.

New York Tribune, 5 October 1920.

North, Jean. "It's No Joke to Be Funny." *Photoplay* 28 (June 1925): 86, 126–27.

Orsini, Mario. "Le candide follie di Harry Langdon." *Filmcritica* (Rome) 23 (April–May 1972): 187–92.

Pittsburgh Telegraph, 17 July 1917.

Schonert, Vernon L. "Harry Langdon." *Films in Review* 18 (October 1967): 470–85.

Simsolo, Noel. "L'Athlète Incomplet (The Strong Man)." *Image et Son* (Paris) no. 269 (Summer 1973): 9–13.

Spokane Spokesman-Review, 19 February; 31 December 1917.

Stein, Elliott. "Capra Counts His Oscars." *Sight and Sound* 41 (Summer 1972): 162–64.

Tournes, André. "Harry Langdon." *Jeune Cinéma* (Paris) no. 51 (December 1970–January 1971): 14–18.

Town Topics (New York), 4 October 1920.

Truscott, Harold. "Harry Langdon." *The Silent Picture* (London) no. 13 (Winter–Spring 1972): 2–17.

Variety, 24 February 1906–28 April 1923; 5 October; 23 November 1927; 4 January 1928.

Vitoux, Frédéric. "Harry Langdon et Frank Capra." *Positif* (Paris) no. 133 (December 1971): 25–32.

Waller, Tom. "Langdon's 'Three's a Crowd' Ready on August 26th." *Moving Picture World* 87 (13 August 1927): 450–52.

———. "'Long Pants' Promises to Be Harry Langdon's Greatest Film." *Moving Picture World* 84 (22 January 1927): 263–66.

Washington Star, 7 May 1912.

Watz, Edward. "Langdon—Silent and Sound, Part 2." *Classic Film Collector* no. 47 (Summer 1975): 50–52.

———. "Langdon, the Unsung Genius." *Classic Film Collector* no. 43 (Summer 1974): 33, 38–39.

———. "The Strong Man." *Classic Film Collector* no. 50 (Spring 1976): 46–47.

Index

"After the Ball," 18, 22, 45–46, 113, 167, 169, 170, 172
L'Age du Cinéma, 54
Agee, James, 13, 54, 140–41, 192
All Night Long, 43, 52, 63, 65, 79–81, 93, 107, 135, 168, 222, 226
American Tragedy, An, 219
Arnold, Edward, 47
Astor, Gertrude, 7, *87*
Auriol, Jean-George, 55

Back Stage, 138
Balloonatic, The, 138–39
Bazin, André, 127
Behind the Screen, 201
Belmore, Lionel, *100*
Bennett, Alma, 68, *91, 94, 221*
Bernds, Edward, 7, 39
Billboard, 20, 22–25, 27, 32–33, 46, 167
Bonner, Priscilla, 7, *74*
Boobs in the Wood, 20, 41, 60–61, 71, 74, 121, 141, 217
Breton, André, 82
Brockwell, Gladys, *220*
Brownlow, Kevin, 13
Brunelin, Andre G., 55
Brunius, J.-B., 55

Campbell, Eric, 200
Capra, Frank, 7, 11–15, 17, 20, 22–24, 35, 38, 43–44, 46–47, 83, 156, 183–84, 205–7
Cat's Meow, The, 41, 81
Champion, The, 201
Chaplin, Charles, 15, 34–36, 44, 48, 110–13, 117, 129, 182–83, 189, 199, 200–203
Chase, The, 211, 226
Chaser, The, 12, 50, 58–59, 70, 73, 76, 77, 84, *85, 122,* 140–41, 156, *158,* 170, 172, 174, 176, *177, 178, 179,* 181, 183, 186, 206, *207, 208, 209, 210, 211,* 215, *216,* 217, *219, 222, 223*

Chavance, 55
Chevallier, Jacques, 56
Cinéma 60, 55
Circus, The, 111, 200–201, 203–4
City Lights, 112, 201–2
Cocteau, Jean, 82
College, 110
Columbia Pictures, 39, 49, 52
Counsel on de Fence, 52
Coursodon, Jean-Pierre, 54
Cure, The, 200

Darro, Frankie, *220*
Dawson, Doris, 75, *101, 114, 115, 185*
Delons, André, 55
Dent, Vernon, 46, 217
de Ramey, Pierre, *221*
Desire Under the Elms, 215
Dreiser, Theodore, 35, 182
Durgnat, Raymond, 56

Educational Pictures, 49, 52
Edwards, Harry, 13, 35, 38
Eisenstein, Sergei M., 169
Electric House, The, 138
Evans, Madge, *50*

Feet First, 190
Feet of Mud, 42, 67, 79, 81, 93, 106, 148, 156, 169
Fiddlesticks, 20, 43, 71, 151, 164, 183
Finney, Edward, 7
First National Pictures, 12, 24, 27, 49, 183–87
For Heaven's Sake, 191
Francisco, Betty, *88*
Fred Karno Company, 200
Freud, Sigmund, 104

Gas Masks, 169
General, The, 138, 194–95, 197–99
Gilbert, Douglas, 25
Gill, Sam, 13

Index

Gilliatt, Penelope, 54
Gilson, Paul, 55
Girl Shy, 191
Goldfayn, Georges, 54
Gold Rush, The, 200–202
Granger, Dorothy, 7
Great Dictator, The, 201
Gribbon, Harry, 35
Gus Sun vaudeville circuit, 24

Hallelujah, I'm a Bum, 49, 50
Hal Roach Comedies, 30, 48, 49
Hansom Cabman, The, 45, 81
Harry Langdon Corporation, 12–13, 183, 206
Hayward, Helen, *207, 208, 210*
Heart Trouble, 12, 75, *98, 99, 100, 101, 113, 114, 115, 117, 136, 160, 161, 171, 172, 173*, 182–83, *185, 186, 187*, 206
Hiatt, Ruth, 7
High and Dizzy, 190
His First Flame, 11, 57, 65, 67, 69, 79, 121, 135, 183, 206, 213, 215
His Marriage Wow, 20, 61, 67, 71–72, 77, 81, 106–7, 109, 123, 125, 135, 148–49, 151–52, 157, 159, 168–69, 191, 213, 222
His New Mama, 38, 44, 215
Hitchhiker, The, 52
Horace Greeley, Jr., 35
Hurlock, Madeline, 44, 45

Image et Son, 56
Immigrant, The, 112
It's a Wonderful Life, 47

Jamison, Bud, *122*
Jeune Cinéma, 56, 82
Jim Jam Jems, 22–23, 27
"Johnny's New Car," 18, 20, *21*, 22, 24–25, *26*, 33, 46, 167, 170, 181
Jokes and Their Relation to the Unconscious, 104
Jones, Dick, 38

Keaton, Buster, 92, 110, 129, 138–39, 143, 166, 189–90, 194–99
Keefe, Cornelius, *97*
Keith-Orpheum vaudeville circuit, 24, 25
Kerr, Walter, 14, 24, 56–57
King of Comedy, 12, 44, 206
Kyrou, Ado, 55–56

Lahue, Kalton C., 13
Langdon, Cecil, 18
Langdon, Donald A., 7
Langdon, Harry, Jr., 52, 187
Langdon, Helen Walton, 50–51, 187
Langdon, James (Tully), 18
Langdon, Mabel Sheldon, *51*, 52, 187
Langdon, Rose Frances, 17, 18, *23*, 50
Laurel and Hardy, 215
Laurie, Joe, Jr., 24
Leary, Richard, 14, 24, 55–56
Leather Necker, The, 52
Lesser, Sol, 35
Lloyd, Harold, 34, 110, 129, 137–41, 143, 183, 189, 190–94, 196, 199
London, Babe, *218*
Long Pants, 12, 52, 60–61, 64, 66–67, *68*, 69, 71, 73, 75, 80, 84, 86, *88*, 89, 90, *91*, 93, *94*, 104–6, 111, 117, 123, 132–33, 135, 141, 149, 156–57, 159, 165, 169, 184, 201, 203–4, 206, 213, 215, 217–18, *218, 220, 221*, 223
Look Out Below, 190
The Luck of the Foolish, 20, 35
Lucky Stars, 41, 65–66, 71, 79, 107, 109, 121–24, 141, 150, 152, 157, 162–64, 168, 190, 213, 215, 226

McCaffrey, Donald W., 13, 54
McConnell, Gladys, 7, *95*, 102, *174, 176, 177, 207, 208, 209, 210, 222, 223*
Mack Sennett Comedies, 28, 34
McLean, Douglas, 185
Majestic Theater, Chicago, 25, *26*, 27
Maltin, Leonard, 52
Martin, Quinn, 173
Mast, Gerald, 14, 54
Meet John Doe, 47
Metropolis, 82
Mr. Smith Goes to Washington, 47
Modern Times, 111, 199, 200
Mozhukin, Ivan, 131
Murnau, F. W., 127
Mutual Pictures, 202

Name above the Title, The, 12, 20, 47, 206
Never Weaken, 200
"Night in an English Music Hall, A," 202
"Night on the Boulevard, A," 18, *19*, 20, 24–25, 32, 162, 170, 181

One A.M., 203
O'Neill, Eugene, 215
Orpheum Theater, Los Angeles, 25

Orpheum Theater, Reading, 27
Orpheum Theater, San Francisco, 25, 27
Orpheum vaudeville circuit, 25–26, 37

Palace Theater, New York City, 24–25, 27, 50
Paleface, The, 166
Pantages vaudeville circuit, 24, 27
Paramount Pictures, 49, 181
Pathé Pictures, 35, 183
Pawnshop, The, 112, 200, 202
Pay Day, 200
Pelswick, Rose, 174
Picking Peaches, 35, *36*
Pierrot, *39*
Plain Clothes, 81
Playhouse, The, 92
Poague, Leland A., 14
Principal Pictures Corporation, 35
Prisoner of Japan, 209
Putting Pants on Philip, 215

Randall, Ed, 21
Remember When, 42–43, 45, 59–60, 63, 70–71, 104–5, 122–24, 140–41, 156, 159, 164–65, 169
Renoir, Jean, 127
Revue du Cinéma, La, 55
Rink, The, 112, 200
Ripley, Arthur, 11–13, 15, 17, 35, 38, 44, 47, 183, 205–7, 209–11, *212,* 213, 227
Riverside Theater, New York City, 20, 21
Roach, Hal, 7, 38–39, 182
Robinson, David, 13, 54
Roscoe, Alan, *220*
Rossellini, Roberto, 127

Safety Last, 139, 141, 143, 190, 192–94, 196
Saturday Afternoon, 41–42, 58–62, 64–68, 72, 79, 84, 104–8, 122–25, 140–41, 144, 148–49, 151, 156–57, 168–69, 213, 215, 222
Schonert, Vernon L., 13
Sea Squawk, The, 42, 45, 59, 81, 148, 215
Sennett, Mack, 11–13, 15, 17, 23–25, 27, 33, 35–46, 49, 51, 57, 81, 113, 128, 138, 156–57, 162, 182–84, 205–6
Seven Chances, 166, 195
Shanghaied Lovers, 36, 38, 44, 81
Sherlock Junior, 92–93
Show Girl, The, 27
Sky Boy, 48
Smile Please, 35
Smith, Chester, 174, 176

Soldier Man, 41–42, 60–61, 63–65, 67, 69, 79, 81, 84, 89, *90,* 93, 106, 141, 149, 156, 159, 168–69, 183, 213, 220, 222
Stein, Elliott, 14
Strong Man, The, 12, 20, 46–47, 52, 55, 58, *59,* 60, *61,* 62–63, 66–69, 72–73, 74, 75–76, 79–81, 83–84, 86, *87,* 88–89, 93–94, 104, *105, 106,* 107–8, 110–12, *116,* 119–22, 124–25, 134–35, 137, 141, 145, 149, *150,* 152, *153, 154, 155, 157,* 159, 168–69, 173, 183, 201, 203–4, 206, 213, *214,* 217, 222
Sue My Lawyer, 52
Sullivan and Considine vaudeville circuit, 24
Swanson, Gloria, *34*

Technicolor, 90, *91,* 221
Three's a Crowd, 12, *31,* 50, 55–56, 59, 64, 66, 69, 72, 76–79, 86, 89, 90, 94, *95, 96, 97,* 98, 100–102, 112, 121, 125, *130,* 133, 142–43, 148–50, 156–57, *158,* 169–70, 172–73, *175, 176, 180,* 181, 184–86, 204, 206, 220–22, *224, 225*
Thunder Road, 209–11, 226
Tournes, André, 56, 82
Tramp, The, 117, 202–3, 227
Tramp, Tramp, Tramp, 12, 47, 57–58, 60–64, 66–69, 71–72, 75–76, 78–79, 81, 83, 93, 104, 107, 109, 122–26, 133–37, 140, 142, 148, 151–55, 157, 165, 168–69, 191, 195–96, 201, 203
Treadwell, Bill, 13

United Artists Pictures, 50

Variety, 17, 20, 22, 24–25, 27, 46, 172, 183
Vaughn, Alberta, *36*
Vigo, Jean, 78
Voice in the Wind, 210–11, 226

Waldron, J. A., 28
Warner Brothers Pictures, 187
Waterfront, 209
Watts, Richard, Jr., 183
Welles, Orson, 127
Western Vaudeville Managers' Association, 24
White, Jules, 7
White Wing's Bride, The, 35
Wyler, William, 127

You Can't Take It with You, 47

Zero for Conduct, 78